Caught in the CROSS-Fire

ALSO BY MICHAEL K. WILSON . . .

The Lives of the Wise in an Anti-God World. Daniel 1–6

The Future for God's People in a Conflict-Ravaged World. Daniel 7–12

Changing Lanes, Crossing Cultures. Equipping Christians & Churches for Ministry in a Culturally Diverse Society (co-authored with Andrew Schachtel and Choon-Hwa Lim; short-listed for 2017 Australian Christian Book of the Year)

Caught in the CROSS-Fire

Combatting the World, the Flesh, and the Devil

MICHAEL KENNETH WILSON

RESOURCE *Publications* · Eugene, Oregon

CAUGHT IN THE CROSS-FIRE
Combatting the World, the Flesh, and the Devil

Copyright © 2025 Michael Kenneth Wilson. All rights reserved. Except for brief quotations in critical publications or reviews, no part of this book may be reproduced in any manner without prior written permission from the publisher. Write: Permissions, Wipf and Stock Publishers, 199 W. 8th Ave., Suite 3, Eugene, OR 97401.

Resource Publications
An Imprint of Wipf and Stock Publishers
199 W. 8th Ave., Suite 3
Eugene, OR 97401

www.wipfandstock.com

paperback isbn: 979-8-3852-4449-2
hardcover isbn: 979-8-3852-4450-8
ebook isbn: 979-8-3852-4451-5
version number 07/24/25

Unless otherwise stated, all Biblical quotations are from the Holy Bible, New International Version, NIV. Copyright© 1973, 1978, 1984, 2011 by Biblica, Inc. Used by permission of Zondervan. All rights reserved worldwide. www.zondervan.com The "NIV" and "New International Version" are trademarks registered in the United States Patent and Trademark Office by Biblica, Inc.

Contents

Author's Note | vii
Introduction | xiii

Chapter One: The Horror of War | 1
Chapter Two: War of the Words | 6
Chapter Three: Facing Inhuman Enemies | 21
Chapter Four: Facing Human Enemies | 45
Chapter Five: Facing Inner Enemies | 85
Chapter Six: Facing Fabricated Enemies | 121
Chapter Seven: Facing the Last Enemy | 145
Chapter Eight: Facing Enemies Together | 152
Chapter Nine: "More Than Conquerors" | 163
Chapter Ten: When War is No More | 180

Questions and Answers | 189
Glossary of Names: Who's Who | 195
Glossary of Terms | 201
Bibliography | 207

Author's Note

FIRST, A WORD ABOUT the title. This is a world ravaged by conflict. There is conflict at multiple levels, in families, in communities, in government, in sport, between nations, and so on. Christians live in the midst of such conflict and, indeed, they often find that they themselves are in the firing line. Conflict as experienced by the Lord's people may result from what is happening around them, but it is exacerbated by inescapable inner conflict. But, precisely because of what our wonderful Lord has achieved for us, we can think of ourselves as being "caught in the CROSS-fire." We face all forms of conflict as those who preach Christ crucified, as those crucified with Christ, as those who, identified with Jesus in his death, have died to sin, the law, and the elemental spiritual forces of this world and who no longer live for ourselves but for him who died for us and was raised again. That is what we have been "caught" up in by grace.

Secondly, what is involved in developing a sound biblical approach to the various forms of conflict we experience?

In this respect, some make much of what they call "spiritual warfare," though often this involves a very limited and circumscribed perspective. For example, the Wikipedia article on "Spiritual warfare" reads:

> Spiritual warfare is the Christian concept of taking a stand against preternatural evil forces. It is based on the belief in evil spirits which are able to intervene in human affairs. Various Christian groups have adopted practices to repel such forces, as based on their doctrine of Christian demonology. Prayer is a common form of spiritual warfare among Christians. Other practices may include exorcisms, laying-on of hands, fasting, or anointing with oil.

AUTHOR'S NOTE

With this article is an inset of a painting by Luca Giordano depicting the archangel Michael (strangely labelled "St Michael") defeating Lucifer's army.[1]

Now go to amazon.com. Enter "spiritual warfare." You will find a plethora of books on this subject, many simply titled "Spiritual Warfare." But in addition we find such titles as:

John Eckhardt, *Deliverance and Spiritual Warfare*.

Scott Meade, *Spiritual Warfare: Fighting Demons*.

Karl Payne, *Spiritual Warfare: Christians, Demonization and Deliverance*.

Ron M. Phillips, *Everyone's Guide to Demons and Spiritual Warfare*.

Michael S. B. Reid, *Strategic Level Spiritual Warfare*.

Jhordan Solomone, *Spiritual Warfare: Fighting Demons that attack your Mind*.

Jonathan Steele, *Spiritual Warfare: My Warfare with Demonic Spirits*.

C. Peter Wagner, *Territorial Spirits*.

Illustrative of the limited manner in which the term "spiritual warfare" is typically used is Sam Storms's 2001 book *Understanding Spiritual Warfare*. This is subtitled "A Comprehensive Guide." Evidently, for Storms "spiritual warfare" is entirely about combatting that which is Satanic and demonic: Part 1: Learning about the Demonic; Part 2: The Threat of the Demonic; Part 3: Responding to the Demonic.

Scott Moreau reports that in the informal polls he has conducted about "spiritual warfare," more than 50 percent of North American Christians had read one or more of Frank Peretti's novels, which graphically depict angels and demons fiercely battling over schools, towns, and whole territories.[2]

Clearly, there is a strong and common view that first and foremost Christians are in conflict with Satan and the demonic, with the term "spiritual warfare" often used with this primarily in mind.

---

1. The website *Catholic Online* illustrates how the labeling of the archangel as "Saint" represents traditional Catholic terminology. See http://www.catholic.org/saints/saint.php?saint_id=308 (Viewed 13/10/16). This language may be based on such texts as Jude 14 where angels are called God's "holy ones" (*hagiai*), an appellation elsewhere applied to God's people and translated as "saints."

2. Moreau, "Gaining Perspective."

But "spiritual warfare" language often involves a serious misreading of the Bible, leading to ways of dealing with the demonic that are not sanctioned in Scripture, along with a largely one-dimensional understanding of the nature of the conflicts experienced by the Lord's people.

There is indeed a demonic dimension to the inescapable conflict that Christians experience. But there are other dimensions. So it is that Christians have often spoken of "the world, the flesh, and the devil" as their enemies, the so-called "unholy trinity"—the "darkness" of John's Gospel.[3]

THE REALM OF THE DEMONIC

Evil spirits or demons are for real and are commanded by the devil, Satan.[4]

FALLEN HUMAN NATURE

When Paul speaks of "the flesh," he has in mind the reality that there is a propensity for evil that is deeply embedded within every human being.

CORRUPTED HUMAN SOCIETY

When the New Testament uses "the world" to denote an enemy, it has in mind "human society as a source of evil,"[5] "the cultural ethos, the social arrangements, the habits of life that follow upon the corrupting of human nature."[6]

---

3. See Jung, "Divine Warrior," iii, 111–15, 151, 157, 165–67, 179–80, 187, 191, 201, 215–16, 251, 253, 255–56, 272 ("The enemy to be defeated is the power of sin, which is the weapon of darkness that keeps God's people in bondage and exile"), 274, 278, 281–84, 286, 288 ("The darkness stands metaphorically for the threefold entity of sin, the world and the devil"), 291, 295.

4. The connection between Satan and demons is not apparent in the Old Testament. There is extra-biblical Jewish literature that makes this association, e.g. *1 Enoch* (variously identifies a leading fallen angel as Shemihazah or Azazel or Satan), the *Book of Jubilees* (Beliar and Mastema) and the Qumran Literature (especially Belial). See Jung, "Divine Warrior, 57–91.

5. See Bauckham, "Nature of Evil," 16. James K. A. Smith ventures, "disordered cultural systems of a fallen world 'under the sway of the evil one,'" referencing 1 John 5:19. Smith, "How (Not) To Change the World."

6. Wells, *God in the Wasteland*, 35. Wells describes "the world" as "the life of unredeemed humanity," adding: "It encompasses the cognitive horizons of the fallen, their appetites, the way they order their life, their priorities, their behavior, what they really *want*, and what they will do to get it. It encompasses the set of social arrangements, the

AUTHOR'S NOTE

These three foes are not separate categories but often collude, making the conflict complex and multifaceted. Christians must give full weight to each dimension and appreciate the full force of demonic, individual, and corporate evil.[7]

Frederick McCubbin produced two of Australia's greatest paintings, "Down on His Luck" (1889) and "The Pioneer" (1904). The first depicts an unsuccessful gold prospector, deep in thought, bemoaning his misfortune. The second involves three progressive panels which begin with a pioneering couple trying to make a living for themselves on the land, followed by cleared land and the growth of the family, and finishing with a grave but with the evidence of emerging urbanization. These paintings contributed to the myth of "the Aussie battler," a term which came into vogue during the economic depression of the 1890s. The Aussie battler was someone who struggled for survival and refused to give in.

Christians are under attack on all sides, from the world, the flesh, and the devil. We are called to be battlers. But there is one major difference between the Christian battler and the Aussie battler. We are not struggling for survival. In many contexts this may seem to be the case, but, as we shall see, this is far from being the reality.

But we will continue to battle against evil in our inner personal lives, in our relationships, in the church, and in the sin-distorted structures and systems that comprise our society: cultural, educational, recreational, political, economic, and religious.[8]

This complexity of evil cautions against thinking that if we can name the sources of evil then we can relax somewhat now that we have them in our sights. As Tom Wright comments,

> The whole point . . . is that evil is nameless and slimy and formless and seeps in . . . It does this with individuals, with societies, with churches and communities. . . sometimes working through earthly power structures and sometimes not . . . Sometimes it works through isolated individuals and sometimes takes grip

---

public context in which fallen life is lived out," 39.

7. Moreau rightly steers away from the common tendency to balance out these sources of evil, insisting rather that the extremes must be held in tension. Moreau, *Essentials*, 14–15.

8. Moreau identifies five fronts on which spiritual warfare is waged: (1) Personal; (2) Interpersonal or "each other"; (3) the local church; (4) systemic ("domination systems that make up our society"); and (5) cosmic (the unseen battle between demons and angels). *Essentials*, 18–19.

AUTHOR'S NOTE

of whole communities. So we can never be sure we have completely nailed it.[9]

Wright perceptively observes that it was as though September 11 had suddenly revealed to an enlightened world that there was still some evil out there. He recalls how at that time Tony Blair at the Labour Conference treated evil as a containable entity, to be confronted and dealt with in the Middle East and in part of Africa. As Wright reflected, it was "as though the post-Enlightenment world had created this lovely, happy, Edenic state and suddenly a snake had come into it. So let's blip it on the head and then everything will be alright. This is amazingly trivial and therefore very dangerous."

It is a common modern error to treat spiritual warfare as though it were essentially a metaphysical battle between a good God and his angels on the one side and the evil devil and his angels on the other. This abstracting of "the devil" from "the world" and "the flesh" is most unfortunate. It does not center the problem of evil in the right place. This book serves as a corrective to such distorted thinking.

Nor should we think that the world, the flesh, and the devil are the most dangerous forces confronting people on earth.

TV screens flash before our eyes the face of a man who has escaped from prison. Then there's the warning: If you see him just ring the police. Don't approach him because he's considered "armed and dangerous."

There are those who warn people to have nothing to do with Christians and their dogmas. Christians are dangerous people. They do not contribute to social cohesion in our pluralistic society with their insistence on Jesus as the only way. How dogmatic! How arrogant! How intolerant! Their slavish anti-intellectual commitment to an outdated book makes them the deniers of basic human rights—the rights of women over their own bodies, the rights of consenting adults to have sexual relations outside of marriage, the rights of men to have sex with men, and women with women. Christians brainwash vulnerable children with archaic ideas that are based on blind faith rather than solid evidence worthy of our modern scientific age. Christians exploit people's fears about what lies beyond the grave. Instead of affirming people they encourage an unhealthy and undignified self-image with their teaching on human depravity. Christians are misogynistic wowsers who have little if anything to contribute to ethics and social life.

9. Watch "N. T. Wright on Satan and Evil 3."

AUTHOR'S NOTE

One response would be to expose the evil and destructive nature of secular humanism. Another approach might give example upon example, from country after country, of Christians, without retaliation, enduring abuse, discrimination, torture, and cruel deaths. This is hardly special pleading. This is sober reality. Christians are soft targets precisely because they don't fight back. Wolves describing sheep as dangerous? How preposterous, we might think.

During the Australian "Festival of Dangerous Ideas" in 2013 a Q and A show asked panelists, Which dangerous idea has the greatest potential to change the world for the better? An atheist homosexual proposed making abortion mandatory for thirty years to reduce the population. Germaine Greer proposed freedom. However, Peter Hitchens startled everyone by saying, "The most dangerous idea in human history and philosophy remains the belief that Jesus Christ was the Son of God and rose from the dead and that is the most dangerous idea you will ever encounter."

Evidently somewhat nonplussed by this response, the compere asked, "Why dangerous?" Hitchens replied,

> Because it alters the whole of human behaviour and all our responsibilities. It turns the universe from a meaningless chaos into a designed place in which there is justice and there is hope and, therefore, we all have a duty to discover the nature of that justice and work towards that hope. It alters us all. If we reject it, it alters us all as well. It is incredibly dangerous. It's why so many people turn against it.[10]

As those who believe in Jesus as their risen, living Lord, Christians represent the most dangerous force people will ever face. We may be under attack, assailed on all sides. But evil, whatever form it takes, cannot prevail against us. Read this book and you will discover why.

---

10. Jensen, "Most Dangerous Idea."

Introduction

"There is a war between the rich and poor
A war between the man and the woman
There is a war between the ones who say there is a war
And the ones who say that there isn't."

LEONARD COHEN

Don't mention the war." So says Basil Fawlty, the character immortalized by John Cleese in the sixth episode of the sitcom *Fawlty Towers* aired in 1975. This episode was called "The Germans." The scene is a fictional hotel in Torquay, run by Basil Fawlty and his wife. At one point Basil has been knocked out and has just returned to the hotel from hospital, still concussed and confused. Thinking of his German guests Basil warns his staff, "Don't mention the war," but his own mind is so full of it that when he is speaking with his German guests he refers to the war in almost everything he says. When one of his guests begins to weep Fawlty blames his guests for starting it. When this is denied Fawlty responds, "Yes you did, you invaded Poland." Fawlty then impersonates Adolf Hitler, doing his version of the goose-step, the marching style popularly associated with Hitler's German troops. When Fawlty is knocked out again, following yet more expressions of his own mental disorder, one of the German guests asks, "However did they win?"

"Don't mention the war"? Well, it's actually a sign of mental disorder, of missing the bleeding obvious, if we can't see that the whole world

INTRODUCTION

is at war. This is not imagination running wild. This is ultimate warfare and all people on earth are caught up in it, whether they like it or not. As for Christians, we find ourselves constantly under attack, ever battling evil in all its guises.

Chapter One

The Horror of War

"In nuclear war, all men are cremated equal."
DEXTER GORDON

WAR IS HORRIFIC. ON battlefields teenagers and youths in their twenties are blown to bits and maimed for life. Women and children are used as shields. Children are abducted and forced to become brutal, merciless soldiers. Terrorists behead victims slowly with knives and crucify children.

War is monstrous. War shatters the delusion that people are basically good and decent and able to live in harmony with all others. In war nice people become monsters. War exposes the immense evil of humankind and the impossibility of ever having a world at peace.

War is merciless. Civilian casualties are no longer collateral damage. Modern war targets civilian populations. Homes and families and population centers are intentionally destroyed. The dogs of war snap at the heels of traumatized people fleeing for their lives.

War is inevitable. There are no wars to end wars. As our Lord warned us, there will continue to be wars and rumors of wars until he returns in glory. The same human evil and confusion that causes people to fight each other in marriage, in families, in the workplace, and in the law courts is the same human evil and confusion that will pitch nations and ethnic peoples and religious groups against each other.

WAR AND THE IMAGE OF GOD

People are not only fallen creatures—sinful and confused. They continue to be those made in the image and likeness of God. This image has been massively damaged, but like the ruins of the Acropolis, there is that which still stands and gives us glimpses of the glory that once was. War is a theater in which not only horrendous human evil is projected onto the screen of human history. We also see extraordinary and profound displays of human sacrifice and nobility.

But war blows thick heavy clouds over the land and snuffs out the sun. Courage and compassion are but pinpricks of light amid oppressive darkness. Terror and dread fill people's hearts—fear for ourselves and those we love.

WAR AND ETERNITY

Jesus warned his disciples not to fear those who kill the body but cannot kill the soul. Rather, he said, we are to fear the one, namely God, who can destroy both body and soul in hell.[1] Think of this together with Paul's declaration "that our present sufferings are not worth comparing with the glory that will be revealed in us."[2] The "us" here are the sons and daughters of God. But what these two complementary perspectives instill in "us" is the realization that the eternal trumps that which is here and now.

Take note! Terrifying wars that bring immense physical, emotional, and psychological suffering in their wake are dwarfed by the eternal damage to human souls inflicted in the war that has never ceased since evil first entered this now fallen world. Way back in 1661 William Gurnall rightly remarked that in comparison with this war, the most brutal war ever fought by people is "but sport and child's play."[3]

The carnage of this war is often invisible to the human eye. Where is the blood and gore? Where are the amputees and the horribly disfigured?

---

1. Matthew 10:28.
2. Romans 8:18.
3. Gurnall, *Christian in Complete Armour*, 2.

Because we do not see such things and do not see the reality which lies beyond the grave it is easy to assume that Christian talk of spiritual warfare is a case of "let's pretend." Is this a time for an honesty that admits that spiritual warfare is not so much a chilling reality as an extravagant use of the imagination to justify the perpetuation of the whole Christian enterprise, involving sheer speculation about the afterlife?

WAR AND THE AFTERLIFE

So, then, much depends on how you answer one fundamental question: What will happen to us after we physically die?

There are of course a great many people who avoid the question and push it to the back of their minds, as though it were a matter no more serious than deferring payment of that not so important bill received in the mail. There are those who have persuaded themselves that when our bodies die we no longer continue to exist. There are Hindus and Buddhists who believe they will come back either to this world or another realm in some other form, whether human, animal, or something else altogether. There are those who confuse near-death experiences with what truly lies beyond death, so that some, for example, referring to experiences of seeing light and feeling love, reassure themselves that whatever lies beyond death is nothing to be feared and dreaded.

In modern pluralistic societies, especially in the West, the very exposure to different views and beliefs leads many to suppose that it's just a matter of opinion. There is no right view. People are entitled to believe whatever they want to believe. Sometimes such thinking is tied to an underlying assumption that in the end nobody really knows what happens after death.

But plain common sense tells us that something happens to us after death. We can't all be right. It is not opinion or viewpoint that determines what that something is. It will be what it will be. But what is that something? Is it possible to know?

Yes it is! We can know for certain that as the writer to the Hebrews states, "after death comes judgment." We can be sure of this because it is based on something that happened in history—the bodily resurrection of Jesus Christ from the dead. This is not religious dogma. This cannot be dismissed as just what Christians believe. No! This is as much an historical fact as the Battle of Hastings in 1066 or the assassination of Franz

Ferdinand on June 28, 1914. If this is not an historical fact then the entire edifice of Christianity is a house of cards. As Paul declared in his letter to the Corinthians, if Jesus did not rise bodily from the dead then the faith of Christians is pointless and we are of all people most to be pitied.[4]

Jesus rose from the dead. Mock this claim if you will. But given the millions upon millions of people throughout history who have based their lives on this, at least give us the courtesy of using the same criteria to test the evidential basis for this claim as you would for any other purported historical event.

The climax of Paul's address to the Athenian Areopagus is this declaration: "God has set a day when he will judge the world with justice by the man he has appointed. And he has given proof of this by raising him from the dead" (Acts 17:31).

Because Jesus did rise from the dead—a demonstrable fact of history—we know that death is not the end. There will come a day of judgment when all will be judged by God with justice by Jesus Christ.

Read the Gospels for yourself. Jesus told his disciples not only that he would be executed and rise from the dead, but also that he would return to judge the world. Jesus also told parables which looked ahead to what happens after death. He not only said that he would separate all people into sheep and goats—those to be admitted into paradise and those to be thrown into hell[5]—but he repeatedly warned people about the horror of dying and going to hell.[6]

The road is narrow that leads to life in paradise and relatively few travel this path. But the road is wide and broad that leads to destruction and many follow the masses along this fatal highway. So said Jesus.[7] Of course, when we take into account the many billions of people who have lived and died and are alive today, then we recognize that the "few" is still a vast multitude, as the book of Revelation well recognizes.[8] But the tragic reality is that the vast majority of people in our world face eternal destruction. Spiritual warfare is horrific.

---

4. 1 Corinthians 15:17–19.
5. Matthew 25:31–46.
6. For example, Matthew 13:36–43, 47–50; 18:7–9.
7. Matthew 7:13–14.
8. Revelation 7:9.

MISSION DEBRIEF

- **Characteristics of War.** It is horrific, monstrous, merciless, and inevitable.
- **Image of God.** While people are fallen, sinful, and in a state of confusion, they continue to be creatures made in God's image. In war we see both horrendous human evil and magnificent nobility and self-sacrifice.
- **Ultimate Fear.** God is to be feared far more than any of the fears people experience in wartime.
- **Ultimate Horror.** Though largely invisible, the horrors of spiritual warfare far exceed those experienced in earthly war.
- **Jesus's Resurrection.** The historical reality of Jesus's resurrection proves that death is not the end and that he will decide the eternal destiny of everyone who has ever lived.
- **Fate of the Majority.** While a great number of people will enjoy the richness of eternal life, the vast majority face eternal destruction.

GATHERING INTELLIGENCE

Read Matthew 13:36–43 (The Parable of the Weeds)

1. The human race is composed of two kinds of people. How does Jesus describe the essential nature of each type?
2. What role does Jesus play in history?
3. How does Jesus describe the reality that awaits each of the two kinds of people in our world?

Chapter Two

War of the Words

"Coming out of his mouth is a sharp sword with which to strike down the nations."

REVELATION 19:15

THERE IS THEN A war being waged which almost never makes the news. There are no dramatic film clips that will show the devastation wreaked by this ongoing conflict. No photos of a small naked Vietnamese girl with a face contorted in terror as she runs for her life away from the horrors of war. No images of dead bodies strewn along the road following a massive bomb blast. So, when we speak of the immense damage to human life brought about by this hidden war it seems to many that this is just words, words, words.

THE MOST POWERFUL OF WEAPONS

Ah, but not mere human words. The words we speak are actually weapons of immense power. So, Paul comments:

> For though we live in the world, we do not wage war as the world does. The weapons we fight with are not the weapons of the world. On the contrary, they have divine power to demolish strongholds. We demolish arguments and every pretension that sets itself up against the knowledge of God, and we take captive every thought to make it obedient to Christ" (2 Corinthians 10:3–5).

There you have it! Christians who follow in Paul's footsteps are waging war. And we do so with weapons "that have divine power to demolish strongholds." Here Paul is doubtless thinking of the enormous siege engines built in his own day which enabled the Romans to destroy massive fortresses. If Paul were living today he may well have used imagery relating to the destructive power of WMDs, weapons of mass destruction.

But do observe that the weapons used by Christians are not at all like this world's weapons. These weapons are composed of words, words that "demolish arguments." Words that attack all the human stratagems for suppressing knowledge of God. Words that capture thinking opposed to the lordship of Christ, and that compel obedience to Christ. Words with divine power.

The Word of God always communicated via human words. The Word of God which is living and active and sharper than any double-edged sword or any commando knife. A word with such cutting power that it can slice between joints and the soft, fatty vascular tissue located in the interior cavities of bones.[1] This word slices between soul and spirit. Just as the giant war machines of Paul's day knocked down the walls of a town and left its inhabitants exposed and vulnerable, so the Word of God, the gospel, demolishes human defenses constructed to shut God out. And, having torn down these walls, it exposes and judges the hidden thoughts and intentions and motivation of the heart.[2]

A WAR OVER WORDS

H. G. Wells wrote *The War of the Worlds*, a classic sci-fi story about war between humanity and extra-terrestrial beings. As we will see, this is closer to the truth than many might think. For the new humanity God is creating is at war with evil angelic powers from heavenly realms.

---

1. Hebrews 4:12.
2. Hebrews 4:13.

However, this conflict is not merely the War of the Worlds. It is also the War of the Words.

One of the major strategies employed in war is the laying of mines. For many years after a war we hear of children blown to pieces or living as amputees because they trod on an undiscovered mine. But in the war of words the focus is not upon the minefield, but the mindfield. For it is in the mind that the greatest battle is raging.

Yes, Satan does use persecution in all its forms to attack God's people. However, first he must instill hatred and animosity in the minds of those who will persecute the followers of Christ. And, indeed, his ultimate goal in persecution is not simply to wreak havoc among Christians, but to use persecution to engender fear and emotional and mental instability in order to destroy their faith. So, our spiritual enemies know full well that the mind is the major battlefield.[3] On this field of battle words have explosive and devastating power.

Think back to how this war began. Read Genesis 3 for yourself. The crafty snake, identified as Satan in the New Testament,[4] takes up words spoken by God, asking the woman, "Did God really say, 'You must not eat from any tree in the garden?'" The woman responds by citing God's words, but her Scripture memory is a bit off because she adds words God did not include, namely "and you must not touch it." The snake then tells the woman that God was lying when he said that they would die if they ate the fruit of the tree of the knowledge of good and evil. He tells her that God only said this to prevent them from becoming like him, sharing his knowledge of good and evil.

It is these words that play on Eve's mind and arouse in her the desire to eat the forbidden fruit, leading to the Fall and all the devastation that has followed that fateful decision. Adam was with her at the time, listening to his wife, and following suit. From this point on, people find themselves to be in conflict with God and estranged from him—conditions mirrored in their now complicated relations with each other.

---

3. There is no biblical evidence that Satan can read our minds, though even humans can be highly perceptive in working out what others are thinking. Whatever the abilities of demons may be in this respect we need to heed Moreau's advice: "fill your mind with godly thoughts so completely that they will not *want* to know what you're thinking!" *Essentials*, 155.

4. 2 Corinthians 11:3; Revelation 20:2.

HIS-STORY: OBEYING GOD'S WORD

We have all fallen down the mind-shaft and its slithery walls frustrate any attempt to climb our way out. With Genesis 3 in mind, Paul describes how our estrangement from God inevitably leads to our thinking becoming futile and our foolish hearts being darkened.[5] Such is the depth of our confusion that our attempts to escape our predicament only result in digging ourselves into a deeper hole.

It follows from this that we are reading the Bible upside down if we think it is a moralistic book telling us what we must do to escape our moral plight. Besides, much more has been damaged by the Fall than merely the human ability to distinguish good from evil. The physical world itself has also been damaged. Humans, and other creatures, are not merely the victims of war but also of natural disasters—floods, earthquakes, landslides, hurricanes, tsunamis, deadly diseases, and so on. At times even the natural environment is hostile to human life.

It was human disobedience to God's Word that set all of this disorder in motion. It is human obedience to God's Word that sets it all right. It is as the New Adam that Jesus obediently clings to and cites God's Word in the face of Satan's temptations.[6] So Paul reminds us that "through the disobedience of the one man (Adam) the many were made sinners," while, by contrast, "through the obedience of the one man (Jesus) the many will be made righteous."[7] And, as Paul goes on to explain, when the glory of those who have been declared righteous, "the sons of God," is ultimately revealed, then "the creation itself will be liberated from its bondage to decay and brought into the glorious freedom of the children of God."[8]

Jesus's entire life was a life of obedience, but without doubt Paul was particularly thinking of the central expression of Jesus's obedience on the cross at Calvary. This was the "one act of righteousness" that results in the justification that "brings life for all men," in contrast with "the one trespass" of Adam that brought "condemnation for all men."[9] There are

---

5. Romans 1:21.

6. Luke 4:1–13. See especially verses 4, 8 and 12, noting that this narrative immediately follows on from the genealogical climax that Jesus is "the son of Adam, the son of God" (3:38). Moreau shows how Jesus's response to Satan's temptations illustrates what it means to engage the truth. *Essentials*, 34–40.

7. Romans 5:19.

8. See Romans 8:18–20.

9. Romans 5:18.

a number of reasons why, in order to deal with the problem of evil, it was imperative that the Word become flesh, why the eternal Son of God should become fully man, namely because:

- God is a faithful creator. He created people to image him and he will fulfill his creation purpose.
- In creating people in his image God formed a unique bond between himself and human beings.
- People can only become what they were created to be by being in union with the One they must image.
- The creation of a new humanity that images God involves forming a people who will in due course render perfect obedience to God.
- Such human beings can only come to render perfect obedience by being united with the One they must image.
- Such is the state of fallen human nature that people have estranged themselves from the One they must image and are incapable of seeing him as he is and therefore being like him.
- God must act to reveal himself as he really is (as the One to be imaged) and to unite people to himself.
- But God is perfectly holy and just and will not and cannot unite disobedient people with himself.
- Only a human being who is perfectly obedient can enjoy perfect union with God and image him.
- Since no human is capable of being perfectly obedient, God, in the person of Christ, clothed himself with our humanity.
- Jesus is the Image of God *par excellence*, the New Man, the perfect human being who has rendered perfect obedience to his Father as one who was not merely fully God but also, more pointedly, as one who was fully human and yet in perfect union with God.
- Jesus now acts as mediator between God and humanity. People who are united with Christ are united with God through him.

In particular, Jesus's act of obedience on the cross, for all united with him, results in complete forgiveness for all sins—past, present and future—while also initiating the process by which all such humans are transformed into the image and likeness of God.

The resurrection of Jesus from the dead also results in a radical difference between two representatives of humanity—"the first man Adam . . . a living being" and Jesus as "the last Adam, a life-giving spirit." That is, as our resurrected Lord, Jesus now indwells his people in the person of the Holy Spirit and thus empowers us, so that "as we have borne the likeness of the earthly man, so shall we bear the likeness of the man from heaven."[10]

As Watkin points out, modernity is informed by four disastrous prejudices concerning the nature of ultimate reality, namely that it is: ahistorical, universal, abstract, impersonal.[11] This way of looking at reality, among other things, necessarily fails to come to grips with evil which is very much an historical, particular, non-abstract, and highly personal phenomenon. Notably, the incarnation in addressing the problem of evil evinces all four of these features, each of them a scandal for those who worship the truth-replacing idol of modernity.

A biblical understanding of what is involved in countering the world, the flesh, and the devil must place at the very center Jesus's supreme and decisive act of obedience on the cross. In the Garden of Gethsemane Jesus exhorted his disciples, saying, "Pray that you will not fall into temptation (testing)." Then he himself prayed, "Father, if you are willing, take this cup from me; yet not my will, but yours be done." In context, then, we see Jesus himself facing the severest time of temptation or testing he had ever experienced. Significantly, while he was in a state of anguish, "he prayed more earnestly, and his sweat was like great drops of blood falling to the ground."[12]

Jesus was waging war on his knees while his disciples slept. It is Jesus's perfect obedience to God's Word and his continuing work as the only mediator between God and humanity that protects and empowers God's people in all our weakness.

WORDS THAT TERRIFY

God never gave up on humanity. He promised Abraham that his descendants would become a great nation. In the first instance that great Abrahamic nation is to be identified with Old Testament Israel and those

---

10. See 1 Corinthians 15:45–49.
11. Watkin, *Biblical Critical Thinking*, 345–46.
12. See Luke 22:39–46.

relatively few non-Jewish people like Rahab and Ruth who were incorporated into the nation. God made a covenant, a special pact with Israel and at its heart this involved what people have dubbed "the Ten Commandments." But in the Old Testament itself they are simply called "the Ten Words."

These Ten Words were heard by Israel at Mount Sinai. Early in the book of Numbers we are told there were over 600,000 Israelite men counted by Moses. Something extraordinary and utterly unique in history happened at Sinai, quite apart from all the dramatic phenomena that accompanied God's self-revelation. What I am referring to is this—God spoke audibly and directly to an entire nation. Somewhere in the order of two and a half million people heard God, the creator of the universe, speak to them.[13]

They were already frightened by the thunder and lightning, the presence of a thick ominous cloud over the mountain and the sound as of a very loud trumpet blast. We are told, understandably enough, "Everyone in the camp trembled." But it then became even scarier. Next the entire mountain "was covered with smoke, because the LORD descended on it in fire." Then the mountain itself shook violently and the trumpet sound grew louder and louder. If the people were trembling before this, imagine how terrified they would have been at this point. Could it be even more frightening than this? Well, yes, it could and it was. For then comes the grand climax. What comes next utterly scares them out of their wits.

We simply read, "Then Moses spoke and the voice of God answered him." That's it! But if you had been there at the time then you too would have shaken in your shoes to hear the voice of the living God, the creator of the universe, the one who simply said, "Let there be light" and there was light.

Winner of *The Voice Australia 2015* competition was 16-year-old Ellie Drennan, singing Sinead O'Connor's *Nothing Compares To You* in the finale. But there is no voice in the universe that can begin to compete with the voice of God. The psalmist speaks of the voice of the Lord splitting cedar trees and stripping forests and shaking the desert.[14] When God

---

13. Scholars debate the numbers and especially the sense of the Hebrew word translated as "thousand." However, at this point in history, scholarly research has not necessitated a revision of these figures which continue to be adopted in almost all modern English translations. Whatever, it remains true that at Sinai God directly addressed an entire nation of people at one and the same time.

14. See Psalm 29.

spoke at Mount Sinai the people of Israel were in the presence of one with whom nothing and nobody compares.

Afterwards, those deeply frightened people came to Moses and spoke plainly to him:

> This great fire will consume us, and we will die if we hear the voice of the LORD our God any longer. For what mortal man has ever heard the voice of the living God speaking out of fire, as we have, and survived"? (Deuteronomy 5:25–26)

So, they tell Moses that from this point on he needs to be the one who alone hears God speak.

The subordination of terrifying phenomena to the Word of God should serve as a warning against those who place undue emphasis on so called miraculous "power encounters."[15] The supreme source of power lies in the immense authority of God's Word. So, when our risen Lord declared that all authority in heaven and on earth had been given to him, he immediately shows that the power this represents is not channeled through signs and wonders but through teaching disciples all that Jesus has commanded.[16]

HATED WORDS

Satan cannot speak words that have creative power. He cannot utter any words that have anything like commensurate power. But he will do everything he possibly can to oppose, undermine, distort, and prevent the verbal communication of the gospel, the news concerning what God has done in history in and through Jesus to accomplish his kingly purposes.

There was the time when Paul and Barnabas were on the island of Paphos. The proconsul sent for them because he wanted to hear "the word

---

15. Kraft discriminates between truth, allegiance, and power encounters. He reasons, "Knowledge . . . is the appropriate antidote for ignorance and / or error. Spiritual power is what is needed when the problem is satanic captivity, harassment or temptation. Allegiance / commitment to Jesus Christ, then, is what is needed to replace any other allegiance that a person has made primary in their life." Kraft, "Allegiance, Truth and Power." However, the Sinai context involves all three of these dimensions occurring simultaneously. This is a truth encounter which is the ultimate power encounter and which at the same time demands ultimate allegiance from the hearers.

16. Matthew 28:18–20. It was John Wimber in particular who influenced many to hold an unbalanced view of the role of miracles in advancing the kingdom of God. God does indeed use signs and wonders but we must never forget that the primary locus of power and authority is vested in his Word.

of God," that is, the gospel. But he had an attendant, a Jewish sorcerer and false prophet named Elymas who "opposed them and tried to turn the proconsul from the faith."[17] Paul, filled with the Holy Spirit, told Elymas to his face that he was "a child of the devil and an enemy of everything that is right," telling him that he was "full of all kinds of deceit and trickery." He then told Elymas that God was going to strike him blind, and so it happened.

Elymas illustrates satanic opposition to the gospel. Paul knew the power of the creator of the universe is vested in the gospel message—a power to save people from eternal disaster.[18]

WORDS THAT SAVE

But, from a human standpoint, the expression and outworking of this power is strange and not at all obvious. Paul recognizes, "The message of the cross is foolishness to those who are perishing, but to us who are being saved it is the power of God."[19] So convinced of this is Paul that he makes this the main focus of his ministry. This causes him to point out to the Corinthian Christians that he had not personally performed many baptisms because "Christ did not send me to baptize, but to preach the gospel—not with words of human wisdom, lest the cross of Christ be emptied of its power."[20]

When the gospel is faithfully proclaimed then words of immense power to transform lives are being spoken. This is so because these are words of divine wisdom. The death of Christ makes absolutely no sense to anybody unless the Lord switches on the light inside their darkened hearts.

We should not be surprised that so many reject the gospel message. In no way should we conclude from this that the gospel lacks power. All of us who know the Lord and have seen the way in which he has transformed our lives and those of other Christians know there is only one explanation to give for this—the power of the gospel.

17. Acts 13:8.
18. Romans 1:16.
19. 1 Corinthians 1:18.
20. 1 Corinthians 1:17.

WORDS THAT DON'T SAVE ALL

In the book of Isaiah we read:

> As the rain and the snow come down from heaven, and do not return to it without watering the earth and making it bud and flourish, so that it yields seed for the sower and bread for the eater, so is my word that goes out from my mouth: It will not return to me empty, but will accomplish what I desire and achieve the purpose for which I sent it" (Isaiah 55:10–11).

If God's word always succeeds in its purpose then why don't all people believe when they hear the gospel? Isn't this proof that the gospel lacks power and efficacy?

There are three things that we can say about this:

- The exercise of God's power is not hey presto. It's not magic. Yes, God's call is irresistible. But God does not make light of our own responsibility in the matter. It is not a simple matter of reprogramming the computer. People are not automatons. The proclamation of the gospel is accompanied with the exhortation to repent.[21] In response to the hearing of the gospel we have a responsibility to acknowledge there is something fundamentally wrong in our lives; that we have seriously violated our relationship with God; that from here on we need to live lives that please and honor God. The reality is that most people are not willing to respond in this way and place their lives in the Lord's hands.

- God's Word does infallibly accomplish its purpose, even when people spurn or ignore what they are told in the gospel communication. It is a sobering reality that it is not God's intent to have mercy on all. That's what Paul communicates in Romans 9 when he says, for example, "God has mercy on whom he wants to have mercy, and he hardens whom he wants to harden."

Many Christians, let alone unbelievers, have difficulty with this clear teaching. Yes, it is perfectly true that God does not want anyone to perish.[22] Indeed, although God is filled with indignation at every instance of evil that occurs on earth, he restrains himself from intervening to end all evil, because he is continuing to give people opportunity to repent, to

---

21. For example, Acts 2:37–38.
22. 2 Peter 3:9.

get their relationship with him and their lives in order. But there is also the matter of justice.

JUSTICE AND ELECTION

Justice? Well, yes. This is precisely Paul's point as he reviews history and observes that God does not choose everyone to be his people. Significantly, in the light of our current discussion, Paul introduces this theme by saying, "It is not as though God's word had failed. For not all who are descended from Israel are Israel. Nor because they are his descendants are they all Abraham's children" (Romans 9:6–7).

JUSTICE AND MERCY

Paul continues in this vein, noting how God chooses some but not others. What is the natural human response to all this? We all know what it is: "It's not fair." And it is precisely this response that Paul repudiates: "What then shall we say? Is God unjust? Not at all! For he says to Moses, 'I will have mercy on whom I have mercy, and I will have compassion on whom I have compassion.' It does not, therefore, depend on man's desire or effort, but on God's mercy" (Romans 9:14–16).

JUSTICE AND DESERVING

Those who respond, "It's not fair" have a fundamental misunderstanding concerning the interplay of justice and mercy. When people say this they betray the fact that they are assuming people deserve to be granted admittance into God's eternal kingdom and spared eternal punishment. "Why did you choose him and not me? I deserve to be chosen just as much as him!" But that's Paul's essential point. Justice is only preserved if God's exercise of mercy does not depend on "man's desire or effort," that is, only if people are undeserving. Justice is scuttled if God is obligated to have mercy on everyone. But the previous sentence is a nonsense sentence anyway. It's a contradiction in terms to speak of being obligated to have mercy.

JUSTICE AND JUDGMENT

I remember a time when my late wife and I were praying about the plight of Christians who were being tortured and butchered for their faith, often in horrific ways. The prayer guide we were using asked us to pray for all their persecutors, that they would be brought to repentance and forgiveness.

It may shock some Christians to hear this, but I have a problem with that. I can't pray that way, nor do I think I should. To begin with, I don't have the faith to pray such a prayer. That is, I don't believe for a moment God would answer such a prayer. Oh, but don't I just need to have more "faith"? Should I shut my eyes tight, clench my fists and screw myself up to believe what my reason tells me is nonsense?

No! Besides, faith is faith in God. Praying with faith is praying in a way that reflects my knowledge of who God is. And I know God is a God of justice. His justice demands that such persecutors be punished for the terrible atrocities they commit. But what I do pray is that in the midst of justice he will show mercy. So, I don't pray that all those who persecute will be saved, as the prayer guide was asking me to do. In the early church there were many who persecuted Christians, but we don't hear of many of them turning to Christ. But God in his mercy did lay his hand on Paul who was among the foremost of the church's persecutors. I pray that among all those who persecute Christians there will be some upon whom the Lord lays his saving hand. Justice and mercy—it is so important to get the balance right.

JUSTICE AND GRACE

As I said, in considering the relationship between justice and mercy we are dealing with a very sober and, indeed, rightly disturbing reality. The early chapters of Romans labor the point that every single one of us deserves to be eternally punished and separated from God and his kingdom without hope of reprieve. In fact, if only we could see ourselves as God sees us, it would be utterly amazing if God chose to have mercy on even one human being. And, given that we all deserve eternal punishment we would not have any right to complain if God did choose to rescue only one person from the sinking ship of fallen humanity. But we are assured that in the glorious new kingdom there will be a vast multitude, beyond numbering, of people whom God will have rescued from every nation, tribe, people, and language. That's grace, amazing grace!

THE GOSPEL AND PERSONAL RESPONSE

But don't get yourself tied up in knots about whether God has chosen you or not. God doesn't want you to perish. His grace is held out to you. So, the ball is in your court. Simply accept that Jesus did indeed rise from the dead and now is Lord. Ask him to forgive you for all the ways you have wronged him. Surrender your life to him. If you genuinely respond in this way then you have just confirmed that God has indeed chosen you. Only the power of the gospel can create such faith in you and lead you to make such a profound commitment.

THE GOSPEL AND TWO TYPES OF PEOPLE

So, the gospel does have immense power, but it is a scary power. As Paul thinks about this ministry of proclaiming the gospel he thanks God "who always leads us in triumphal procession in Christ."[23] His very next thought is that to preach the gospel is actually to tell people about how wonderful Jesus is. So, he continues: "and through us spreads the fragrance of the knowledge of him." But, still remembering that he is marching in a victory parade he observes, "For we are to God the aroma of Christ among those who are being saved and those who are perishing."

Whoa! We've met that phrase before—"those who are being saved and those who are perishing." There are two types of people in our world. Those whom God is drawing to himself and those whom he is not. Paul, still thinking about the impact of his ministry of proclaiming Christ, concludes: "To one we are the smell of death, to the other, the fragrance of life. And who is equal to such a task?"

Get the point? When we tell people about Jesus—the "task"—we are being used as instruments through whom God saves people. But the message we proclaim also is used by God to seal the fate of those who think the Christian message stinks. So, God's Word always works powerfully to accomplish God's purpose.

---

23. 2 Corinthians 2:14.

THE SAVING POWER OF GOD'S WORD OFTEN INVOLVES A PROCESS

When we don't see people being converted by our communication of the gospel we need to recognize the process of which Paul speaks—"those who are being saved."[24] Think of how these words apply to those who are yet to acknowledge Jesus as their Lord. Such a response to gospel truth doesn't usually happen in one hit. For most people it is a case of hearing the gospel, perhaps in bits and pieces, over a period of time before it sinks in. Our own attempts to communicate the gospel are often but links in the chain.

A last point to add to the above is that when we don't see people converted by our sharing of Christ it reminds us of a core fact: that the gospel is the power of salvation, not us.

Jesus is at God's right hand. He is victorious. He is ruling. Whatever may be the contrary appearances we are marching in his triumphal procession and we are speaking out words that have immense power, words that will be used to save and transform the lives of countless numbers of people. We have an enemy who will do all he can to neutralize the power of those words. We are indeed locked in battle in the war of the words.

MISSION DEBRIEF

- **The Ultimate Weapon.** Christians wield a weapon of incomparable power—God's Word.

- **God's Word and Human Defenses.** God's Word has the power to break down all human defenses designed to keep him out.

- **The MINDfield.** Satanic opposition, in seeking to deflect the otherwise irresistible power of God's Word, concentrates its attacks, as it has always done, on the human mind.

- **Jesus's Perfect Obedience.** Jesus's act of obedience to God's Word as the perfect man, supremely on the cross, is central to God's work of setting things right.

---

24. This phrase involves the understanding that God's work of salvation continues in the lives of those who have already come under the lordship of Christ, even though "there is no condemnation for those who are in Christ Jesus" (Rom 8:1). The phrase also describes God's work in those he is bringing to the point when they will acknowledge Jesus as their Lord.

- **Frightening Communication.** An entire nation, the Israelites, were terrified to hear God's voice address them audibly, when he gave them the Ten Words.
- **Effective Power.** It often appears that Satanic opposition to and human resistance to our communication of the gospel is a denial of its irresistible power. But this is not so. The gospel is not magic; it does infallibly accomplish God's purpose, whether in effecting salvation or destruction; its impact is often realized gradually rather than instantly; and saving power is not vested in us and our efforts, but in the gospel itself.

GATHERING INTELLIGENCE

Read Acts 13:44–52

1. How and why did Jewish hearers express their hostility towards the Word of God communicated by Paul?
2. What reason is given for the positive response to God's Word on the part of Gentile hearers?
3. Did the hostility of Jewish opponents and their success in effecting the expulsion of Paul and Barnabas indicate God's Word was lacking in power? Explain your answer.

[NB. There is no hint of anti-Semitism here. Remember that Paul and Barnabas and the vast majority of believers at this time were themselves Jewish.]

Chapter Three

Facing Inhuman Enemies

"It is perilous to study too deeply the arts of the Enemy, for good or for ill."
GANDALF THE GREY (J. R. R. TOLKIEN, *LORD OF THE RINGS*).

CHRISTIANS ARE AT WAR. It is horrific. Far more so than the wars that shed rivers of blood on human soil. God sent us his own Son whose own blood soaked into the earth beneath a hideous cross. Yet he rose from death, the ultimate warrior possessing incomparable might. We, as soldiers in his army, have also been given a weapon to use which is of immense, matchless power. Humans, for all their scientific genius and enterprise, will never be able to produce a weapon that is of compatible power. That weapon is the Word of God, the gospel, the message about Jesus—who he is, what he has done and what he means for our lives and indeed the whole creation here, and now, and forevermore.

But who are we fighting? Who is the enemy?

EXTRA-TERRESTRIAL INVADERS

Paul identifies one of our main enemies as he rounds off what he has been saying in his letter to the Ephesians: "For our struggle is not against flesh and blood, but against the rulers, against the authorities, against the powers of this dark world and against the spiritual forces of evil in the heavenly realms" (Ephesians 6:12). He goes on to urge Christians to "take up the shield of faith, with which you can extinguish all the flaming arrows of the evil one."

The "evil one" is none other than Satan and "the spiritual forces of evil" are the demonic forces led by Satan.[1] Some influential theologians have pooh-poohed belief in such beings. So, Friedrich Schleiermacher treated the doctrine of angels as a childish belief. He opined that the doctrine of the devil was "so unstable that we cannot expect anyone to be convinced of its truth." Believing God himself to be the cause of evil, he treated Satan and demons as but personifications of evil thoughts opposed to the good.[2] He further thought that the teaching of Jesus and the apostles concerning Satan and demons was a matter of accommodating popular beliefs of the time. Similarly, David Strauss insisted, "If the modern idea of God and conception of the world are right, there cannot possibly be beings of this kind."[3]

By contrast, the Bible treats such beings as very real personalities.[4] The Pharisees called Satan "the prince of demons."[5] It is such demons who are the "rulers," the "authorities," the "powers of this dark world" of which Paul is speaking. Paul calls Satan "the god of this age."[6] Jesus called him "the prince of this world."[7] Whether people realize it or not,

---

1. As a warning against overstating the role of Satan and demons it should be noted that in the Old Testament neither Satan nor demons receive significant mention. In the Old Testament "satan" is typically a human adversary (1 Sam 29:4; 2 Sam 19:23; 1 Kgs 5:4, 11:14, 23, 25; Ps 109:6). Notably, at one point the angel of the Lord becomes a "satan," an adversary (Num 22:22). It is at 1 Chronicles 21:1, Job 1–2 and Zechariah 3:1–2 that we start to develop a picture of a celestial adversary of God's people.

2. Hendrikus Berkhof stated, "One can even doubt whether Paul conceived of the Powers as personal beings. In any case this aspect is so secondary that it makes little difference whether he did or not. He may be using personifications." Cited by MacDonald, "Personal or Impersonal," 1.

3. See Allison, "You Asked."

4. It is extremely difficult to succinctly summarize what Karl Barth has in mind when he speaks of demons. His concept of evil is inextricably linked with his notion of *Das Nichtige*, inadequately translated as "nothingness." In refusing to see them as fallen angels and rather viewing them as the necessary expression and outworking of *das Nichtige*, emerging from God's "No!," Barth never unequivocally treats them as having personal intent as free rational beings. See Smith, "Church Militant," 161, 174–84.

5. For example, Matthew 9:34.

6. 2 Corinthians 4:4.

7. John 12:31; 14:30; 16:11.

all people outside of Christ follow the ways of this world and so follow and do the will of the devil, "the ruler of the kingdom of the air, the spirit who is now at work in those who are disobedient."[8]

Attend a church at random on a Sunday and there's a good chance you will find yourself praying the familiar "Lord's Prayer." You start with "Our Father in heaven" and you end with "deliver us from the evil one."[9] Well, that's how it is translated in many Bible translations. But you will find some translations that have "deliver us from evil" and that's often how we are taught to say it in church. However, it is highly probable that Jesus was teaching us, as his disciples, to pray for rescue from Satan. In Matthew's Gospel this prayer is fused to the words "And lead us not into temptation." The last time we came across "temptation" in this Gospel it concerned Jesus being tempted by Satan, not by abstract evil. Clearly, as Jesus's prayer makes plain, Jesus saw this evil angelic being as a very real threat to the wellbeing of his followers.

In 2016 China completed the construction of the world's largest telescope, eclipsing the Arecibo telescope in Puerto Rico. At an estimated cost of $US185m, the dish, located in SW China, is 500 metres wide, the size of thirty football fields. This telescope will map the distribution of hydrogen in our galaxy and beyond and may enable the detection of gravitational waves. But Peng Bo, the director of the NAO Radio Astronomy Technology Laboratory, speaks of the telescope's greatly enhanced ability to discover alien life in outer space and it is this possibility that excited particular interest.[10]

It is ironic when those who are convinced that there are extra-terrestrial beings elsewhere in the universe scoff or belittle the biblical portrayal of spiritual beings as the stuff of myth and legend. Science fiction movies imagine wars with alien beings and invasion of our planet by vastly more powerful extra-terrestrial beings. But the Bible teaches that the stuff of sci-fi imagination is in fact sober reality. Earth has been invaded to the point that Satan is described as "the god of this age," such is his hidden power over the lives of all who do not know the true and living God and bow the knee before our Lord Jesus.

---

8. Ephesians 2:2. Ancients thought of the air as the dwelling place of evil spirits. So Beliar is called "an aerial spirit" (*Testament of Benjamin* 3:4). There are also magical texts that protect people from "every demon in the air" by calling on "the one who is in charge of the air." See Boyd, *God at War*, 274.

9. Matthew 6:9–13.

10. See Hunt, "China's Giant Space Telescope."

As Moreau points out, hidden assumptions concerning the purported activity of spirits inform the thinking and behavior of Christians at opposite ends of the spectrum. Those who downplay such activity, the secular-minded, assume, "If I did not personally see it, it should be questioned." By contrast, those who take such activity seriously, the spiritistic, presuppose, "If someone reliable says it happened, it must be true." The secular-minded believer assumes spirits now operate differently than in biblical times, whereas the spiritist sees no change. Local explanations of spirit activity in spiritistic societies are regarded as being fundamentally flawed by secular-minded Christians but as fundamentally correct by spiritistic Christians. Psychosocial explanations trump spiritual explanations in the minds of secularistic believers, while the reverse is the case for spiritistic believers.[11]

Clinton Arnold helpfully points out, "The cloistered existence of the Western university tends to isolate Western academics from the realities that many Third World people experience on a regular basis."[12]

We do need to avoid not only being over-cynical but also being overly credulous. But make no mistake about it, evil spirits are for real.

THE PROMISE OF VICTORY

Satan's first appearance in the Bible is in the third chapter of Genesis in the guise of a snake. The most extensive reference to Satan in the Old Testament is in Job 1, which some regard as the oldest.[13] There Satan seeks to put God on trial and to effect the destruction of Job.[14] The Bible does not present any clear and indisputable information as to how Satan came to make himself God's enemy.[15] As is so often the case, where the

---

11. This is derived from a PowerPoint presentation which Scott Moreau graciously gave to me at a Brisbane School of Theology Conference ("Not Against Flesh and Blood. The Christian and the Powers") on July 28, 2018.
12. Arnold, *Powers of Darkness*, 181.
13. See Boyd, *God at War*, 144.
14. Boyd, *God at War*, 147.
15. Isaiah 14:1–23 and Ezekiel 28 are passages often believed to refer to the initial fall of Satan. This is speculative though Boyd finds some credence in such views, see *God at War*, 157–62. The fall of Satan is necessarily presupposed in that "the heavens" of Genesis 1:1 include the realm of God and angels and the original creation is "very good." One spurious view is that of Wink who maintained that Satan's fall did not occur in time but in the human psyche (Smith, "Church Militant," 210). There are also those who read Genesis 3 as simultaneously involving the fall of Satan.

Bible is silent speculation is rife. Cyprian supposed that it was "jealousy and malevolent envy" that caused Satan to rebel against God, aroused at the sight of human beings being created in God's image.[16]

The battle lines were first drawn at the time our first parents heeded the voice of the snake, that is, Satan. God told the snake that from that time on he would put enmity between him and the woman.[17] He adds that there will also be enmity between the offspring or seed of the snake and the offspring of the woman. But this will culminate in the offspring of the woman crushing the head of Satan, though Satan will strike the heel of the woman's offspring.

A HUMAN VICTOR

This is an extraordinary promise to make so early in the Bible. It is saying that a human being, someone descended from Eve, will be the one who utterly and conclusively defeats and destroys Satan, even though bitten by the snake.

Remember that God created people to rule over what he had created. The reason Satan is presented in Genesis 3 as a snake is because this illustrates two things. One, it shows how drastically human identity, as those created in God's image, has been damaged. For now, instead of human beings serving their creator by ruling over creatures, they are effectively under the thumb of a creature. In a passage that alludes to the Genesis 3 story at many levels, Paul reflects that all people, not merely Gentiles, have "exchanged the truth about God for a lie and worshiped and served the creature rather than the creator, who is blessed forever. Amen."[18]

But the Fall, as the sin of our first parents is often called, did not take God by surprise. God created people in his image and likeness and his creation purpose cannot be thwarted. So central to the biblical story is God's work of creating a new humanity.

We need to understand that all of us entertain thoughts, utter words, and engage in behavior that radically dehumanizes us. This is the inevitable consequence of refusing to live lives that image God, bearing and reflecting his likeness. For it is only when we live as those created

---

16. See Allison, *You Asked*.

17. Genesis 3:15.

18. Romans 1:25. I've used here the ESV translation because "creature" is to be preferred to the NIV rendering "created things."

in God's image that we are authentically human. Our suppression of the knowledge of God dehumanizes us. Restoration of the image is the ultimate work of humanization. Involved in this grand restoration of human dignity is our need to regain mastery over other creatures. This includes mastery over Satan.

JESUS, THE HUMAN VICTOR

In his Gospel, Luke has his own slant on the significance of the time when Satan tempted Jesus in the wilderness. When Matthew tells this story he is primarily comparing Satan's testing of Jesus with the way the nation of Israel was tested in the desert during their forty years of wandering.[19] In Matthew's Gospel Jesus is the embodiment of all that Israel, God's people, should be.

Immediately before Luke tells this same story he presents us with a genealogy which shows that ultimately Jesus is "the son of Adam, the son of God."[20] This means that when we read Luke's version of the testing of Jesus by Satan we are being encouraged to see Jesus as the embodiment of all that Adam should have been and, therefore, as the representative and head of a new humanity. To the extent that Luke, like Matthew, echoes the testing of Israel in the desert it is with the implication that Israel was called to be the new humanity and that this destiny is fulfilled in their Messiah, the Christ. Jesus is "the image of the invisible God,"[21] and his victory over Satan is proof positive of this.

DIVIDED ALLEGIANCES

The New Testament certainly understands that Jesus is that promised descendant of Eve and that it is he who has defeated Satan and will ultimately and completely destroy him. However, although "the offspring of the woman" is particularly fulfilled in Jesus, it is not exclusively fulfilled by him. Take stock of what Paul says, as he closes his great letter to the Romans, "The God of peace will soon crush Satan under your feet."[22]

---

19. Matthew 4:1–11 compare Deuteronomy 8:25.
20. Luke 3:38.
21. Colossians 1:15.
22. Romans 16:20.

Here Paul is plainly recalling the promise made in Genesis 3. But now he is identifying Christians in general with the offspring of the woman.

Paul is not the only one to do this. In his first letter the Apostle John, having exhorted Christians to love one another, warns: "Do not be like Cain, who belonged to the evil one and murdered his brother."[23] John considered Cain to be an example of the offspring of the snake and, therefore, implicitly viewed Abel as the offspring of the woman.

When Jesus called his religious opponents a "brood of vipers" he may well have been implying that they were the seed of the snake.[24] On one occasion Jesus did not pull any punches, telling them: "You belong to your father, the devil, and you want to carry out your father's desires. He was a murderer from the beginning, not holding to the truth, for there is no truth in him. When he lies, he speaks his native language, for he is a liar and the father of lies" (John 8:44).

The book of Esther is an unusual book because God is not mentioned in it. However, it presupposes the wonderful providence of God. At the other end of the scale, there is no mention of Satan when Cain killed Abel, but this account follows on from God's declaration that there will be enmity between the snake and the woman. John therefore drew the right conclusion in saying that Cain murdered his brother because he (Cain) belonged to the evil one. Jesus too points us back to this event when he states that Satan "was a murderer from the beginning." So, when he tells his opponents that the devil is their father he was probably alluding to those embryonic words concerning the conflict between Satan and the seed of the woman.

Paul does say we are not contending against flesh and blood but against demonic forces. But, of course, he says this precisely because it seems as though it is flesh and blood, people like ourselves, who are the enemy. In so many societies, it is people, in their ignorance and hatred, who discriminate against God's people in education and the work-place, dispossess them of their property, bring false accusations against them, imprison them unjustly, torture and kill them. It is people who introduce seductive yet destructive ideas in churches and cause immense damage to Christian lives and communities.

---

23. 1 John 3:12.
24. For example, Matthew 3:7; 12:34.

THE PUPPET-MASTER

Yes, people are responsible for what they think, say, and do and will be held to account on the Day of Judgment. But when Christians experience opposition there is a very real sense in which the strings are being pulled by Satan. For it is he who "has blinded the minds of unbelievers, so that they cannot see the light of the gospel of the glory of Christ, who is the image of God."[25] Arnold makes an important point here: "Even in Christian ministry the spiritual dimension is often ignored. Ineffective evangelism, for example, is often attributed to a lack of training or persuasive skill rather than powerful demonic hindrance."[26]

Paul warns the Corinthian Christians that they seem gullible enough to accept the teaching of someone who preaches a different Jesus than the one presented in the apostolic gospel. But his fear is "that just as Eve was deceived by the serpent's cunning, your minds may somehow be led astray from your sincere and pure devotion to Christ" (2 Corinthians 11:4).

A TARGETED PEOPLE

Jesus foresaw the dire relational consequences of following him when he told his disciples: "Do not suppose that I have come to bring peace to the earth. I did not come to bring peace, but a sword. For I have come to turn a man against his father, a daughter against her mother, a daughter-in-law against her mother-in-law—a man's enemies will be the members of his own household" (Matthew 10:34–36).

Time and again, in place after place around the world, those who decide to follow Jesus are told they have brought shame to their families. They are often tossed out of their families and told never to return. A woman may be locked in a room and left to live the rest of her life in solitary confinement unless she renounces her faith. It is common for family members to be beaten and sometimes they are even killed by their own flesh and blood.

In collective societies identity is very much tied up with meeting the norms and expectations of the group or community. A whole community can turn against the new believer. An Algerian friend told me what happened after he gave his life to Christ. He was chased through

---

25. 2 Corinthians 4:4.
26. *Powers of Darkness*, 148.

the marketplace by his best friend who was wielding a hatchet with full intent to kill him.

It is people, "flesh and blood," who persecute Christians in these ways and demand that they renounce their faith, often resorting to cruel and brutal ways of bringing this about. But with such persecution in mind, Peter exhorts: "Be sober-minded; be watchful. Your adversary the devil prowls around like a roaring lion, seeking someone to devour. Resist him, firm in your faith, knowing that the same kinds of suffering are being experienced by your brotherhood throughout the world. And after you have suffered a little while, the God of all grace, who has called you to his eternal glory in Christ, will himself restore, confirm, strengthen, and establish you. To him be the dominion forever and ever. Amen" (1 Peter 5:8–11).

Yes, it is people who persecute the saints, but, when we boil it all down, we must remember that the real enemy is Satan who is seeking to use the opposition of family members and others to undermine and destroy our faith.

SATANIC POLITICS

This also pertains to persecution led by the State and other governing authorities.[27] In the book of Revelation, John, following Daniel 7, casts blasphemous anti-God human authorities as an evil beast that wages war on the saints.[28] In fact, the book of Daniel has more to say about what really lies behind political events that threaten the wellbeing of God's people.

Daniel 10 is a most instructive chapter. It begins with God imparting a revelation to Daniel that "concerned a great war." The effect of this revelatory vision is to cause Daniel to mourn for three weeks. This is consistent with a major theme in the book of Daniel: a disturbing look into

---

27. This *personal* linkage of the demonic with political realities is at odds with Wink's flawed assumption: "As long as these Powers were thought of personalistically . . . reduced to the categories of individualism . . . belief in the demonic had no political categories. But once we recognize that these spiritual forces are the interiority of earthly institutions or structures or systems, then the social dimension of the gospel becomes immediately evident." Cited by MacDonald, "Personal or Impersonal," 1. Wink's de-personalization of demons creates the opposite error, that of confusing the demonic with such political structures and systems. It also involves the objectionable notion that "although they may be evil, they can nevertheless be redeemed and transformed." Ferdinando, *Message of Spiritual Warfare*, 5.

28. Revelation 13.

the future that involves terrible suffering for God's people. So it is in this case. Daniel is given a window into the future and it fills him with dread and grief.

Daniel was living at a pivotal point in history. God's people had already experienced immense suffering. Not only the city of Jerusalem but even the temple of God had been destroyed and they, God's people—those not butchered by the Babylonians—had been made exiles from their own land, forced to live in the land of Babylon where they were mocked and scorned for their religion. But now, as God had promised through Jeremiah, God's people were going to go back to their land to rebuild their city and temple. Daniel, however, sees that much as he and his people may wish it to be otherwise, even more terrible suffering for God's people lies around the corner of history. In the book of Daniel there is particular anticipation of the horrific blasphemy and atrocities to be perpetrated by Antiochus IV Epiphanes in the period centering on AD 164. But Daniel's vision of God's people experiencing terrible future sufferings involves the rest of history, right through to the time when all authority will be given to "the one like a son of man" and "the saints," God's people, whom he represents.[29]

In Daniel 10 Daniel has an amazing visionary experience in which he sees the central combatant in the great war. This person is so glorious that Daniel loses all strength, turns deathly pale and is rendered utterly helpless. The language used to describe this person is very similar to that used in Ezekiel 1 and evidently describes the Lord himself.

The bringing of this vision, we are informed, is delayed for twenty-one days precisely because this person has himself been delayed for twenty-one days. This plainly corresponds to the three weeks of Daniel's mourning. This delay occurs because in a conflict waged between angelic beings this glorious one was resisted by the so-called "prince of the Persian kingdom."[30] But the Lord is now able to come and appear to Daniel in this vision because the archangel Michael, "the great prince who protects [Daniel's] people," has taken his place in contending against the angelic being who, we can surmise, is seeking to make sure Persian

---

29. Daniel 7:13–14.

30. It goes beyond the text to conclude that the "prince of Persia" was an angel assigned by God to Persia but who has now become demonized, *contra* Boyd, *God at War*, 137. We should also note a line of interpretation that argues the prince of Persia and the prince of Greece are human. See Priest, et al., "Missiological Syncretism," 73

political policy will not permit the Israelites to return to their land and rebuild Jerusalem and the temple.

Given the limitless disparity between the Lord's power and that of demonic angelic powers we should not think that this passage is implying that demonic forces have the ability to match the Lord's strength. At most the passage as it stands suggests that God's will allows for the persistence of evil angelic powers. The very fact that the passage goes on to confidently foretell the future in precise terms clearly implies the absolute sovereignty of God.

But we are being encouraged to see this conflict between angelic princes or authorities as a very real ongoing war. At this point in history the nations of most relevance to Israel's immediate future, its resettlement and reconstruction, were Persia and Greece. Clearly, there were evil angelic powers trying to make sure that these nations would act against the interests of God's people.

TERRITORIAL SPIRITS?

In ancient times, people were polytheists, worshiping many gods. Each city-state or nation had a specific deity for protection. For instance, the moon god Sin protected Ur, Abraham's city, and Marduk was Babylon's deity.[31] Some believe Daniel 10 substitutes these protective deities with guardian angels for nations.[32] Certain Christians attempt to identify and combat territorial spirits by declaring the victory of Christ. In the 1980s, groups like Lydia Fellowship supported practices such as "breaking ley-lines," "taking the high places," and "prayer marches" to combat these spirits.[33] The March for Jesus Movement also accepted this view.[34]

---

31. Other tutelary deities include Ishtar (Nineveh), Nekhbet (Nekheb, Upper Egypt), Wadjet (Buto, Lower Egypt), and Melqart (Tyre).

32. Deuteronomy 32:9 is sometimes read as indicating that each nation has an angelic power assigned to it. This is a speculative conclusion and is not clearly demanded by what the text itself says. See, for example, Boyd, *God at War,* 134.

33. See Taylor, "The cutting edge." Though not focused on a particular spirit, the late medieval processions that churches conducted on Rogation Day bears some affinity with such practices. Such processions, involving handbells, banners, and the parish cross, "beat the bounds" of the parish, seeking "to drive out of the community the evil spirits who created division between neighbors and sickness in man and beast." Smith, "Church Militant," 39.

34. Charismatic songwriter for the March for Jesus, Graham Kendrick, saw spiritual warfare, understood as combatting territorial spirits, as a major aim of the March. Smith cites Kendrick: "Satan has the real estate of villages, towns and cities overshadowed by

Although there is a gift for distinguishing between God's Spirit and evil spirits, identifying territorial spirits is a highly dubious practice.[35]

Lowe observes that "the exorcism of territorial spirits is a growing practice around the globe, including among evangelicals in America." He recalls Christians traveling to a foreign city where they aggressively prayed, naming and binding demons that they believed ruled over particular areas of the city so as to enable powerful gospel ministry.[36]

"Strategic-level spiritual warfare" (SLSW), as championed by Peter Wagner, seeks to "deactivate" territorial spirits, provoking them to manifest themselves by "warfare prayer" (aggressive or violent prayer). This often involves addressing the demons while speaking in tongues.[37] Wagner claimed such confrontation of territorial spirits introduces a "spiritual technology"[38] that will generate the greatest burst of missiological power since the modern Protestant missions movement which began

---

ruling spirits which work untiringly at his command to bring about his malevolent will . . . ruining lives which God intended for joy, happiness and true worship." Smith, "Church Militant," 67, 68 and n.136.

35. See 1 Corinthians 12:10.

36. There are those who engage in "spiritual mapping," seeking to discover the location and activities of various demons, their names, and power. See Gardner, "Spiritual Warfare," 6. In Wagner's *Engaging the Enemy* we find examples of such naming: "the spirit of religiosity—Nashville," "the spirit of pleasure—Orlando," "the spirit of unrighteous trade—London," "the strongman of bondage—Annapolis," "the spirit of unrighteous greed—San Francisco" (McDonald, "Review of Engaging the Enemy"). Riddlebarger observes, "Although there are many Christians who have not abandoned the inner cities, for many in the spiritual warfare crowd even the solution to street crime, drugs, and prostitution is to be found in taking authority over the demonic forces that control a particular geographical area. The superstitious character of all this was pointed out by one of my seminary professors, who cynically remarked, 'So what if they bind the demon prince of Pasadena; he just moves his operations over to Duarte' (a neighboring city)." Riddlebarger, "This Present Paranoia," 279.

37. Wagner discriminates between "ground-level spiritual warfare"—exorcising demons from people—"occult-level spiritual warfare—dealing with shamans, New Age channelers, occult practitioners, witches and warlocks, satanist priests, fortune-tellers, etc.—and "strategic-level spiritual warfare," that is, the most ominous level dealing with territorial spirits. See Gardner, "Spiritual Warfare," 6.

38. Not only does evicting and binding territorial spirits lack biblical warrant, but it also places too much stress on technique and effectiveness. Moreau (2000). In *Essentials*, Moreau's overview of the language of binding in the New Testament leads him to conclude that we cannot bind Satan in the sense of constraining him from all activities, otherwise Peter's exhortations to remain alert to his attacks wouldn't make sense. But we can bind Satan in the sense of "limiting, hindering, constraining, and even stopping his work in the lives of others," through only a legitimate exercise of Christ's authority. Moreau, *Essentials*, 60–161.

with William Carey.[39] Taylor explains, such "warfare prayer" has been more acceptably redubbed "strategic-level intercession," though with no significant change in underlying philosophy.[40]

Such practices have sometimes been supplemented by "identificational repentance."[41] So a group of Christians, assuming they are acting in a representative capacity, stop at various points during a walk, to repent on behalf of others for past national sins.[42] So, for example, they might apologize to Muslims for past atrocities committed during the Crusades. Anglo-Saxon Christians might apologize to Celts, or Scandinavians visiting Britain might apologize for the Vikings. Taylor wryly comments: "The failure of aristocrats to attend these meetings presumably accounted for the absence of apologies for past Norman brutality! Certainly, with my ethnic background, I was left wondering which part of me should apologise to which other part—and for what!"[43]

It is an over-reading of Daniel 10 to conclude that each "nation" has its own territorial spirit or demon which controls it. This is an animistic notion opposed to God's sovereign control over all geographically situated peoples and nations.[44] Paul does speak of contending against "rulers" in the heavenly places, but he never associates demonic angelic beings with specific nations or territories. Yes, Satan offered Jesus all the

---

39. See Moreau, *Essentials*.

40. Taylor, *Cutting Edge*.

41. With respect to sins committed by deceased persons against deceased persons, such as the slave trade, such matters are addressed when living persons, claiming to represent the perpetrators, repent for the sin once committed to representatives of the victims. This involves: (1) Identifying the national sin; (2) Confessing the sin corporately and asking God for forgiveness; (3) Applying Christ's blood; (4) Taking steps of obedience and repairing the damage, e.g. by changing laws or paying appropriate compensation. Moreau, *Essentials*.

42. Lynn Green of YWAM began the Reconciliation Walk to incorporate the ideas of identificational repentance and prayer journeys and this included walking and praying in the lands crossed by the Crusaders. Moreau, *Essentials*.

43. Taylor remarks, "Although we cannot repent of sins we did not commit, it is worth keeping in mind that vocally disassociating oneself from others' malpractice can sometimes be helpful in evangelism. This is one way in which we can demolish some of the stereotyping that blocks the reception of our message."

44. The Old Testament makes it abundantly clear that it is a lie to think that the gods of the nations really control their territories or to suppose God has less control in certain places. As the book of Daniel makes lucid, God is very much sovereign over Babylon and indeed declares, "The Most High is sovereign over the kingdoms of men and gives them to anyone he wishes" (Dan 4:25, 32). See Priest et al., "Missiological Syncretism," 74–75.

kingdoms of the world, saying, "I will give you all their authority and splendor, for it has been given to me, and I can give it to anyone I want to."[45] But this text says nothing about how demonic angelic powers are organized with respect to Satan's control of human kingdoms.

Furthermore, Daniel 10 does not indicate that Babylon, Persia, and Greece had permanent territorial spirits. The implication is simply that when Persian or Greek foreign policy conflicted with the will of God for his people, these nations were manipulated by unseen demonic rulers. Additionally, Daniel 10 provides no encouragement for human involvement in this angelic conflict.[46]

The book of Revelation speaks of Satan having his throne in Pergamum and living in this city.[47] But this language must not be interpreted as proving the presence of a territorial spirit. If one is to adopt such an approach then one has to be at least consistent! The text speaks of "Satan," not a demon living there. Since John speaks of Satan also being present in Smyrna, Philadelphia, and Thyatira it is quite apparent that he does not intend to limit Satan's circle of operations to any particular geographical area.[48] In the cases of Smyrna and Philadelphia the references are to Jewish efforts to stir up persecution against believers. In this way their synagogues carried out Satan's evil ends. The official cult center for emperor worship in Asia was located in Pergamum and this is why it is regarded as the center of Satan's activity in this region.

Greenlee observes that belief in territorial spirits involves confusing ontological reality (what the Bible declares as "really real") with phenomenological reality (what is perceived by people to be real).[49] Breshears highlights two major concerns arising from this false teaching. First, "the

---

45. Luke 4:6.

46. Breshears observes that while Daniel 10 does involve territorial identification of certain angels, it "does not support any sort of human involvement in angelic warfare. Far from finding Daniel involved in warfare prayer, discerning and praying against regional spirits, we find him frustrated in the absence of response to his prayer to God. Daniel is wholly unaware of angelic warfare until the angel's apologetic explanation for the slowness of God's response to his prayer . . . There is no hint of discerning, binding or praying against cosmic evil spirits." Breshears, "Body of Christ," 14.

47. Revelation 2:12–13.

48. See Revelation 2:9; 3:9; and 2:24 respectively.

49. Greenlee, "Territorial Spirits Reconsidered," 507. Greenlee states, "despite the presence of territorial spirits in the belief systems both of Jews and Gentiles, phenomenological reality, they are not recognized ontologically nor do we find clear examples of Jesus or any Christian engaging in prayer or otherwise acting to depose a spirit on a territorial basis" (510).

emphasis on discerning information about demons—including their names, hierarchies and functions—is akin to a pagan, magical worldview where discerning a name gives one control over such a being."[50] Secondly, in treating prayer as a warfare weapon it ceases to be family fellowship that "brings communion and intimacy with God as well as unity to the body."[51]

In Ephesians 6, he adds, prayer "is not a work the armed believer does but the attitude of the believer as the armor is put on."[52] Prayer is here associated with being alert, the essential need of a soldier.[53] However, while Breshears is right to reject the particular way in which proponents of territorial spirits treat prayer as a weapon of warfare, it is arguably used as such in Ephesians 6, though in a very different way. The context is one of treating the church as the embodiment of the Divine Warrior who, as such, is called upon to assist Paul in his struggle to proclaim the gospel, just as Yahweh as Divine Warrior came to the aid of Israel.[54]

There is a further concern with the ideology of territorial spirits. As Greenlee points out: "spirits claiming a territorial domain have lost their control through military conquest, political changes, immigration, the building of a canal, the imposition of colonial government structures, and land reform, all with the clear link to cessation of veneration of the spirit."[55]

Proponents of strategic-level warfare are making a colossal and foolish mistake. Their biblically unwarranted focus on territorial spirits diverts attention from the real evil that must be addressed, human hearts and wills that are committed to venerating such spirits.[56] Once this is

---

50. See too Moreau, *Gaining Perspective*.

51. Moreau comments, "the orientation towards prayer as smart bombs vs scud missiles borrows too heavily on what Walter Wink explored as the myth of redemptive violence that pervades human cultures. Prayer was not intended to be a vehicle of violence, but a means of fellowship, growth, and strength. One danger of an attitude of 'spiritual violence' is that we may become the very thing we are fighting against!" *Gaining Perspective*.

52. *The Body of Christ*, 15–16.

53. Boyd, *God at War*, 282.

54. See Gombis, "Triumph of God in Christ," 3.

55. *Territorial Spirits Reconsidered*, 512.

56. Moreau comments on the danger: "that we detach demons from people, which de-emphasizes our own participation in the rebellion against God . . . by and large the enemy is externalized, enabling us to avoid responsibility for our sin." Greenlee observes how "Jews who entered into the system of the knowledge of names of and authority granted to the 'angels of the nations' helped to lay the base of Gnosticism." Greenlee, "Territorial Spirits Reconsidered," 513.

recognized then the real remedy becomes apparent: the transformation of people through the proclamation of the gospel.

UNDERSTANDING DEMONIC ACTIVITY

In one intriguing passage Jesus rebukes the "wicked and adulterous generation" of his own day: "When an impure spirit comes out of a person, it goes through arid places seeking rest and does not find it. Then it says, 'I will return to the house I left.' When it arrives, it finds the house unoccupied, swept clean and put in order. Then it goes and takes with it seven other spirits more wicked than itself, and they go in and live there. And the final condition of that person is worse than the first. That is how it will be with this wicked generation" (Matthew 12:43–45).

As the last sentence indicates, Jesus is using this example to illustrate the nature of his contemporary generation. The preceding context has involved Jesus exorcising, that is, casting out demons. The Pharisees rationalized their continued opposition to Jesus with what Jesus revealed as crazy logic. They told themselves, "It is only by Beelzebub, the prince of demons, that this fellow drives out demons." What Jesus says about seven demons replacing one demon must be understood against this background. Jesus's ministry has involved opposing Satan, casting out, as it were, the evil spirit from this generation. But by regarding none other than Jesus himself as evil, the Pharisees show how profoundly they themselves are committed to evil, thereby pointing ahead to the even greater degree of evil that will grip this generation in the future. That is, by opposing Jesus's actions against Satan the religious leaders were necessarily inviting Satan to have an even greater foothold on the nation in the future. In the same way, the more a society persecutes the followers of Jesus, the more they invite the devil to dictate what constitutes acceptable behavior.

Still, don't miss the underlying implication from the example Jesus uses. Demons possess people. There is one case where a legion of demons is expelled from a man and enters a herd of pigs.[57] The Gospels speak of

---

57. See Mark 5:1–20. From a Jewish viewpoint it was highly appropriate that unclean spirits should enter unclean animals, pigs. Hooker takes it that "Mark believed that when the demons were expelled by Jesus they had to find another home—if not in the pigs, then perhaps in another human being; better that unclean animals should be destroyed than another man or woman! Probably, then, Mark supposed that the destruction of the pigs involved the destruction of their tenants—otherwise, the demons would move on and do damage elsewhere. The prophetic words of the demoniac in chapter 1 are fulfilled: Jesus has come to destroy the whole army of unclean spirits.

demons possessing people, but it is difficult to find any clearcut biblical examples of demons occupying or possessing territories or social and cultural structures, though some have supposed that Paul's concept of "principalities and powers" includes such a concept.[58]

The insightful observations of David Stevens are worthy of note:

> A marked difference stands between the nature of Daniel's prayer and what is presently termed "strategic-level intercession." Daniel never sought the names of these cosmic powers nor did he employ their names in his intercession—a practice more in keeping with occultic arts. In fact there is no indication that Daniel was aware of what was taking place in the heavenlies during his three week period of prayer and fasting. It is not until after this period that Daniel received revelation about the identity of the angels engaged in this heavenly struggle. And even then, the only angel who was named was Michael (10:13), who fought on behalf of Israel. The evil angelic princes of Persia and Greece were identified by their generic titles.[59]

Stevens also points out: "Daniel did not engage in aggressive prayer against such powers with the expectation of 'binding' or 'evicting' them. The prophet did not pray against cosmic powers but for the people of God and the fulfillment of God's redemptive purposes (cf. Eph. 6:18–20). Apparently Daniel's focus in prayer was not on the celestial warfare in the heavenlies, but on the promises of God (Dan. 10:12; cf. Jer. 25:11; 29:10) and their fulfillment on the terrestrial scene."[60]

Another sober assessment is provided by David Pawson who observes: "One striking feature of engagement with demons by Jesus and

---

Hooker, *Message of Mark*. Luke's version the demons beg Jesus not to order them to go into the Abyss (8:31). The waters into which they were plunged would have been viewed as the gateway to the Abyss. Leaney, *The Gospel According to St Luke*.

58. Here I concur with John Stott: "The addition 'in heavenly realms' in the Ephesians passages, and the antithesis to 'flesh and blood' in Eph. 6:10, not to mention the world-wide extent of the powers' influence, seem to me to fit the concept of supernatural beings much more readily, although of course such beings can and do use structures as well as individuals as media of their ministry." Stott, *Cross of Christ*, 271, n. 11.

59. Stevens, 2000. "Daniel 10," 429–30.

60. Similarly, in commenting on 1 Peter 5:8–9, Derek Tidball observes, "There is no mention of challenging territorial spirits in cosmic spiritual warfare, no mention of special prayer walks, or particular acts of deliverance." Tidball, *The Message of Holiness*, 258–59. Given the context, I assume that when Tidball speaks of "special prayer walks" he is thinking of this as a strategy for directly attacking Satan. I certainly would encourage Christians walking around neighbourhoods and praying for people and society as they do so.

others in the New Testament is that they never took the initiative. They never went looking for them. Only when demons manifested themselves were they confronted and banished and even then not always immediately, as if their interference was a distraction (Acts 16:18)."[61]

There are actually far fewer direct confrontations with demons in the New Testament that many would think. The Gospel authors often tell the same story from different perspectives. In fact, apart from general statements about how Jesus cast out demons in association with his healing miracles, there are fewer than ten instances of Jesus directly confronting demons, and only five instances recorded in the book of Acts.[62]

HEAVENLY POWER PLAY

In the intensely graphic book of Revelation, John picks up the same overall thought being conveyed in Daniel 10: "And there was war in heaven. Michael and his angels fought against the dragon, and the dragon and his angels fought back. But he was not strong enough, and they lost their place in heaven" (Revelation 12:7).

All over the world we see from time to time government policies and legislation being enacted that are opposed to the values and beliefs of Christians and sometimes deliberately discriminating against them. We should not be surprised by such developments. They are a reflection of the great war, the great battle being fought in the heavenly places which predetermines what happens on earth.

It is encouraging to know that there are immensely powerful heavenly armies deployed by God to defend and fight for his people. Before the spectacular fall of Jericho we are told that Joshua "looked up and saw a man standing in front of him with a drawn sword in his hand."[63] Joshua falls on his face when he realizes this is none other than the "commander of the army of the LORD," that is, the "angel of the LORD" who is God in human

---

61. Cited by Wakely, "A Critical Look," 152–62. Smith summarizes a number of dangers arising from a paranoid dualism, supernatural deception, or inexperience, namely (1) failing to see "that those claiming to have an evil spirit most often did not"; (2) "casting out non-existent demons can leave damaging feelings of guilt"; (3) "some can wrongly minister with never-ending lists of demons"; (4) "there can be a lack of clear spiritual authority in this ministry"; (5) "there can be a lack of common sense, or the use of strange practices lacking proportion and decency"; BUT also (6) "refusing to act." Smith, "Church Militant," 99.

62. Observed by Moreau, *Essentials*, 61.

63. Joshua 5:13.

appearance. By the way, we should note that when angels appear to people in the Bible it is almost always, if not always, in human guise.

Another suggestive incident concerns a time when early in his reign David is seeking to get the better of Philistine enemies. David inquires of God as to what he should do. He is told, "Do not go straight up, but circle around behind them and attack them in front of the poplar trees. As soon as you hear the sound of marching in the tops of the poplar trees, move quickly, because that will mean the Lord has gone out in front of you to strike the Philistine army" (2 Samuel 5:23).

As you may have gathered by now, when David hears "the sound of marching in the tops of the poplar trees" he is really hearing the marching of God's great heavenly army going forth to defeat the Philistines. We can see implied here what is brought out more clearly in Daniel 10 and even more explicitly in the book of Revelation: the earthly contest between David's soldiers and the Philistine soldiers is the outworking of the more profound conflict between God's mighty angels and the opposing demonic angels seeking to use the Philistines to oppress and destroy God's people.

Along the same lines we might recall the time when the king of Aram sent an army with horses and chariots to encircle the city where Elisha was staying.[64] It was the king's intent to force the city to hand over Elisha to him to prevent him from continuing, by prophetic inspiration, to thwart the king's strategies to defeat Israel in war. Elisha's servant is distressed when he sees these considerable forces encircling the city. But Elisha prays that God will open his eyes and suddenly he looked "and saw the hills full of horses and chariots of fire all around Elisha," confirming Elisha's words of reassurance, "Do not be afraid. Those who are with us are more than those who are with them." Next Elisha prays and the entire Aramean forces are struck with blindness, just as visiting angels in human form struck all the men of Sodom with blindness to rescue Lot and his family from their malice.[65]

MISMATCHED OPPONENTS

The book of Ephesians begins and ends with an exposure of reality in "the heavenly realms." On the one hand, God is to be praised because he "has blessed us in the heavenly realms with every spiritual blessing

---

64. 2 Kings 6:8–23.
65. Genesis 19:11.

in Christ." On the other hand, there are "spiritual forces of evil in the heavenly realms" against whom we struggle.

Following the resurrection of Jesus from the dead, God has "seated him at his right hand in the heavenly realms, far above all rule and authority, power and dominion, and every title that can be given, not only in the present age but also in the one to come."[66] It follows that when we read about Satanic forces in the heavenly realms we are in no way to think that essential reality is dualistic, with forces of good and evil being roughly matched. Nor should we suppose, as, for example, Greg Boyd does, that Satan is able at times to thwart God's plans. It is notable that in Boyd's books there is minimal reflection on the significance of Christ's resurrection. Note those words "far above." Satan's power is utterly dwarfed and trivialized by that of Jesus.

But what we must not miss is the fact that Paul is praying that we Christians will know and grasp this reality. He prays we will know "his incomparably great power for us who believe. That power is like the working of his mighty strength, which he exerted in Christ when he raised him from the dead and seated him at his right hand in the heavenly realms." So, when Paul urges us to "be strong in the Lord and in his mighty power" he is referring to immense, immeasurable might on an almost unimaginable scale.[67]

We Christians, therefore, have enormous power and might, by virtue of our relationship with our risen and ascended Lord. It follows that in Ephesians 6 it is not us, but Satan who is fighting in a desperate fashion. He is the one who is fighting a lost cause. His situation is hopeless. He is a doomed foe. But knowing his time is short he is filled with fury and he will inflict as much damage as we allow him. "As we allow him" are the key words. For it is only when we fail to arm ourselves as Paul commands that we let Satan have his way with us.

SHAMEFUL TACTICS

Paul wrote his letter to the Ephesians from a Roman prison. How ironic that he should speak of Christians being so irresistibly strong, with

---

66. Ephesians 1:20–21.

67. There is much to commend Gombis's (2005) reading of Ephesians: God's triumph over the powers ruling the present evil age (1:20–23), the triumphs of God in Christ (2:1–22); Paul's ironic participation in this triumph (3:2–13); the church's participation in this triumph (4:1—6:9). Gombis, "Triumph of God in Christ," 4.

himself and they participating in Christ's triumph over the principalities and powers,[68] when his imprisonment was an expression of his own apparent weakness under the authority and might of the then world's greatest superpower. Immediately after Paul reminds Christians that they are invincible when strong in the Lord and clad in gospel armour he asks them to pray that he himself would be given God-imparted words to "fearlessly make known the mystery of the gospel, for which I am an ambassador in chains."[69] It is important here to see how Paul regards himself. As he explains earlier in the letter, God has given him a special role "to preach to the Gentiles the unsearchable riches of Christ, and to make plain to everyone the administration of this mystery." Do we see the point?

From time to time countries will find themselves in sharp disagreement with each other. One nation may call in the ambassador of the country it is displeased with. Perhaps relations may sour to the point where the ambassador will be sent packing to his own nation and the embassy will be closed down. But it would be an act of war to imprison an ambassador.

Yet that is precisely what the Romans did, without of course realizing the gravity of what they had done. God is the living and true God and Paul was his unique ambassador, sent from the heavenly government to the nations of this world to set before them the claims of Jesus as Lord of the universe. The humiliating and degrading imprisonment of Paul was an insult to God. Further, this aligns the Roman authorities with the shameful, dishonorable way in which Satan conducts warfare against God's people.

Paul's way of portraying the conflict between Christians and Satanic forces probably taps into Greek and Roman beliefs concerning honorable and dishonorable ways of conducting battle. The heroic and honorable way to conduct battle is to openly match strength against strength. Many would have regarded it as shameful to avoid fighting man-to-man, but instead to seek to win by shameful, deceitful means. The only way Satan can inflict

---

68. "It is through Paul's preaching that God calls the church into being, which then points to the triumph of God by demonstrating his manifold wisdom to the powers ruling the present evil age (3:10). Even in apparent defeat, God demonstrates his triumph." Gombis, "Triumph of God in Christ," 6. He adds, "The powers have ordered the present evil age in such a way as to exacerbate the divisions within humanity created by the Law (2:11–12). God confounds the powers, however, by creating in Christ one unified, multi-racial body consisting of formerly divided groups of people. And it is the existence of the church as such a body set within the hostile environment of the present evil age that proclaims to them the wisdom of God." Gombis, "Triumph of God in Christ," 97–98.

69. Ephesians 6:20.

damage upon God's people is through his schemes, by acting as a disgraceful fighter who resorts to shameful tactics involving deceit. Satan cannot match strength with strength. Satan avoids fighting at close quarters and instead resorts to firing missiles from a distance ("flaming arrows").

HIS DOOM IS SURE

Arguably, in a highly symbolic form, Revelation 20 summarizes much of what we have been saying above. It describes Satan as the one who deceives the nations, gathering them for battle to encircle and destroy God's people. Personally, I take this to be descriptive of the entire course of history from the time of Christ till Jesus returns. Revelation 20 goes on to describe the ultimate fate of the implacably evil adversary of God's people: "But fire came down from heaven and devoured them. And the devil, who deceived them, was thrown into the lake of burning sulphur, where the beast and the false prophet had been thrown. They will be tormented day and night for ever and ever" (Revelation 20:9b–10.)

This looks forward to the time when all evil is completely destroyed and once and for all removed as a threat to God's people. For everlasting destruction awaits the evil one and the main expressions of his evil, namely anti-God human authorities ("the beast"), and all institutions and people that justify and promote the evils done by human authorities against God's people ("the false prophet").

Ironically, Satan's fate was sealed when the greatest of deceivers fooled himself. For he was defeated when he thought he had won his greatest victory. It was when he succeeded in effecting Jesus's death that he himself received the death blow, the fatal wound that spells his certain end.

When Jesus remained silent before Pilate, this scared and exasperated Roman official said to Jesus, "Do you refuse to speak to me? Don't you realize I have power either to free you or to crucify you?"[70] With words that remind us of the inseparable link between anti-God human authority and underlying demonic power Jesus responded, "You would have no power over me if it were not given to you from above. Therefore the one who handed me over to you is guilty of a greater sin" (John 19:11).

It was Satan who handed Jesus over to Pilate though he did so by filling Judas's heart to betray Jesus and using human agents to effect Jesus's

---

70. John 19:10.

arrest.[71] Peter was rebuked by Jesus for swiping off the ear of one of the high priest's servants with his sword. So much for Jesus's need of human agencies to meet physical force with physical force. Jesus told Peter, "Do you think I cannot call on my Father, and he will at once put at my disposal more than twelve legions of angels?"[72]

But no! Jesus did not need to call upon masses of angels to defeat his foe. He achieved this in the most counter-intuitive way possible. He willingly submitted himself to torture and an agonizing death.[73] However, remember how God said it would be a human being, offspring of the woman, who would bring about the final destruction of the snake, the evil one. And the restoration of people as the image and likeness of God required that this victory be won by a human being. And this is precisely what happened on the cross, the locus of Christ's glorification and victory when he overcame the world, casting out the ruler of the world and taking away the sin of the world.[74] Accordingly, in the letter to the Hebrews it is explained: "Since the children have flesh and blood, he too shared in their humanity so that by his death he might break the power of him who holds the power of death—that is, the devil."[75]

MISSION DEBRIEF

- **Reality of Demonic Hostility.** Believers are pitched in battle against Satan and demonic forces that are very real.
- **Satan's Control over the Unsaved.** Fallen people are dehumanized by their failure to live lives that image God and this involves being subject to Satan's control and influence.
- **Image of God and Victory over Satan.** God's program is to create a new humanity in his image and likeness and this involves mastery over Satan, first realized when Jesus as "the image of the invisible God" was victorious over Satan as initially promised in Genesis 3.

71. John 13:27.
72. Matthew 26:53.
73. Jung proposes that when Isaiah 52:13 says the Suffering Servant "will be raised and lifted up and highly exalted" it means that the New Exodus, involving glorious divine victory, will be effected through the suffering and death of the Servant. All of this is a modification of the divine warrior as displayed in Exodus 15, for now the enemy is not a military power but sin. Jung, "Divine Warrior," 35–42.
74. See John 1:29; 12:31–32; 16:33.
75. Hebrews 2:14.

- **Demonic Opposition to Believers.** Just as Cain killed Abel so believers as "the seed of the woman" find themselves opposed by "the seed of the serpent," people whose hostility towards Christians is due to Satan's deceit.
- **Vehicles of Persecution.** It is common for such opposition to come from family members. But political structures will also be used by Satan to persecute God's people.
- **Danger of Animistic Thinking and Practice.** Many Christians have been duped into believing and practicing something never taught or encouraged in the Bible, namely that effective spiritual warfare involves identifying and directly opposing territorial spirits. This is a species of Christian animism.
- **Don't Seek Confrontation with Demons.** Demons do possess people but Christians are not to go looking for demons to confront.
- **Angelic Protection.** Mighty angelic forces are deployed by God to defend and fight for his people.
- **Superior Power of Believers.** Christians by virtue of their union with Christ have immense power. Satan is a doomed foe and can only inflict as much damage as Christians allow him to. Because he cannot match strength against strength, he resorts to shameful, deceitful tactics.
- **The Decisive Victory of the Cross.** It was on the cross that Jesus, fully sharing our humanity, conclusively defeated Satan and sealed his inevitable doom.

GATHERING INTELLIGENCE

Read 2 Corinthians 11:1–4, 13–15

1. What is Satan's objective?
2. How does Satan seek to achieve his foul purpose?
3. Why might Christians be susceptible to accepting a false gospel?
4. How are we to recognize those who are communicating a false gospel?
5. How can and should Christians protect themselves from this form of Satanic deception?

Chapter Four

Facing Human Enemies

"If the Tiber rises as high as the city walls, if the Nile does not send its waters up over the fields, if the heavens give no rain, if there is an earthquake, if there is famine or pestilence, straightway the cry is, 'Away with the Christians to the lion!'"

TERTULLIAN, *APOLOGY*.

SPIRITUAL WARFARE INVOLVES HORRIFIC eternal destruction. True followers of Christ have been conscripted to fight in this great war that has been waged since our first parents listened to words of deceit, words of war. The enemy against whom we fight is a vicious angelic being filled with malice and intent to undermine our faith and destroy us. He, along with demonic forces at his command, works through human agents and human institutions to attain his evil ends. However, behind the scenes he is outmatched by a vastly superior angelic army. He is already a defeated foe, vanquished at the cross. When God has fulfilled his great new creation purpose in history our adversary will be destroyed, the war will end, and eternal peace will be ushered in.

But what of the humans whom Satan uses in one way or another to shape a world, an environment, and cultures which at some basic level are hostile to the knowledge of God?¹ How should God's people respond and relate to the people around them?

RELIGIOUS VIOLENCE

Religious Violence in General

Following the devastating attack on the Twin Towers in 2001 many connected violence not merely with Islam but with religion in general. Scholars often argue that religion legitimates violence. Some contend that violence is primarily inspired by religion. Some again would identify monotheism as the major culprit. But one has only to think of the millions upon millions slaughtered under the tyrannical rules of such despots as Stalin, Hitler, and Pol Pot to see how foolish it is to think that if there were no religion people would be much more peace-loving. There is a fundamental failure here to see that violence is an inevitable outworking of the radical evil that lurks in every human heart.²

God told Cain that sin was like a predatory beast crouching at his door, poised to destroy him and that he must master this beast.³ Unable to control his anger, Cain killed his brother Abel in a cold, calculated manner. It is true that the occasion for this was provided by religion. Abel offered his sacrifice by faith and God therefore accepted it, while Cain's sacrifice was not offered in this way and was therefore not favored by God.⁴ Notwithstanding this religious dimension, the fact is that religion as such had very little to do with what followed. Later in the chapter

---

1. There is a significant difference between the way the Synoptic Gospels portray the conflict between Jesus and Satan and the way this is done in John's Gospel. In the latter, as Jung points out, "there is no direct encounter between them. In the Fourth Gospel it is always through human instrument that the devil attempts to attack Jesus." Jung, "Divine Warrior," vi.

2. As Matthew Rowley says, it is not that "religion poisons everything" (*contra* Christopher Hitchens), but "people poison everything." Rowley, "Epistemology of Sacralized Violence," 64. Rowley affirms the validity of Cavanaugh's critique of Charles Kimball. Kimball identifies five "warning signs" of when religion is likely to turn violent: (1) absolute truth claims; (2) blind obedience; (3) the establishment of an "ideal" time; (4) the belief that the end justifies the means; (5) the declaration of holy war. Cavanaugh rightly points out that these same criteria apply to secular ideologies, providing a framework for understanding the circumstances under which any institution or ideology becomes evil. Rowley, "Epistemology of Sacralized Violence," 63, n.2.

3. Genesis 4:7.

4. Hebrews 11:4.

Lamech boasted of killing a man for wounding him, with no hint of religion being involved.[5] Indeed, this incident is particularly significant because it caps a list of cultural traditions that can be traced back to Cain's descendants: living in tents and raising livestock, the playing of musical instruments, and the manufacture of metal tools. For all his evil Cain remained a man made in God's image. His descendants and all people who have ever been born evidence this reality in their creativity. However, this lineage also perpetuated the tradition of violent retribution.

These days domestic violence is much in the news and it would be a silly person indeed who claimed that every time a man bashed his wife or partner it was because of his religion. Still, it can hardly be doubted that religion and violence are no strangers. But there is no scholarly consensus concerning the relationship between religion and violence. It is an extremely complex matter. There is a multitude of factors that play a part in fomenting religious violence. Let's consider some major connections between religion and violence.

Religious violence and power

Religious people can become violent when their power is threatened. Jewish religious leaders resented the threat posed by Jesus and finally succeeded in killing him as they had long sought to do.

Religious violence and stereotyping

Some religious violence follows upon treating a person or group as the cause of a perceived crisis or tragic state of affairs. When Danish cartoons lampooned Muhammad a significant number of people, especially Christians, were targeted by enraged Muslims, on the erroneous assumption that all Westerners are Christians.

Religious violence and morality

Many who perpetrate religious violence which slaughters non-combatant men, women, and children sincerely believe that they are doing what is right and acceptable. Typically, this will involve religious teaching,

---

5. Genesis 4:23–24.

whether understood truly or in a distorted manner, that justifies treating people as sub-human or worthy of destruction.

Religious Violence in Islam

A 15-year-old Muslim boy comes out of the Parramatta mosque dressed in black Islamic garb with a gun. He heads for the police station, shoots and kills a police employee and is shot dead himself. Immediately, police stations increase their security arrangements. Meanwhile some call for a moratorium on Muslim migration and the already existent gap between the broader Australian community and the Muslim community widens still further. A significant number of young Muslims left Australia to join the extremist Daish (ISIS) forces,[6] who shocked the world with gruesome videos showing executioners slowly cutting off the heads of live captives with knives.

Around the world there are many examples of religious violence being perpetrated by non-Muslims. Indeed, in Myanmar minority Muslims themselves are sometimes the victims of terrible violence. However, the statistical evidence is overwhelming that the vast bulk of contemporary religious violence is perpetrated by Muslims. Often this violence is a case of Muslim against Muslim; for example, Sunni against Shiite, though Christians are often in the firing line. The sheer scale of Muslim violence flies in the face of propaganda attempts to present Islam as a religion of peace, notwithstanding the fact that a large majority of Muslims are peaceable. I will not address the question as to whether Islam is essentially violent or not. What cannot be doubted is that there is a legitimate place for violence in Islam. Violence is very much a part of the beginnings of Islam and its original development with, for example, three of the first four caliphs being killed. In our contemporary world we see that whatever political, social, and economic factors may also be at play, appeal is frequently made to the Qur'an and Hadith to justify violent acts.

It is not possible for me to give to this sensitive and crucial issue the space it deserves. But any fair-minded treatment must discriminate between Muslims as people and Islam. It also must avoid treating Islam as

---

6. This movement is variously labelled. Daesh stands for Al-Dawlah Al-Islamiyah fe Al-Iraq wa Al-Sham (the Islamic State of Iraq and Syria, or Sham). It is also referred to as ISIL or ISIS. Those who belong to the group like to call themselves the Khilafat (Caliphate), hence "Islamic State" (IS).

a monolithic whole. Integrity also requires that we avoid comparing the worst in Islam with the best in Christianity.

What we can say is that traditional Islam sees the people of the world as living in either of two spheres. Some Muslims live in territory which is controlled by Muslims who uphold Sharia law. Such countries are deemed to be part of what is variously called Dar al-Islam, "the House of Islam," or Dar al-Salam, "the House of Peace," or Dar al-Tawhid, "the House of [Islamic] Monotheism." Other Muslims live in territory controlled by non-Muslims. Significantly, this is deemed to be "the House of War" (Dar al-Harb). Islam means "submission" and history shows the continuing force of traditional Islam in the minds of the many who are seeking to force conquered people to submit to their understanding of the Qur'an, the Hadith, and Sharia law.

Religious Violence in Christendom

In his book *God is Not Great* Christopher Hitchens wrote, "The Bible may, indeed does, contain a warrant for trafficking in humans, for ethnic cleansing, for slavery, for bride-price, and for indiscriminate massacre, but we are not bound by any of it because it was put together by crude, uncultured human mammals."[7]

Christians and Violence

I will briefly consider the role of violence in the Bible. There is a necessary place for violence in a fallen world. Christians are essentially called to be non-violent peacemakers,[8] though not pacifists. God grants the State legitimate use of violence to punish evil and reward good. Therefore, Christians can serve as police officers or soldiers and may use force to oppose or restrain evil when justified. Early Christians served as soldiers in the Roman army by the second century AD. The New Testament includes Roman soldiers without condemning their profession. Indeed, when soldiers asked John the Baptist what they should do to produce fruit in keeping with repentance, he told them to refrain from extortion and making false accusations, not to stop being soldiers.[9]

---

7. Hitchens, *God Is Not Great*, 102.
8. Matthew 5:9.
9. Luke 3:14.

I warned against comparing the worst in Islam with the best in Christianity. There is no escaping the fact that throughout history there have been appalling examples of professing Christians resorting to violence or approving of such violence to achieve their ends. Contrary to revisionist histories, it was never idyllic for minorities to live under Muslim rule, not even in Spain. Minorities under Muslim rule have always been treated as *dhimmis* and as such have typically experienced severe discrimination and humiliation. However, it must be conceded that in so-called Christian nations minorities, especially the Jews, were often treated in at least comparable ways.

Christian violence is especially associated with the Inquisition, the Crusades, Wars of Religion, anti-Semitism, and the mistreatment of slaves and colonial subjects. The evaluation of so-called Christian violence throughout history is by no means as cut and dried as some moderns may suppose. For example, there is a popular modern narrative, unfortunately accepted by many Christians in their naivety, that the Crusades describes a period of history when, as Rodney Stark summarizes it, "an expansionist, imperialistic Christendom brutalized, looted, and colonized a tolerant and peaceful Islam."[10] This is nonsense, though there is no doubt that professing Christians did indeed commit some shocking atrocities during this period.

There have been many shameful instances of violence throughout history perpetrated by professing Christians. Too often the lives and conduct of professing Christians have been more shaped and driven by culture and ethnic allegiance than by the faith taught by Christ. For example, though we need to have a balanced understanding of the political realities of the time, a good deal of the religious motivation for the Crusades involved appealing to values at odds with biblical thought, for example "pilgrimage, avenging affronts to the clan's honor and the idea that works of penance are instrumental to salvation."[11]

Illegitimate Use of the Bible to Justify Violence

Collins observes, "While it is true that both Bible and Qur'an admit of various readings and emphases, and that terrorist hermeneutics can be

---

10. See Stark's demolition of various myths concerning the crusades: Stark, *God's Battalions*.
11. Doriani, "Speech that Launched the Crusades."

seen as a case of the devil citing Scripture for his purpose, it is also true that the devil does not have to work very hard to find biblical precedents for the legitimation of violence."[12]

Contrary to Collins, such legitimations typically involve the lamentable mishandling of biblical texts that have been used to justify Christian violence. When Jesus said, "I did not come to bring peace but a sword," he plainly meant, as the preceding context had made palpably clear, that families and others would turn against those who decided to follow him.[13] The "sword" metaphorically stands for the violence that would be wielded against Christians, not by Christians. But this has not stopped some from wresting Jesus's words from their context and making this instead a pretext for Christians to use violence.

The Bible has been grossly mishandled in other respects. Through the Methodist Samuel Leigh's efforts, the first person specifically appointed as a missionary to Aborigines in Australia, the Rev. William Walker of the Wesleyan Missionary Society (WMS), arrived from England in 1821. He was, on his arrival, only twenty-one years old and said to be of exceptional intelligence, of lively personality, and an outstanding preacher. He married Elizabeth Hassall in 1823. Walker stated at the outset the theological stance that was to be the essential view of many missionaries. Aborigines were descendants of Ham and under a curse. They were "the progeny of him who was cursed to be a servant of servants to his brethren," but they were also "about to stretch out their hands unto God."[14]

In the wider context of the Pentateuch the cursing of Canaan, not Ham, anticipates Israelite invasion of the land of Canaan. It is a completely misguided interpretation of this context to regard Australia's indigenous people, or those of African or Arabic descent, as descendants of Ham. In an appalling abuse of this text, the enslavement of Canaan was construed as justification for enslaving people of African descent.[15] Jefferson Davis, president of the Confederate States during the American

---

12. Collins, "Zeal of Phinehas," 3.

13. Matthew 10:34.

14. Harris, *One Blood*, 47.

15. The Babylonian Talmud encouraged this view by claiming, "Ham was smitten in his skin." According to this same source Noah is said to have told Ham, "Your seed will be ugly and dark-skinned." In 1706 the Puritan Cotton Mather, going along with the prevailing consensus of the time wrote, "Suppose these wretched Negroes to be the offspring of Ham," but added the parentheses: "which yet is not so very certain" (from *The Negro Christianized*). See Weiner, "This 'Miserable African.'"

Civil War, understood slavery not only to be sanctioned by the Bible but permanently established by divine decree.

Christian theologian Paul Althaus described the rise of the Nazi Party as "a year of grace from God's hand" and regarded the rise of Hitler as a "gift and as God's."[16] He even called this an "Easter moment" for the German people and its church. He believed God would use the Nazis to effect the "resurrection" of Germany. He did not go as far as some other German Christians did who called Hitler a new "Messiah" and thought of Nazi Germany as a "new Israel." But he did see National Socialism as embodying the union of faith and Volk, of gospel and national identity. At the root of Althaus's fatal syncretism lay his racist views. He regarded marriage, family, race, and "Volk" as God's order of creation. He even saw Volk, the German nation, as an arena of revelation and wrote: "We champion the cause of the preservation of the purity of the Volk and of our Race."[17]

Historical foundations for apartheid policy go back to the Great Trek of the Dutch, which began in 1835. The Dutch, seeking to escape from British rule, became convinced that as a people they were analogous to Israel as depicted at the time of the Exodus in the Old Testament. They saw in their trek the hand of God delivering them just as he delivered Israel in the wilderness. Just as Cromwell had equated the Catholics of Ireland as Canaanites and as Cotton Mather equated Native American tribes with Amalekites, so the Boers similarly viewed the hostile black nations they had to conquer as akin to the Amalekite and Philistine enemies faced by Israel at the time of the conquest.[18] Following the Battle of Blood River, when the Dutch defeated the Zulus, they entered into a solemn covenant with God, in which they regarded the Transvaal and Orange Free State as their promised land which, they believed, God had given to them as their inheritance. They saw themselves as a divinely chosen people, a divinely elected nation.[19]

Christian Violence and Religious Freedom

Christian violence is especially regrettable when it is a denial of religious freedom and presupposes that it is legitimate to use coercion and even

---

16. Schwarz, "Paul Althaus," 36.
17. Stott, *Issues Facing Christians Today*, 199.
18. Collins, "Zeal of Phinehas," 13–14.
19. See Stott, *Issues Facing Christians Today*, 199.

violence to make people Christians, or punish heretics and other non-Christian minorities. Tragically, it was a great Christian thinker, who has contributed so much good, who also opened the door to incalculable harm when he changed his mind and sanctioned the use of force to make people become Christians. I am speaking of Augustine of Hippo.[20]

Prior to the fourth century Christian leaders had spoken clearly about the importance of religious freedom. So Tertullian stated, "It is assuredly no part of religion to compel religion—to which free-will and not force should lead us."[21] Similarly, Lactantius, an advisor to the Roman emperor Constantine, declared, "There is no occasion for violence and injury, for religion cannot be imposed by force; the matter must be carried on by words rather than by blows, that the will may be affected . . . We do not entice, as they say; but we teach, we prove, we show."[22]

Emperor Constantine shared the view of religious toleration and sought to perpetuate it. In the fourth century, he stopped persecuting Christians, legalized Christianity, and began favoring it. Constantine ended violence against Christians, prompting upper-class men to join the church. He abolished house churches, made Sunday a day of rest, and exempted churches from taxes. By Constantine's time, churches had about six million adherents, roughly 10 percent of the imperial population. Subsequent emperors, except for Julian's brief reign, regarded themselves as Christians. By AD 380, between a third and half of the Roman Empire's population belonged to the Christian church. During this time, some Christians committed acts of violence, destroying buildings and images, and occasionally resorting to murder and intimidation.

Emperor Theodosius I (379–95) chose violence with an edict in 382 that appointed inquisitors to prevent secret assemblies of heretics. In 395, Gaza's Christians elected Porphyry as bishop, who sought the emperor's military support to convert the masses. Soldiers were sent to destroy Gaza's temples by force and fire. When citizens protested, soldiers beat them with clubs. Some Christians chanted psalms, proclaiming "Christ has conquered!"

And then came the most critical wrong step of all—Augustine's defense of "just persecution" by Christians against non-Christians. Tissue-thin argumentation from Scripture was used to justify this. Augustine

---

20. See Kreider, "Violence and Mission." Much of the content of this section is drawn from Kreider's excellent summary.

21. *To Scapula* II.4 in Schaff, *Anti-Nicene Fathers*. Vol 3.

22. *The Divine Institutes* 5.20 in Schaff, *Anti-Nicene Fathers*. Vol 7.

took the view that God had used coercion to make Paul repent on the Damascus Road and also appealed to the Parable of the Great Banquet which ends with the master telling his servants, "Go out to the roads and country lanes, and make them come in, so that my house will be full."[23]

Augustine's theory of just persecution has had highly unfortunate consequences. So Kreider observes, "Augustine's rationalization of the use of force changed mission; violence, justified by the most formative theologian in Western history, could now be a legitimate instrument of mission."[24]

A PLACE FOR VIOLENCE

It would be irresponsible for us to skirt over Old Testament material and simply focus on what the New Testament requires of God's people. Clearly, there is a radical difference between what God required of his people in Old Testament times and what is now required of his people following the life and work of Christ.

There are two ways in which God's people treated other people that have caused considerable angst for many Christians, let alone unbelievers:

- God's command to forcibly drive Canaanites out of the land of Canaan, which includes commands to annihilate populations—men, women, and children.[25]

- The apparent biblical legitimation of imprecations, that is, curses, against people considered as enemies.

Both matters raise a fundamental issue—the place of violence in the lives of God's people in the Old Testament.

---

23. Luke 14:15–24, especially verse 23.
24. Kreider, "Violence and Mission," 5.
25. Regarding the driving out of Canaanites: (1) Expressions of God's intent: Exod 23:28–31; 33:2; 34:11, 24; Lev 18:24; 20:23; Num 32:21; 33:55; Deut 4:27, 38; 7:1, 22; 9:3–5; 11:23; 18:12; 33:27; Josh 3:10; 13:6; 23:5, 9, 13; 2 Kgs 16:3; 17:8, 11; 21:2; 2 Chr 20:7; 33:2; (2) God's often unfulfilled expectation that the Israelites will drive out the inhabitants of the land: Exod 23:31; Num 33:55; Deut 9:3; 12:29; 19:1; Josh 12:13; 13:13; 14:12; 17:13; 18; Judg 1:19–33; (3) God's command to drive out the inhabitants of the land: Num 33:52; (4) Israel's failure leads to God ceasing to drive out the Canaanites: Josh 23:13; Judg 2:3, 21, 23. Regarding the annihilation of Canaanites: (1) Language expressing God's intent: Exod 23:23; Deut 19:1; (2) God's command that the Israelites annihilate Canaanites: Deut 7:1–2, 23–24; 9:1–3; 20:16–18.

Violence and the Removal of Evil

The starting point is to recognize that the removal of evil necessarily requires violent action. The great flood of Genesis 6 is an extreme example of God acting violently to remove human evil. The rationale for this is presented as follows:

> The Lord saw how great the wickedness of the human race had become on the earth, and that every inclination of the thoughts of the human heart was only evil all the time. The Lord regretted that he had made human beings on the earth, and his heart was deeply troubled. So the Lord said, "I will wipe from the face of the earth the human race I have created—and with them the animals, the birds and the creatures that move along the ground—for I regret that I have made them." But Noah found favor in the eyes of the Lord (Genesis 6:5–8).

When reading the Old Testament, remember that it often points ahead to future events. The Genesis narratives often have this aim, like the story of Joseph in Egypt, who is unjustly treated and then exalted, foreshadowing God's plan for his people. Similarly, the flood narrative shows God's intent to remove evil entirely, anticipating the ultimate act of judgment on the Day of the Lord.

This is made crystal clear by Paul as he considers the persecutions and trials being endured by Christian believers:

> All this is evidence that God's judgment is right, and as a result you will be counted worthy of the kingdom of God, for which you are suffering. God is just: he will pay back trouble to those who trouble you and give relief to you who are troubled, and to us as well. This will happen when the Lord Jesus is revealed from heaven in blazing fire with his powerful angels. He will punish those who do not know God and do not obey the gospel of our Lord Jesus. They will be punished with everlasting destruction and shut out from the presence of the Lord and from the glory of his might on the day he comes to be glorified in his holy people and to be marveled at among all those who have believed. This includes you, because you believed our testimony to you (2 Thessalonians 1:4–10).

When Jesus returns in great glory there will be vengeance and, this text insists, such vengeance is proof that "God is just." Justice demands vengeance, hence the extreme violence of the Day of Judgment, violence that will far eclipse the violence involved in the Great Flood and which certainly goes way beyond the violence involved in the conquest of Canaan by the Israelites. On that day all who do not know God and who do not obey the gospel will suffer eternal destruction in a state of permanent exile from God's presence.

Justice and Violence

We need to be clear that justice demands vengeance, "payback." The reason we don't see this clearly is because we are only too aware that justice is not usually well-served when people avenge themselves for perceived or actual wrongs done to them.

David is often remembered as a great biblical hero, but the narrative reveals serious flaws in his character before his adultery with Bathsheba and the murder of her husband, Uriah. When Saul was trying to kill David, David and his men protected the shepherds of Nabal, a wealthy man. David expected provisions in return, but Nabal insulted him. David intended to kill Nabal's household out of revenge, but Nabal's wife, Abigail, brought provisions and convinced David to reconsider, reasoning: "When the Lord has fulfilled for my lord every good thing he promised concerning him and has appointed him ruler over Israel, my lord will not have on his conscience the staggering burden of needless bloodshed or of having avenged himself" (1 Samuel 25:30–31).

Citing the book of Deuteronomy, Paul tells Christians, "Do not take revenge, my friends, but leave room for God's wrath, for it is written: 'It is mine to avenge; I will repay,' says the Lord" (Romans 12:19).

Let's pause and come to terms with the fundamental nature of true justice. True justice occurs when everybody gets what they deserve.

But here's the rub. What people think they deserve and what they actually deserve are two very different things. I'm not just thinking of the terrorists who slaughter hundreds or thousands and imagine their god will reward them for this. I'm talking about something that applies to every person on the face of the planet. To you. To me.

The Satisfaction of Justice

God will create a new humanity to live in a new heavens and a new earth. There will be no evil whatsoever in this new creation. At face value this means not one of us will ever experience this paradise. We are all disqualified.

God's plan includes qualifying people to join a great community, similar to a registration process. This is called justification in the New Testament. In the Greek, the words for "justification" and "justice" are closely related, as, indeed, these English words themselves clearly suggest. When God justifies someone to be part of this community, he upholds his justice.

Because God is perfectly just there is nothing we can do or appeal to in ourselves that will "bribe" him into looking the other way. I mean, get real! We all make light of our own moral problems by saying such things as, "Well, nobody's perfect." But in doing so we compare ourselves with one another and reassure ourselves by thinking, "I haven't murdered anyone or committed child abuse or any major crime. I'm not such a bad person." However, what we don't do is take seriously God's standard of morality. And so we live with this crazy fantasy that on the Day of Judgment we can rock up to God and say, "In the light of my generally decent moral behavior please overlook that time when I . . ." Wink, wink, nudge, nudge. Is that how we imagine we will be able to talk to the Judge of all the earth? In your dreams, maybe, but, if so, it will end up being your worst nightmare.

So, God's plan to form a new humanity requires that all our morally corrupt thoughts, attitudes, words, and deeds be forgiven and the slate wiped clean and yet in a way that does not involve God looking the other way. If justice is to be satisfied he needs to be able to look at you directly and see that there is no retribution warranted in your case. How is this possible?

Well, the thing is that Jesus died on the cross for enemies of God, people like you and me. He took my punishment on himself so that I wouldn't have to face it myself, but in the context of a broader work of God in my life. This broader work involves the Holy Spirit dwelling within us, inspiring us to aspire to be the individuals God intended us to be at creation. The Holy Spirit guides us towards committing ourselves to being transformed into God's image and likeness, progressively becoming more like Jesus Christ. This transformation is an ongoing and sometimes challenging process, but it will be completed when Jesus returns.[26] At that time, we, along with a multitude of people from every nation, tribe,

---

26. Philippians 1:6.

people, and language, will be transformed into the likeness of Jesus. It is because this holds such significance for me that I embrace Jesus as the substitute whom God provided out of his love.

Our Ultimate Act of Violence

But take stock of the above. It would be so easy, wouldn't it, to see God as simply the one who dishes out the violence on the Day of Judgment, as indeed he will. However, now turn the lens of your camera and focus on the cross. Take a long hard look. For that is not just a man suffering immense agony. This is God himself who hangs there, agonizingly struggling for every next breath.

Slow down. Be in no doubt about this. The most monstrous act of violence ever committed in human history anywhere in the world was perpetrated on that dark day. This was God who was mocked, and spat upon, and punched, and flogged within an inch of his life before the nails were driven into his raw, quivering flesh. And you and I share in the responsibility for this crime above all crimes. We are complicit in murder and sadism, you and I. Make no mistake about it.

On February 13, 2008, Prime Minister Kevin Rudd, on behalf of Australians, publicly apologized to Indigenous Australians for the "stolen generations"—Aboriginal children forcibly removed from their families. Some believed this apology was necessary, while others felt they were not responsible for past actions, even if those actions were taken by their ancestors.

In collective societies, history is seen as a shared experience, binding contemporary generations to past events. There is a tendency to rewrite history to downplay or justify ancestral wrongdoings, leading to a distorted view of one's own history. Just think, for example, of how many Muslim societies have developed a convenient history that justifies a one-eyed view of what happened during the period of the Crusades.

But in asking you, like me, to see ourselves as complicit in Jesus's death I am not just appealing to a sense of collective evil, as valid as this may be.

In the nineteenth century, African-American slaves in the US composed a well-known spiritual hymn that begins with the question: "Were you there when they crucified my Lord?" Peter Marshall, a former chaplain to the US Senate, once delivered a notable sermon with the same title. Were you there when they crucified my Lord? I was. I was complicit. Jesus did not just die for his contemporaries. He died for me.

GOD'S RESPONSE TO EVIL AND VIOLENCE

All Lives Belong to God

Job tragically lost all ten of his children in a disaster sanctioned by God. Job's response was to worship, saying, "Naked I came from my mother's womb, and naked I will depart. The Lord gave and the Lord has taken away; may the name of the Lord be praised." Notably, "In all this, Job did not sin by charging God with wrongdoing."

Job had grasped the truth conveyed by the opening words of Psalm 24, words that profoundly undermine all human claims to entitlement: "The earth is the Lord's, and everything in it, the world, and all who live in it."

Understand this: My life is not truly mine but belongs to my creator. There is no such thing as inherent immortality. Life is not an inherent right, but a privilege, blessing, and gift.

Many people view our bodies as biological machines that function on their own, with death marking total breakdown. How many truly believe that all life comes from God and depend on him for every heartbeat and breath?

As Elihu reflected, "The Spirit of God has made me; the breath of the Almighty gives me life" (Job 33:4). Elihu also observes, "If it were [God's] intention and he withdrew his spirit and breath, all humanity would perish together and mankind would return to the dust" (Job 34:14–15).

People often fail to understand that all life comes from God and that he has the right to take it away due to our immense evil. The Great Flood in Genesis illustrates this point, showing God's response to human depravity.

We Fail to Honor and Thank God for our Lives

Despite Noah's survival via the ark, human hearts remained evil. God then vowed never to destroy all living creatures by water again, despite "every inclination of the human heart [being] evil from childhood" (Genesis 8:21).

We struggle to accept how the Bible views our morality. We imagine a spectrum with evil figures like Hitler and Stalin at one end and decent individuals at the other. In this view, even atheists can be highly moral, along with many who live as if God is irrelevant or marginal. In Romans 1 Paul disabuses us of this fatally flawed understanding of the human moral condition. Some years back, when my wife was alive, we visited a family. Their ten-year-old was a delightful, sweet young girl. Years later, then aged 16, that same girl had become an objectionable spoilt brat. She was rude and disrespectful to her ever-obliging parents, demanding that they do what she wanted and never showing an ounce of gratitude for anything they did for her, which was in fact a great deal.

In Romans 1 Paul paints a portrait of your heart, of mine. God is our creator. Deep down, even though many are in a state of denial, we all know this. He is the source of all the goodness we experience in life because whether we admit it or not we are living in a God-created world. Yet we think, speak, and act as spoilt brats. Or, as Paul puts it, "For although they [all people] knew God, they neither glorified him as God nor gave thanks to him, but their thinking became futile and their foolish hearts were darkened" (Romans 1:21).

Have you ever considered that it is because of a generous creator that we continue to exist? Often, we fail to honor or express gratitude to our creator, and instead treat other things and people as more important. We are behaving like spoilt brats when we see ourselves as entitled to demand that God treat us as we want to be treated.

Only when we see that God is fully within his rights to destroy sinful human beings can we begin to understand the conquest which, in fact, foreshadows the ultimate dispensing of divine violence that will occur on the Day of Judgment, when all evil is removed from God's radically renewed universe by the eternal and, yes, violent removal of all evildoers.

THE CONQUEST AND THE CREATION OF A NEW HUMANITY

Above, we alluded to the way in which major events in biblical history have an eschatological bent. It is vital to see that this is very much the case with the conquest.

Think back to the Garden. In particular notice the language used to describe man's role when he was "put" in the Garden (Genesis 2:15).[27] Later, we see this term used for manna, Aaron's linen garments, and

---

27. See Sailhamer, *Pentateuch*, 100.

representative tribal staffs being "put" in the Most Holy Place, plus the basket of first fruits "put" in the presence of God.[28] The "putting" of Adam in the Garden is God setting him apart to serve him in his presence. Indeed, this verse uses additional language that makes it clear that the man was put in the Garden to do the "work" of a priest by "guarding" the sanctity of the Garden. These same two terms are later used to describe the "work" of the Levites in "taking care" of all the furnishings of the tabernacle (Numbers 3:7–8). Of course, Adam and Eve failed to "guard" the Garden: that is, they failed to drive out evil from the Garden. As a result, they themselves, as evildoers, are driven out of the Garden. But the Garden still needs to be guarded and consequently we read: "After he drove the man out, he placed on the east side of the Garden of Eden cherubim and a flaming sword flashing back and forth to guard the way to the tree of life" (Genesis 3:24). Yes, that word "guard" is precisely the same word initially used to denote what God put the man in the Garden to do.[29]

All well and good, but what does this have to do with the conquest? The point is that God intends for his people collectively to be a new "Man," that is, the embodiment of a new humanity which he will place in a new version of the Garden of Eden, namely the land of Canaan. As "a kingdom of priests" (Exodus 19:6), it will be their responsibility to drive evil out of this new "garden"; otherwise, they are warned, like Adam and Eve, they will themselves be driven out. And, of course, this is precisely what eventually happened, when God drove his people out into exile in Assyria and Babylon respectively.

The eschatological significance of the conquest is this. As a faithful creator, God is committed to forming a new humanity, free of evil, that forevermore will live in a garden paradise from which all evil has been driven, never to return. It is confident expectation of the ultimate realization of this with which the Bible ends (Revelation 21–22).

Consequently, the violence involved in the conquest underscores a fundamental truth. The driving out of evil from God's universe necessitates the use of violence, precisely what the dreadful Day of Judgment will involve. At the time of the conquest, God called upon his people to be a new humanity, demonstrating their willingness to do that which is necessary to bring about a world from which evil has been driven out.

28. Exodus 16:33–34; Leviticus 16:23; Numbers 17:4; Deuteronomy 26:4, 10.

29. Ezekiel sees the king of Tyre as recapitulating what happened in the Garden. It's as though he, having been placed in the Garden as its "guardian cherub" (Ezekiel 28:14), commits such wickedness, that he too, as it were, is driven out from the Garden, significantly dubbed "the holy mount of God."

Violence against the New Humanity

Similar to some detective stories with unexpected twists, the biblical story line also contains surprising elements. During the conquest, the removal of evil required acts of violence by God's people. This historical period highlights how, instead of eliminating the evil from the land, God's people formed prohibited relationships with the Canaanites, resulting in God's people becoming even more evil than the Canaanites themselves. Thus, the biblical account emphasizes that true elimination of evil requires addressing the evil within the human heart.

Ironically, the removal of evil from human hearts is achieved through violence against, not by, the new humanity. Jesus, as the New Adam, embodies this new humanity, and it is violence against him, his crucifixion, that lays the foundation for eradicating evil from the human heart. This process fosters a diverse, new humanity formed progressively from all nations. Ironically, those who belong to this new humanity are victims rather than perpetrators of violence, highlighted in the Sermon on the Mount's closing benedictions: "Blessed are those who are persecuted because of righteousness, for theirs is the kingdom of heaven. Blessed are you when people insult you, persecute you and falsely say all kinds of evil against you because of me. Rejoice and be glad, because great is your reward in heaven, for in the same way they persecuted the prophets who were before you" (Matthew 5:10–12).

With this broader biblical perspective in mind, let's think about this whole issue of violence.

The Necessity of Violence to Remove Evil

Face reality: evil involves violence at different levels—physical, emotional, and psychological abuse. Combatting evil necessitates violence. This is why nations have police and military forces. While they do not completely eliminate evil, they help contain it.

Even if we accept that divine violence is necessary to remove evil, many struggle with the annihilation of entire populations, including women and children. The Israelites sought to pass peacefully through the territories of Kings Sihon and Og. However, these kings responded with aggression, leading to war. Moses recounts that after God delivered these armies into the hands of the Israelites, they destroyed all their cities, including men, women, and children.[30]

In Deuteronomy 20, God instructs the Israelites to treat enemies differently based on their location. For distant enemies, they should seek peace, but if unsuccessful, they may spare women and children and take plunder: "This is how you are to treat all the cities that are at a distance from you and do not belong to the nations nearby" (verse 15). By contrast we read: "However, in the cities of the nations the Lord your God is giving you as an inheritance, do not leave alive anything that breathes. Completely destroy them—the Hittites, Amorites, Canaanites, Perizzites, Hivites and Jebusites—as the Lord your God has commanded you. Otherwise, they will teach you to follow all the detestable things they do in worshiping their gods, and you will sin against the Lord your God" (Deuteronomy 20:16–18).

Notice the rationale, given, as we've seen, that God intends for Canaan to be a new Eden. God's people are being called upon to be utterly ruthless in ensuring that all temptation to do evil is removed from the land. Most of us are naturally repulsed by violence, especially against women and children. However, only in the land of Canaan, and only during a specific historical period, were God's people instructed to do this as that deemed necessary for making Canaan a new Eden.

The Conquest and the Use of "God's Will" to Justify Violence

Collins represents scholars who believe that biblical texts are ideological fictions, not reliable historical accounts of early Israelite history.[31] There are debates about the dates of the Exodus, the Israelite entrance into Canaan, and related archaeological evidence. While the Bible describes Joshua's conquest, some argue that the Israelites did not actually conduct a large-scale slaughter of the Canaanites.

Leaving aside archaeological evidence and questions of historical authenticity, as James Barr observes, "the problem is not whether the narratives are fact or fiction, the problem is that, whether fact or fiction, the ritual destruction is commended."[32]

---

30. Deuteronomy 2:34; 3:6.
31. Collins, "Zeal of Phinehas," 10.
32. Cited by Collins, "Zeal of Phinehas," 11.

Indeed, for debunkers of biblical authority such as Collins and Barr, the view of Scripture as divine revelation is considered "the root of religious violence in the Jewish and Christian traditions." When the Bible is treated as God's Word then its categories become absolute and it is "not subject to negotiation or compromise."[33] So Collins concludes: "The Bible has contributed to violence in the world precisely because it has been taken to confer a degree of certitude that transcends human discussion and argumentation. Perhaps the most constructive thing a biblical critic can do toward lessening the contribution of the Bible to violence in the world, is to show that that certitude is an illusion."[34]

It is important to understand that interpreting the conquest in the Bible as merely an example of people using "God's will" to justify violence is not accurate. For instance, Christopher Hitchens interprets Old Testament violence as suggesting that anything becomes ethically permissible if one believes in an all-powerful God who can decree any action, including acts of extreme violence.

Are Christians called upon to live lives of blind obedience, ready to do whatever they believe God is asking them to do, even if it means committing acts of violence? In Numbers 25 we read how Phinehas the priest was commended by God when he drove a spear through the bodies of an Israelite man and a Midianite woman as they were presumably copulating in the Israelite man's tent. White supremacist Richard Kelly Hoskins took this passage as his word from God, legitimating the banding together of four individuals intent on safeguarding what he considered to constitute true Christian identity. Like Phinehas, the self-dubbed Phinehas Priests set themselves against all that they viewed as immoral including interracial relationships, homosexuality, and abortion. In 1996, for example, they carried out a number of bombings on abortion clinics in the US.

Hitchens's argument is based on the assumption that all religion is created by humans, and any belief that a person or group has in their actions being directed by a deity is a purely subjective delusion. According to him, all Christians are just as deluded as Hoskins, even if their beliefs do not result in extreme actions. Historically, rulers and leaders have often claimed divine approval for acts of violence and war. Notably, however, in the ancient Near East, unlike in Israel, the divine will was typically determined through various forms of divination.[35]

---

33. Collins, "Zeal of Phinehas," 18.
34. Collins, "Zeal of Phinehas," 21.
35. John Walton cited by Rowley, "Epistemology of Sacralized Violence," 79.

Historically, there have been instances where professing Christians have invoked the will of God to justify acts of violence. For example, during the Crusades, the call to arms was met with the crowd's chant "*Deus vult*," meaning "God wills it."[36] Given that the God of the Bible is in fact the true and living God how is one to discriminate between true revelations and false ones? Consider the command given to the Israelites to kill every man, woman, and child in Canaan. It is important to note that Israel was not permitted to kill people under other circumstances. There was no mandate to conquer additional lands or to kill people except for the execution of capital punishment for a limited number of specified crimes and violations. Nevertheless, what distinguishes the Canaanite mandate from the numerous occasions in post-biblical history when professing Christians have claimed God's will in carrying out violent acts?

The Violence of the Conquest as God's Will

Miracles on a grand scale confirm that God's will was behind the Canaan mandate. The parting of the Jordan River for Israel to cross into Canaan and the fall of Jericho's walls are examples, similar to the wonders in Egypt and the Red Sea's parting.[37] These miracles clearly demonstrated God's intention for the Israelites to possess Canaan. This certainty contrasts with other ancient methods of divining the divine will, which lacked objective proof. Unlike subjective visions or spoken words, these extraordinary miracles authenticated God's will beyond doubt.[38]

For many, the command to exterminate all who lived in Canaan is morally offensive. It belongs to much else in the Bible which is deemed to be not worthy of any "God" or of humanity. Greg Boyd, asserting that the cross reveals God as non-violent and that all Scripture points to this conclusion, interprets biblical passages that associate God with violence

---

36. Rowley, "Epistemology of Sacralized Violence," 66.

37. Joshua 3–4.

38. For a full consideration of how attendant miracles make certain the objectivity of God's will for Israel, see Rowley, "Epistemology of Sacralized Violence." As Rowley shows, the epistemology of sacralized violence serves to critique "the claims of those who invoke God's will as a justification in present-day violence" (p.64). As Rowley states, "God desired to safeguard against the misunderstanding of his will: therefore he chose to validate new knowledge with miracles" (p.66).

as reflecting the perspectives of sinful people rather than the true nature of God.[39]

In the second century AD, Marcion gained notoriety by rejecting the Old Testament and accepting only ten of Paul's epistles, and his own abbreviated version of Luke's Gospel. He opposed what he saw to be depictions of a malevolent deity, favoring a benevolent God. Boyd's approach is similar, dismissing violent portrayals of God. Others mitigate problematic passages by emphasizing themes like Deuteronomy's concern for slaves and aliens, or the New Testament's teachings on loving enemies.[40]

God informed Abraham that his offspring would endure slavery and oppression for a period of 400 years in a foreign land. He also revealed that they would depart from that land with substantial wealth before returning to Canaan, the territory that God had pledged to Abraham. God explained to Abraham that "the sin of the Amorites has not yet reached its full measure."[41] The conquest took place as a result of the Canaanite societies in the region having descended into such moral corruption that divine judgment could no longer be withheld.[42]

When faced with extreme evil, it is important to remember the above perspective. The existence of evil is often used to question or doubt God's existence or to suggest he is indifferent and uncaring. While addressing this issue fully would require extensive discussion, biblically-informed believers often find that human atrocities reinforce their faith. They believe that all injustice and evil arouses God's indignation, and that his lack of immediate intervention is due to divine restraint. Amid such malevolence, God gathers a community for himself, creating a new humanity, showing remarkable patience and giving people a chance to repent before it's too late.

Anyway, the ordered destruction of Canaanites in the land was first and foremost God's way of clearing away evil from the land. It was not ethnic cleansing. They were not targeted because of their ethnic identity. Nor was it an attack on religion as such, though in this case religious

---

39. This is a precis of the entire thesis Boyd presents in his book *Cross Vision*.

40. Collins, "Zeal of Phinehas," 19.

41. Genesis 15:16.

42. Scholars such as Collins, who do not accept the Bible as divine revelation, do not take biblical denunciations of the Canaanites at face value and, therefore, refuse to accept that the Canaanites were as evil as the Bible declares them to be. Collins, "Zeal of Phinehas," 10.

views and practices were inseparably linked to evil. For example, one evil was the sacrifice of children to appease deities.

God could have eradicated the entire human population without any human involvement, as demonstrated during the Flood and the destruction of Sodom and Gomorrah. However, it is important to note that natural disasters should not be interpreted as signs of divine wrath directed at those affected. Jesus clarified this misconception by asserting that the Galilean victims of Roman oppression were not greater sinners than their fellow Galileans, and similarly, the eighteen individuals who perished in a tower collapse were not more culpable than others residing in Jerusalem.[43] In fact, Jesus added—and when do people ever really think like this?—that any time we see people dying *en masse* we should take to heart our personal need to repent, to get our lives right with God.

IMPORTANT CONSIDERATIONS IN UNDERSTANDING THE CONQUEST

There is much more that can be said and I recommend reading two chapters devoted to the conquest of Canaan in Paul Copan's book *Is God a Moral Monster?*[44] It is worth noting a few key points made by Copan:

- Response to evil not ethnic identity. Against the notion that the conquest of Canaan was ethnic cleansing note that in the Old Testament God's judgments consistently fall on those who practice evil, whether they are non-Jewish or Jewish, and especially on his own people.

- Equal rights of resident foreigners. The law of Moses treated foreigners legitimately living in the land as having the same legal rights as the native Israelite. Indeed, the Israelites were commanded to love them as themselves.[45]

- Rhetorical language of destruction. The conquest of Canaan was not as broad and brutal as many believe. Copan suggests that the language in the book of Joshua resembles the typical war language used in the ancient Near East and aligns with other military stories from that period. For example, at one point we read that Joshua "left

---

43. Luke 13:1–5.
44. Copan, *Is God a Moral Monster?*, 158–97.
45. Leviticus 19:33–34.

no survivors. He destroyed all who breathed, just as the Lord, the God of Israel, had commanded."[46] But the very closely connected book of Judges begins with the mention of Canaanites who were not driven out and still remained. As Copan explains, Joshua was not being deceptive but simply using language which the people of his day would have understood. Think of the way we might say the All Blacks massacred England in the 2015 Rugby World Cup.

- Location of inhabitants. Copan, following Hess, explains that when Joshua mentions the destruction of every living being in Jericho and Ai, it is important to note that archaeological findings show these cities were mainly military forts and not places where most people lived. Although there were some women like Rahab present, the majority of the population resided in the countryside rather than in these fortified locations. This observation also applies to other Canaanite cities that were attacked.

From Israel's perspective, following God's commands means successfully removing the Canaanites from the land, so killing them may not be needed. Most instructions about how the Israelites should face the Canaanites when they arrive focus on this removal. For example, in Deuteronomy 9:5, driving out these groups fulfills God's promise to Abraham, Isaac, and Jacob. As Sailhamer points out, with the promise of Genesis 12:3 in mind: "in terms of God's ultimate purposes, God's driving the nations out of the land and giving it to Israel was part of God's ongoing plan to bring blessing to all nations, including, ironically, those who were now being driven out of the land."[47]

Still, even allowing for the qualifications presented by Copan, we need to deal with the reality that the sacred ban (*herem*) commanded by God, consistent with what we find elsewhere in the ancient Near East, does involve the complete displacement of the population of Canaan, whether by expulsion or extermination.

The Conquest, Holiness, and Ritual Purity

Ideas are involved here that are at odds with Western beliefs, particularly those concerning what is clean, unclean, and holy. God sees the land of

---

46. Joshua 10:40.
47. Sailhammer, *Pentateuch*, 442.

Canaan as his own property, similar to how a landlord views their house. We often hear stories about tenants who trash the house they are renting. God believes the current residents, the Canaanites, have defiled his land, his property. As a result, he instructs the Israelites to remove them and, if necessary, destroy them.

It is God's clearly expressed intent that his people should be a "holy people," indeed a "royal priesthood,"[48] and that they should treat the whole land as priests living not merely in a house, but in God's house, God's temple.[49] The sacred ban is all about making that which is otherwise merely public or secular, holy. God's purpose is that his holy presence fill the whole land.

To help his people understand his holiness, God established rules about what is clean and unclean. Since God is holy, he cannot be associated with anything unclean. As Athas explains, being "unclean" is akin to being God's enemy, or being in debt to him and to society.[50] Israelites could become unclean by sinning or by coming into contact with something or someone unclean. Even those who were clean and thus in a state of readiness for a personal relationship with God still needed to recognize God's authority over their lives. They did this by offering sacrifices to express the true state of their hearts.

But there's a problem. At this point in history, holiness was only available to Israel. To be in a state of holiness, which involved an intimate, personal relationship with the one true God, one had to be a member of the covenant community, symbolized by circumcision.

In 2017, Australia faced a constitutional crisis when it was revealed that several politicians had not given up their citizenship from other countries, which the constitution requires. Many of them chose to resign. To live in God's house, the temple, that is, the entire land of Canaan, a person needed to be or become part of the covenant community.

When Israel arrived in the promised land, they encountered people who were all unclean. This was mainly due to their strong devotion to other gods and the idols they worshiped. The fundamental integrity of the priestly covenant community is fundamentally compromised if the

---

48. Exodus 19:6.

49. Exodus 15:13, 17: "In your unfailing love you will lead the people you have redeemed. In your strength you will guide them to your holy dwelling... You will bring them in and plant them on the (temple) mountain of your inheritance—the place, O LORD, you made for your dwelling, the sanctuary, O LORD, your hands established."

50. Athas, *Deuteronomy*, 126.

Israelites merely attempt to coexist with the Canaanites on the land. As Athas points out, "Holiness was not contagious."[51] The holiness of the Israelites could not be imparted to the Canaanites solely through the presence of the Israelites in the land. Moreover, Canaanite society was fundamentally at odds with everything that Israel embodied, as the Israelite worldview was incomprehensible to other ancient peoples. This disconnect was so profound that, throughout history, the Israelites frequently failed to honor their own constitution and often reverted to the cultural values and belief systems of the ancient civilizations with which they interacted.

The Conquest and the Nature of Ancient Societies

Athas, recognizing that modern people recoil against the program of social dismantling commanded by God, helpfully presents six considerations that help us to see things from an ancient rather than a modern perspective:

- The lack of institutional infrastructure and technologies.
- The lack of democratic processes and of universal suffrage.
- The lack of any societal basis for championing individual human rights.
- The lack of individual religious expression.
- The lack of any concept of religion as a relative belief.
- The legitimacy of divine judgment against sinful people.

Athas explains how "radical change in a society could not be achieved through the kinds of formal protocols today."[52] Israel's government, like that of all ancient societies, was "from the top, down," meaning that "going to the polls or passing legislation through parliament" could not bring about radical change. Furthermore, in all ancient societies, the tribe or nation—rather than the individual—was "the center of social gravity," meaning that overthrowing a government or expelling specific individuals was insufficient to bring about radical change. Since each tribe or nation was thought to have its own god or gods connected to a

---

51. Athas, *Deuteronomy*, 128.
52. For this and the points that follow see Athas, *Deuteronomy*, 131–35.

specific region in antiquity, it was unthinkable that the Canaanites as a whole would switch their religion, especially since they believed it to be absolute, not relative.

Ultimately, it all boils down to this: God is the earth's judge, and, in rendering judgment, sin is also treated as a collective reality and not merely as an individual issue. Ironically, this is still the case despite the individualism of the contemporary Western world because we are all inherently cultural beings and, despite the fact that many of us like to think of ourselves as free thinkers, we all profoundly adhere to cultural and sub-cultural values and belief systems.[53]

Violent Curses

What about the imprecations or curses I spoke of earlier? There are a number of psalms in which this is so dominant that they have been called imprecatory psalms.[54] Among all the wonderful words of worship and faith found in the psalms we find some very brutal words. Here are just a few examples:

> May the Lord cut off all flattering lips
> and every boastful tongue . . .[55]

> May his children be fatherless
> and his wife a widow.
> May his children be wandering beggars;
> may they be driven from their ruined homes.
> May a creditor seize all he has.
> may strangers plunder the fruits of his labor.
> May no-one extend kindness to him
> or take pity on his fatherless children.
> May his descendants be cut off,
> their names blotted out from the next generation.[56]

It's pretty hard to top this one:

> O Daughter of Babylon,

---

53. "It is more that the culture shapes hearts and minds, than that hearts and minds shape culture" (Hunter) cited by Bjoraker, "How Do Cultures Really Change?"

54. For example, Psalms 12, 35, 52, 69, 70, 83, 109, 129, 137, 140. See too 5:10; 10:15; 17:13; 28:4; 40:14–15; 55:9, 15; 59:12–13; 79:6, 13.

55. Psalm 12:3.

56. Psalm 109:9–13.

> doomed to destruction,
> happy is he who repays you
> for what you have done to us—
> he who seizes your infants
> and dashes them against the rocks.[57]

In the case of this last example, taken from Psalm 137, it is important to realize that a sustained metaphor is being used. In the immediately preceding verse we have the following NIV translation: "Remember, O LORD, what the Edomites did on the day Jerusalem fell. 'Tear it down,' they cried, 'tear it down to its foundations'" (verse 7).

This rendering conveys the broad sense but fails to capture the metaphor used by the psalmist. Here Jerusalem is likened to an unfortunate woman who falls into the hands of lustful enemies who intend to rape her. The verb translated "tear it down" can be understood as "to make nakedness seen," serving as a euphemism for sexual intercourse.[58] According with this, the word "foundations" has a double sense, namely "buttocks." So, the sense is as follows: "Strip her, strip her, exposing her complete nakedness."[59]

In the ancient world, it was common to compare cities to women, as the above illustrates. When the psalmist turns to curse Babylon, that is exactly what is taking place. Babylon is referred to as "Daughter Babylon" or "Mademoiselle Babylon," which does not imply that she has a father but rather presents her as a sophisticated young lady.[60] The curse's language does allude to the ruthless and savage treatment of enemies' children by soldiers up to the present day. However, the metaphor is not about actual children, but rather the "children" of the "woman," which is Babylon, or the people of Babylon.[61]

An understanding of the woman and mother metaphor of Psalm 137 may soften the force of the curse, but it still belongs to a significant number of very harsh utterances. There have been attempts to fudge. One scholar thought when the psalmist said such things he was using "effective" magic against spiritual foes. Another believed these curses should

---

57. Psalm 137:8–9.
58. Stowe, *Song of Exile*, 176.
59. Compare Dahood, *Psalms III, 101–150*, 273.
60. See Goldingay, *Psalms 90–150*, 609.
61. Othmar Keel, cited by Goldingay (*Psalms 90–150*, 610), sees the children as figurative of Babylon's future. The underlying idea, to this mind, is that of putting an end to Babylon's self-renewing domination.

be read as prophetic words presaging the ultimate fate of the wicked. Yet others think this language is just rhetoric, words felt keenly enough, but used as a psychological technique, a catharsis, by those suffering at the hands of others.

However, we must not tolerate such feeble attempts to lessen the impact of these curses. No! The psalmist identifies himself with what he wants in retaliation, and these imprecations are directed at actual, flesh-and-blood people. The Old and New Testament imprecations are not rhetorical; rather, they are prayers for judgment that God has undoubtedly answered and will continue to answer.

If it is naïve to water down such language it is also simplistic to regard them as but unbecoming words of hate and venom. Some interpret such words as proof that the psalmist was not completely reliant on God and was not patiently enduring suffering. Not a few have labelled such imprecations as "unchristian" or "sub-Christian."[62]

When Judas Iscariot died a revolting death Peter quoted curses from two psalms.[63] Peter believed that God had answered such prayers with respect to Judas. Indeed, prior to this Jesus picked up the language of another psalm and uttered the fundamental word of curse on Judas.[64] Jesus uttered woes, that is, curses upon the teachers of the law and the Pharisees.[65] Paul indicated that unbelievers are subject to the curse of the law[66] and he utters a most extreme and emphatic curse on any who would preach another gospel.[67] Indeed Paul utters the following general imprecation: "If anyone does not love the Lord—a curse be on him. Come, O Lord!"[68] It is important to note that none of these New Testament curses is motivated by personal vengeance or vindictiveness, which would be contrary to the New Testament's spirit.

---

62. For example, John Bright speaks of the prayer of Psalm 137 as "sub-Christian," though he expresses sympathy for the psalmist as one who was driven by the savagery experienced during the exile. See Firth, " Cries of the Oppressed," 77. Firth finds Bright's approach deficient in that "it relocates authority away from the text of Scripture itself and onto the person who prays."

63. Acts 1:20. Peter quoted Psalm 69:25 and Psalm 109:8.

64. Matthew 26:23–24. Jesus cited Psalm 41:8–10.

65. Matthew 23.

66. Galatians 3:13.

67. Galatians 1:8–9.

68. 1 Corinthians 16:22.

Curses and God the Lawgiver

What then should we say about the imprecations of the Bible, especially those uttered in the book of Psalms?

Reading something in light of its historical context is always a good idea. When we do this, we discover that the way the law functioned in the country of Israel and other parts of the ancient world differed greatly. Around 1754 BC, when the descendants of Jacob were still residing in Egypt, the sixth of the Babylonian kings, Hammurabi, enacted the Law Code of Hammurabi. In Mesopotamia it was Hammurabi and his officials who administered justice and the punishment of crime. However, in the early years of Israel's history, there were no authorities to take over the private individual's responsibility for atoning for an offense. Under such circumstances, the blood feud operated.

Later on Israel was granted kingship. When the Israelite state seized much more control of local life, blood feuds were curbed. But the private individual still did not regard the State as the custodian of law, even though this was standard in other ancient societies. To do this would be a violation of faith in Israel's God; it would be to divorce all law from the absolute and immediate jurisdiction of God.

Israel had a very different perspective on morality and judgment. The essential thought was that all life belongs to God. In contrast to other ancient law codes such as that of Hammurabi, all law in Israel is much more closely tied to religion; all law is of divine origin. In such a world the individual who has been wronged looks to God to deal with the perpetrators of injustice.[69]

Curses and Outrage

However, more is involved in the imprecatory psalms than the psalmist's nose being put out of joint by unfair treatment; than an experience of injustice exciting a passion for vengeance.

---

69. Firth observes "that the imprecatory psalms are marked by an act of surrender, in which the right to retribution is left to Yahweh," understanding "that justice begins finally to Yahweh." Firth, "Cries of the Oppressed," 81. In the case of Psalm 109, the psalmist is applying the law of false accusation as per Deuteronomy 19:16–19, in response to malicious accusations made against him. As Firth remarks, "What is requested therefore is an expression of justice linked to the outcome that would have applied had the psalmist been convicted, which is in effect an application of the *lex talionis*." Firth, "Cries of the Oppressed," 84.

Think about this sentiment: "Do I not hate those who hate you, O Lord, and abhor those who rise up against you? I have nothing but hatred for them; I count them my enemies."[70]

I know, the language of hate doesn't sound good and demands a comment. But do observe that the psalmist is not motivated by a desire for personal revenge. Rather, he is so outraged that anyone should make themselves the enemies of his God that he counts them his enemies too. The psalmists accept God's right to be the moral governor of the world and therefore deem it to be just and right for him to judge those who do evil.

Curses and the Need for Justice

Let's now go a step further. The Bible involves what we call progressive revelation. As history progresses God's people receive increments of revelatory insight. When the psalmists were composing their psalms they did not know as much as we do now about how God's justice works.

At this stage in history the psalmist did not have a clear concept of the Day of Judgment nor did they have a clear understanding of what form judgment might take after death. Think about the implications of this. For all those vitally concerned to see righteousness rewarded and evil punished, the focus was very much upon seeing God's judgment carried out in this world before people died. This was particularly acute in a world in which human judicial systems frequently failed to deliver justice.

One of the key reasons why Christians can have an entirely different attitude is because we bathe in the light of a fuller revelation brought to us in and by Jesus. We know what will happen after people die and we know there will indeed be an ultimate day of reckoning.

In Israel, people were seen as either righteous or wicked, with little expectation of moving between these categories. The wicked could be warned and threatened,[71] but conversion was rare. Examples like Ruth, Rahab, and Naaman are exceptions. Mostly, conversion applied to righteous individuals who had fallen into sin. The Lord "restores" or "converts" the soul of such who, for a time, wander from the right path.[72] The psalms reflect a pre-gospel era where it was uncommon for salvation

---

70. Psalm 139:21–22.
71. For example, Psalm 2:10.
72. For example, Psalm 19:7; 23:3.

messages to result in the wicked being numbered among the righteous. Thus, eradicating evil focused on destroying its perpetrators.[73]

Curses and Powerlessness

Another consideration arises from the observation that many of the imprecatory psalms are attributed to David.[74] But in understanding David's prayers for vengeance it is important to keep in mind what David said to his enemy Saul: "May the Lord judge between you and me. And may the Lord avenge the wrongs you have done to me, but my hand will not touch you" (1 Samuel 24:12).

Indeed, as Firth concludes from his study of the imprecatory psalms, "In the end, these psalms ask us to take a position of powerlessness and to approach God only from that position."[75]

In this situation David had Saul at his mercy and was able to wreak personal vengeance. However, he refused to do so but left this matter in God's hands. We can be confident that the same faith undergirds David's imprecations in the psalms. David thus foreshadows Jesus's own response to being unjustly made to suffer by wicked people: "When they hurled their insults at him, he did not retaliate; when he suffered, he made no threats. Instead, he entrusted himself to him who judges justly."[76] David, like Jesus, believed vengeance belongs to God.[77]

Many psalms involving curses presuppose that the psalmist felt powerless and helpless in the face of evil and therefore needed to take refuge in God and look to him for redress. The imprecations are not an expression of self-righteous, power-seeking egotism but of immense pain and hurt caused by the evil actions of others. In all cases either the psalmist is helpless to do anything about it other than cry out to the Lord or else, like David with respect to Saul, refuses to take the law into his own hands.

---

73. Psalm 55:15.
74. Psalms 12, 35, 69, 70, 109, 140.
75. Firth, "Cries of the Oppressed," 88.
76. 1 Peter 2:23.
77. Romans 12:19.

Curses and a King's Responsibility

Imprecations uttered by a king have a specialized nature. Many are mouthed by David either as the Lord's anointed or as the reigning king, or, in the case of other psalms, by another monarch. The king has a responsibility before God to build a kingdom of righteousness and, therefore, the utterance of imprecations is an expression of his total commitment, in dependence upon God, to rid his realm of the rebels whose presence and activity undermine this objective and his responsibility to shepherd and protect his people.

So, while Christians worship the same God as the saints of the Old Testament, the context in which they do this is radically different. This has massive implications for the way Christians relate to people who make themselves the enemies of God's people.

The Israelites lived in a theocracy, which is a form of government in which God and his laws were regarded as supreme. Eventually, monarchy was incorporated into this, with the king expected to read God's laws every day and commit himself to implement them. We only have to think of our own nation to recognize that the preservation of our perceived or legislated rights and freedoms requires that action, sometimes involving necessary violence, is needed to deal with those who undermine or threaten those rights and freedoms.

It is right and proper to pray the imprecatory psalms provided that we recognize that love and hate are not necessarily mutually exclusive. Frame explains this well:

> If love is a disposition to seek the good of someone else, and hate is opposition to the values and plans of someone, then it is certainly possible both to love and to hate the same person. For example, it is possible to hate some vicious despot (Adolf Hitler, Josef Stalin, Idi Amin, Pol Pot, Slobodan Milosevic, Saddam Hussein) in the sense of opposing his plans and calling God to judge him, indeed even being emotionally disgusted by his character and actions, while at the same time desiring his conversion.[78]

---

78. Frame, *Systematic Theology*, 271.

Honoring Rightful Authorities

The New Testament orders Christians to submit themselves to governing authorities, recognizing that it is in the providence of God that they have the authority they possess.[79] To rebel against such authority is to rebel against what God has established. The early Christians were never so stupid as to assume that governing authorities would always act in the best interests of the people over whom they ruled. They of all people knew full well that this was often not the case. But they did believe in God's over-arching sovereignty and knew that governing authorities were expected to act for the good of the people. Christians were committed to being the very best of subjects, not merely to avoid punishment, but out of conscience.

Being good subjects or citizens (remembering that not all subjects were Roman citizens) required Christians to honor the king, the emperor. Christians would do this even if the ruler was not worthy of honor. One honors the king because he is the king, not because of his personal character or performance.

In 2003 I represented the Anglican Archbishop of Sydney at a national function for the Australian Federation of Islamic Councils. The then Prime Minister, John Howard, was the speaker. We had all been seated at tables getting to know each other for some time before the Prime Minister made his entrance. On one side of me sat the President of the Islamic Council of Tasmania, a delightful person to talk to. On the other side, sat a female politician (I won't say who or which party she represented). Anyway, when the Prime Minister walked in everyone stood until he took his seat. But as we stood the female politician on my right muttered under her breath, with contemptuous words I could clearly hear, "What are we standing for him for?" I was deeply shocked and offended. I don't know John Howard personally and am not in a position to assess him as a man. But I stood to honor him for the position he held.

One of the Ten Words is to honor our parents. This holds true regardless of how well or poorly our parents have raised us. Since our parents are our parents, we should respect them. When their children convert to Christianity, parents in many parts of the world turn against them. I encountered hostility from my stepfather when I became a Christian at the age of 19. But in many cultures people who devote themselves to Jesus are ostracized, beaten, and sometimes even killed by parents. Clearly, in

---

79. Romans 13:1; 1 Peter 2:13.

hostile situations Christians need to be wise as to what practical measures they will take for their own safety and wellbeing. But the command to honor our parents remains constant, however they may treat us.

Loving Our Enemies

Christians are not encouraged to think of unbelievers as their enemies. However, there are unbelievers who make themselves enemies. The New Testament is remarkably consistent in directing Christians as to the appropriate response to make in such cases. Consider this portion from the famous Sermon on the Mount:

> You have heard that it was said, "Love your neighbor and hate your enemy." But I tell you, love your enemies and pray for those who persecute you, that you may be children of your Father in heaven. He causes his sun to rise on the evil and the good, and sends rain on the righteous and the unrighteous. If you love those who love you, what reward will you get? Are not even the tax collectors doing that? And if you greet only your own people, what are you doing more than others? Do not even pagans do that? Be perfect, therefore, as your heavenly Father is perfect.[80]

When Jesus says, "You have heard that it was said" he is referring to laws given by God to the people of Israel through Moses. Jesus is not implying that he is opposed to what was said. Not for a moment is he saying that his Father got it wrong and he is now setting the record straight. No! Jesus's concern is with the interpretation and application of the law. As Jesus said, when introducing all these reflections on the law:

> I have not come to abolish them but to fulfill them. For truly I tell you, until heaven and earth disappear, not the smallest letter, not the least stroke of a pen, will by any means disappear from the Law until everything is accomplished. Therefore anyone who sets aside one of the least of these commands and teaches others accordingly will be called least in the kingdom of heaven, but whoever practices and teaches these commands will be called great in the kingdom of heaven. For I tell you that unless your righteousness surpasses that of the Pharisees and the teachers of the law, you will certainly not enter the kingdom of heaven.[81]

---

80. Matthew 5:43–48.
81. Matthew 5:17–20.

Now think about the law Jesus was referring to in this particular case: "You have heard that it was said, 'Love your neighbor and hate your enemy.'" This goes back to a command in Leviticus. I will quote it along with the command that immediately precedes it, which you will see is very relevant to the comments Jesus made about what it means to obey the command, "Do not murder": "Do not hate a fellow Israelite in your heart. Rebuke your neighbor frankly so you will not share in their guilt. Do not seek revenge or bear a grudge against anyone among your people, but love your neighbor as yourself. I am the Lord."[82]

Plainly, the command "love your neighbor" derives from here. What about "hate your enemy"? There is nowhere in the Old Testament that commands this. Israelites may have thought it was implied by the command in Leviticus; that it was okay to hate someone who was not a fellow Israelite and to seek revenge or bear a grudge against someone who was not from among their own people. Whatever, Jesus's focus is on amplifying what is implied in the command "Love your neighbor."

Jesus points out that every day, when we see the rising of the sun or the falling of rain, we should see that God cares for all people, both the evil and the good. Therefore, we must learn to love like our Father if we are to honor him and emulate him as his children. That's why we must love our enemies and pray for those who persecute us. This is not how people typically think and speak and act. The followers of Jesus are called to be different and this genuine loving of our enemies lies at the very heart of our distinctiveness.

Paul echoes his Lord when he exhorts, "Bless those who persecute you; bless and do not curse."[83] He goes on to say:

> Do not repay anyone evil for evil. Be careful to do what is right in the eyes of everyone. If it is possible, as far as it depends on you, live at peace with everyone. Do not take revenge, my dear friends, but leave room for God's wrath, for it is written: "It is mine to avenge; I will repay," says the Lord. On the contrary: If your enemy is hungry, feed him; if he is thirsty, give him something to drink. In doing this, you will heap burning coals on his head. Do not be overcome by evil, but overcome evil with good.

---

82. Leviticus 19:17–18.
83. Romans 12:14.

Christians Are Not Doormats

However, all this does not mean that Christians are called to be doormats, which people can just walk over and trample upon. It is a serious misunderstanding of Jesus's teaching to see him as promoting pacifism. Think deeply about this segment from the Sermon on the Mount: "You have heard that it was said, 'Eye for eye, and tooth for tooth.' But I tell you, do not resist an evil person. If anyone slaps you on the right cheek, turn to them the other cheek also. And if anyone wants to sue you and take your shirt, hand over your coat as well. If anyone forces you to go one mile, go with them two miles. Give to the one who asks you, and do not turn away from the one who wants to borrow from you.[84]

"What?" you say! Haven't I just shot myself in the foot? Isn't this passage blatantly commanding Christians to be pacifists and to always avoid violence? Isn't the same plea for pacifism implicit in Jesus's rebuke of Peter when he took up a sword to defend him in the Garden of Gethsemane, when Jesus told him to put away his sword?

Well, think again. "You have heard that it was said," so Jesus begins. These are the same introductory words used for all of the commands Jesus comments on. As we have seen, Jesus does not rubbish these commands or say they are now out of date and need to be replaced. He did not come to abolish the command "Eye for eye, and tooth for tooth."

Let's make sure we have taken this to heart. Consider the first illustration: "You have heard that it was said to the people long ago, 'Do not murder.'" In what follows Jesus urges a deeper understand of the implications of this command. Jesus explains that anger and derogatory words are a violation of what God intended when he issued this command. But Jesus is not abrogating the law which says "Do not murder" for he did not come to abolish it, but to fulfill it.

Similarly with the command "Do not commit adultery" and the other commands which follow. So, when we come to the command "Eye for eye, and tooth for tooth," Jesus is saying, "Yes, this is the law and it still stands. But I tell you do not use this law, as valid as it is, as an excuse to avenge yourself on the one who hurts or exploits you."

Does that bring back memory of those commands we quoted from Leviticus 19? Doesn't it seem as though these were very much in Jesus's mind as he presented these challenges against popular misunderstandings

---

84. Matthew 5:38–42.

of the Jewish law? Here I'm thinking of the words: "Do not seek revenge or bear a grudge against anyone among your people."

It follows that the principle of justice enshrined in the eye / tooth law still applies. If someone burgles my house and he is apprehended by the police, am I required as a Christian to say that I will not press charges? No! It is right and proper for justice to proceed and for the criminal to be tried and convicted in court. If the daughter of a Christian family in Pakistan is gang-raped by Muslim men—tragically not uncommon in that country—then that family has every right to pursue justice in the courts of the land, as elusive as this may be.

Jesus's command therefore calls for discernment. We need to avoid taking vengeance into our own hands. We are to make space for God's wrath, as we read from Paul earlier. Evildoers will most certainly receive their just deserts in due course. However, though we are not to use wrongs committed against us as justification for lashing back, we must also respect and obey the law of justice. For such a law is written not merely for our own benefit but for the good of society. Clearly, letting the burglar go scot-free is no help to the community. Letting rapists go free is to say in effect that it is okay for men to rape women with impunity.

But Jesus goes further than merely saying don't lash back. Not only are we to turn the left cheek if struck on the right one,[85] but to give even more to the one who unjustly treats us, throwing in a coat along with the shirt demanded of us, "going the extra mile," and not using the eye / tooth idea of justice to justify tight-fistedness to those who are in need.

---

85. Malina reads this in the light of his understanding of Mediterranean shame-honor culture. By turning the left cheek the disciple is playing the honor game of challenge and response. Turning the other cheek would normally end the violence. This is because by using the flat of the hand rather than the back of the hand on the right cheek the aggressor has already implied the disciple is someone of commensurate honor, otherwise he would have struck him with the back of his hand. Given this, the aggressor is unlikely to strike the left cheek because an "honorable" opponent does not deserve such an insult. Therefore, Malina assumes that Jesus would only have had in mind someone striking one of his disciples on the right cheek with the flat of the hand. This is so, because if someone had struck with the back of the hand this would communicate inevitable violence which treated the victim with utter contempt. In this case there would be no point in turning the other cheek. Consequently, Malina sees Jesus as recommending a response that has the same shaming effect as what Paul has in mind when he speaks of "heaping burning coals" on the head of one's enemy (Rom 12.20). Summarized by van Aarde, "Paul's Version," 44.

MISSION DEBRIEF

- **Human Nature and Violence.** There are many examples of religious violence, but fallen human nature will express itself in violence whether religiously or non-religiously.

- **Islam and Violence.** There is a legitimate place for violence in Islam, as indicated by its historical origins and texts in the Qur'an and Hadith, and the understanding that people either live in "the House of Islam / Peace" or "The House of War."

- **Government and Violence.** There is a necessary and rightful place for violence in a fallen world, especially for the sake of responsible government.

- **Peacemaking.** Christians are called to be peacemakers, but not pacifists. Yet, tragically, there are shameful historical expressions of "Christian" violence, sometimes rationalized by a lamentable misuse of Scripture.

- **Timing of Violence.** There is a radical difference between what God required of Israel in Old Testament times and what he now requires of his people. Justice demands the obliteration of evil and giving all that evildoers deserve. This necessitates violence—in history (for theocratic Old Testament Israel) and on the Day of Judgment.

- **The Most Horrendous Violence.** The most monstrous act of violence in history occurred when God the Son was tortured and crucified. All human beings are guilty of this crime above all crimes.

- **Valid Old Testament Violence.** Sanctioned Old Testament violence includes the command to annihilate all Canaanites and the imprecatory psalms. Various considerations caution against over-reading these texts.

- **Honoring Authorities.** Christians must honor God-given authorities such as the State and parents even if they are mistreated by them.

- **Justice Not Vengeance.** While loving one's enemies rules out seeking vengeance, it is not incompatible with seeking justice for wrongs committed.

GATHERING INTELLIGENCE

Read Romans 12:9–21

1. How must Christians respond to those who treat them with hostility or who wrong them?

2. There are exhortations in this section that do not deal directly with this (vv.9–13, 15–16). Do they have relevance for the way Christians will respond to mistreatment? If so, why and how?

Read Matthew 5:38–48

3. In what ways do Paul's words in Romans 12 reinforce what Jesus himself taught?

4. What is the Christian understanding of justice and how does it help in responding to mistreatment?

Chapter Five

Facing Inner Enemies

"The worst enemies we have are lodged in our own heart and in our very flesh and blood. They wake, sleep, and live with us, as an evil guest whom we have invited into our house and now we cannot get rid of."

Martin Luther (Ewald Plass, *What Luther Says*).

War is horrific and nowhere is this more so than with respect to the great war that has raged ever since our Fall. The outbreak of hostilities was instigated by the evil one who is intent on wreaking as much damage as he can to God's wonderful creation plan. While our struggles are against him and the forces at his command, we must also respond in godly ways to the human agents he uses in his implacable opposition to the church. We face not only inhuman but also human foes. But, tragically, we are often our own worst enemy. For, yes, we find that we have to fight against our very own selves.

John Frame is known for the way he consistently looks at things from three perspectives.[1] Whenever we try to understand anything we must keep in mind:

---

1. For what follows see *Systematic Theology*, 31, 848–49.

- God's norms and standards (the normative perspective).
- The factual situation or reality independent of our personal experience (the situational perspective).
- Our personal experience (the existential perspective).

For example, to understand what it means to think of God or Jesus as Lord we need to bear in mind:

- The authority of his commands and revealed will (the normative perspective).
- The reality of his control and sovereignty, whatever our personal perceptions may be (the situational perspective).
- Our personal experience as Christians of the Lord's presence with us as he dwells in us and among us (the existential perspective).

A healthy understanding of God's lordship involves appreciating his authority, control, and presence. Let's apply this to our inner struggle with the evil we find within our own persons. A proper understanding of this evil or "sin" will see it as:

- Rejecting the Lord's authority.
- Allowing our lives to be shaped and controlled by persons and factors other than the Lord himself.
- Lacking a personal experience of his presence, whatever other mystical experiences might be confused with this.

What then does it mean for us to live victorious Christian lives, characterized by Christlike goodness and righteousness? Victorious Christians respect our Lord's authority and obey him. We take seriously the fact of his control, the reality of his kingdom and its purposes, and allow this to shape our goals, seeking his glory and the prospering of his kingdom. We also live our lives sensitive to his presence with us, responding to our Lord with faith and love.

PSYCHOLOGICAL PERSPECTIVES[2]

Self-Image and the Demonic

Neil T. Anderson's Freedom in Christ Ministries have helped many and there is indeed much to admire and commend.[3] He rightly stresses the importance of Christians understanding who they are in Christ.[4] However, in the process he sets up a false dichotomy between being sinners and saints, and greatly exaggerates the importance of self-image.[5]

In his ministry Anderson discourages fixation with demons and wants to make sure the focus is very much on Jesus and immersing people in God's Word.[6] Nevertheless, he all too easily attributes to Satanic influence what is really plain sinfulness for which we need to take personal responsibility.[7]

He once surveyed 286 Christian high school students. He listed various "startling responses" as evidence, to his mind, that these children had experienced demonic influence.[8] Anderson considered such evidence to include reports of experiencing a frightening "presence" in one's room (45 percent); harboring bad thoughts about God (59 percent);

---

2. In this book I do not delve much into the various ways of thinking people have that are in conflict with gospel truth. For many examples of this see especially Moreau's book *Essentials of Spiritual Warfare*.

3. See the biographical and background information presented in Carl, "Analysis and Critique," 18–32. See too positive comments made by Powlison, notwithstanding his significant critique of Anderson—Carl, "Analysis and Critique," 223.

4. However, there is a need for greater balance. Anderson insists that the right order is not "who you are is determined by what you do," but rather "what you do is determined by who you are." Anderson, *Victory Over the Darkness*. This is an overstatement. To some degree this resonates with New Testament ethics which urge us to be what we already are in Christ, e.g. "You are the light of the world," so shine and don't put your light under the bushel. However, as Steven J. Cole points out, in his critique of Anderson's position, "Obedience is always right, whether I understand 'who I am in Christ' or not. We grow to understand our identity in Him as we trust and obey (see 2 Pet 1:5–11)." Cole, "Steak and Arsenic."

5. See the critique by Moore and Pyne: "Neil Anderson's Approach," 75–78.

6. Smith, "Church Militant," summarizes Walker's warnings against having a "paranoid universe" mindset as involving "a belief in being constantly under threat from demons, seeing God and Satan as warring over the most trivial issues in people's lives" (p.164), something Anderson wants to avoid. However, the exaggeration of demonic influence, as Smith observes, can "lead to looking for 'strong men' with 'gnosis' and power to protect us and perhaps help to turn us into 'spiritual warriors,'" and unwittingly Anderson appears to have succumbed to this danger.

7. Moore and Pyne "Neil Anderson's Approach," 78–79.

8. Anderson, *Helping Others*, 52.

finding it mentally hard to pray and read the Bible (43 percent); hearing "voices" in one's head, as though a subconscious voice was communicating 69 percent); entertaining thoughts of suicide (22 percent); and feeling that one is different from others and that what works for others doesn't work for "me" (74 percent).

In response Miller observed that while one can't exclude the possibility of Satan having an involvement in such experiences, "so too might human imagination, sinfulness, and emotional/psychological maladjustment."[9] To be fair, Anderson does make room for non-demonic factors to be at play. Whether the above surveyed responses indicated demonic influence among "Christian" students or not, the potential for demonic influence is greatly facilitated by the easy access children have to such pernicious media influences as pornography and violence.

Personal Problems and Generational Curses

One of the issues Anderson rightly addresses is the need to repent from the futile way of life inherited from one's forbears (1 Peter 1:18). However, Anderson's view of the generational transference of sin and curses and even demons smacks more of animistic influence than of a sound biblical understanding.[10] Unfortunately, in some circles we find a species of teaching on generational sins and curses which is highly damaging to a godly psyche and which undermines the gospel. As Priest, Campbell, and Mullen point out, this involves a basic misreading of animism which wrongly presupposes that the views of spirits found in folk religions correspond to the biblical view of spirits.[11]

We live in a world in which it is common for innocent people to become the victims of evil. Suicide bombings are a clear example of this. Tragically, when parents do evil things they often bring great suffering into the lives of their children. Somewhat along the same lines we read in Lamentations 5:7: "Our ancestors sinned and are no more, and we bear their punishment."

We also live in a world where many people believe they are responsible for evils perpetrated before they were born. For example, Hindus and Buddhists who believe in reincarnation and rebirth respectively,

9. Miller, "Neil Anderson."
10. Moore and Pyne "Neil Anderson's Approach," 81–85.
11. See Priest et al., "Missiological Syncretism," 18–19.

hold the view that each person alive today has had innumerable past "lives." For both Hindus and Buddhists to be reincarnated or reborn is itself wrong and their goal is to achieve an ultimate state of mind that will permanently end this cycle of birth, death, rebirth. But in both religions it is believed that karma in some previous existence accounts for the suffering and problems experienced in one's present lifetime and that "I" am in some way responsible for what happened before I was born.

In more recent times some prominent Christian leaders have been teaching something that bears some parallel to this. It was during what Peter Wagner termed the "Third Wave" Charismatic movement of the 1980s that the concept of "breaking curses" gained momentum.[12] Now there are those who teach that many Christians experience a cursed condition that is due to evils perpetrated before they were born. They are thinking of evils done by one's ancestors.[13]

Kenyan Biko Gerro Rading, Editor of Parastatal Africa Magazine, recalls a period in his life when something consistently happened to frustrate him from landing a job. His wife suggested that the problem might lie in his roots. He asks his readers, "Why is it that those who were performing poorly in schools are more successful in life than you, yet you have graduated with distinctions and you have been looking for a job for the last five or more years, to add salt into your injuries even those who were behind you in college are doing better?"

He then tells "us" why this is so, "Brothers and sisters, someone in your lineage sold you out and that's why your life is just there and you think it's normal . . . The truth of the matter is that there is generational curse that was laid upon your lineage and unless you break it then even your children will suffer even more worse than you are."[14]

---

12. Gondwe, "Breaking Curses." Wagner distinguished between a spiritual warfare movement he identified as occurring at the close of the twentieth century ("Third Wave") from two prior movements: the Pentecostal movement at the beginning of the twentieth century and the Charismatic movement in the middle of the twentieth century. Gardner, "Spiritual Warfare," 2.

13. In Buddhism "self" is an illusion, so the "evils" perpetrated before birth, technically speaking, were not committed by oneself and yet "I" am responsible for the sufferings I now experience, especially because a key reason for this condition is that I keep on mistakenly grasping on to this illusory "self." Consequently, the difference between those who attribute a cursed condition to what ancestors did before I was born and the Buddhist view is not as great as might first appear. In both instances there is the sense that I must take responsibility and am in some sense accountable for what not I but others have done before I was born.

14. Rading, "Generational Curses."

There are websites which preach that generational sins and curses constitute a problem of mammoth proportions. On the Above & Beyond Christian Counseling website Don Ibbitson claims that generational curses being passed down through family lines "may be responsible for between one half and two thirds of the issues people deal with"![15] Linda Chance and Karen Kaufman insist, "Many believers are experiencing bondages that evidence generational curses and iniquities."[16] They see alcoholism and disease as common expressions of generational curses rooted in iniquity. A high incidence of premature death in a family over a few generations is given as another example of this.[17] Derek Prince's understanding of generational curses insinuates that almost all Christians are likely to be under one:

> Conversely, any one of the four generations preceding us, by having committed these sins, could be the cause of a curse over us in our generation. Each of us has two parents, four grandparents, eight great-grandparents, and sixteen great-great grandparents. This makes a total of thirty persons, any one of whom might be the cause of a curse over our lives. How many of us would be in a position to guarantee that none of our thirty ancestors was ever involved in any form of idolatry or the occult?[18]

The Bible and Generational Curses

Rading views Exodus 20:5 (= Deuteronomy 5:9) as a text which refers to generational curses, and finds further support in Exodus 34:7 (God "punishes the children and their children for the sin of the parents to the third and fourth generation" = Numbers 14:18).

We read in Exodus 20:4–6: "You shall not make for yourself an image in the form of anything in heaven above or on the earth beneath or in the waters below. You shall not bow down to them or worship them; for I, the Lord your God, am a jealous God, punishing the children for the sin of the parents to the third and fourth generation of those who hate me, but showing love to a thousand generations of those who love me and keep my commandments."

15. Ibbotson, "Generational Curses."
16. Chance and Kaufman, *Signs, Wonders and Miracles*, 56.
17. Chance and Kaufman, *Signs, Wonders and Miracles*, 57.
18. Cited by Bob DeWaay, "Generational Curses."

The key words here are "to the third and fourth generation." This phrase is not only repeated in the parallel presentation of the Decalogue in Deuteronomy 5 but also, as indicated above, at Exodus 34:6–7.[19]

Jonas Clark, who calls himself Apostle Jonas Clark, runs a website entitled "Jonas Clark's Holy Spirit Ministry Training. Experience Something Different." Along with a multitude of others, Clark sees Exodus 20:5–6 as referring to "family curses," that is, "reoccurring problems that steal, kill, and destroy." He explains, "When someone up the family tree gives spirits the right to visit because of iniquity, they come looking for a reason to mess up your life. Take courage. After family curses are exposed, Christ's deliverance is readily available."[20]

Clark next attempts to summarize covenant curses set out in Deuteronomy 28, saying that this provides "a partial list" of family curses. In this way he identifies (1) emotional instability and fear (28:28); (2) hereditary family sickness (28:21, 27, 35); (3) barrenness, impotence, female problems (28:18); (4) family breakdowns, divorce (28:30, 32, 41); (5) lack, poverty, inability to produce (28:17, 29); (6) no ambition, vision, direction (28:29); (7) bondage and slavery (28:43–44).[21] Derek Prince presents a very similar list, also stressing the parallels with Deuteronomy 28. He teaches that if one of these things is happening this may not indicate a generational curse, but "if several of them are true, the diagnosis is pretty obvious."[22]

The idea of generational curses is deeply ingrained in many animistic societies in the so-called Global South (Africa, Latin America, and Asia).[23] But don't be confused by the language used in these biblical texts. These Scriptures have nothing whatsoever to do with pagan notions of generational curses. There is certainly no indication whatsoever of demonic spirits being passed down from one generation to another. Further, these texts are clearly set within the special "contract" or covenant that God entered into with his people, Israel, and it is therefore precarious to lift them out of this particular context and apply them

---

19. Compare Numbers 14:18.
20. Clark, "Battling Generational Family Curse."
21. Similarly Vander Klok, "Breaking Generational Curses."
22. Prince, "Seven Indications."
23. Philip Jenkins observes that in Africa, Asia, and Latin American (the Global South) there are a surprising number of churches that believe the power of evil can span generations. He comments, "For many Christians in the global South . . . the idea of ancestral guilt, of curses spanning generations, is anything but a relic of distant antiquity." Jenkins, *New Faces*, 120.

willy-nilly to Christians today. These Scriptures concern how God will treat his people if they rebel against him by committing idolatry. In the typical Israelite family there would be three of four generations living together in the same household at the same time.[24] Judgment "to the third and fourth generation" was a judgment that fell on such a household. The idea here is not of children being born subsequent to the initial operation of the curse and immediately being under a curse because of the family they were born into.[25] So in Deuteronomy 24:16 we read: "Fathers shall not be put to death for their children, nor children put to death for their fathers; each is to die for his own sin."

Calvin comments,

> But when God declares that He will cast back the iniquity of the fathers into the bosom of the children, He does not mean that He will take vengeance on poor wretches who have never deserved anything of the sort; but that He is at liberty to punish the crimes of the fathers upon their children and descendants, with the proviso that they too may be justly punished, as being the imitators of their fathers. If any should object, that this is nothing more than to repay every one according to his works, we must remember that,—whenever God blinds the children of the ungodly, casts them into a state of reprobation, (*conjicit in sesum reprobum*), and smites them with a spirit of madness or folly, so that they give themselves up to foul desires, and hasten to their final destruction,—in this way the iniquity of the fathers is visited on their children.[26]

---

24. Also pertinent is Sailhamer's observation concerning the preceding context of the Decalogue command in Deuteronomy 5 (see verses 1–5): "It should be noted that according to Deuteronomy 11:2ff., this generation (as children) saw God's glory in Egypt and the second, their children (the present generation), saw the great displays of God's glory. The next generation (the third), however, did not. The importance of placing this reminder at this stage in the narrative can be seen in the fact that the motivation given for the prohibition of idolatry in [sc. vv8–10] is its threat to the children of 'the third and fourth generation' (5:9) . . . Thus the second generation was being called upon to teach God's ways to the third generation" (cf. Deut 6:2). Sailhammer, *Pentateuch*, 436–37.

25. Driver points out: "children are linked to their parents by ties, physical and social, from which they cannot free themselves; and they suffer, not because they are *guilty* of their father's sins, but because by the self-acting operation of natural laws their fathers' sins entail disgrace or misfortune upon them." Cited by Sailhamer, *Pentateuch*, 467.

26. Calvin, *Commentary on Deuteronomy 5:9*.

It will be observed that Calvin's remarks are finely balanced and bridge the poles well. Significantly, Calvin does allow for a sovereign work of God, the effecting of a curse on the lives of those children which explains why they give themselves up to evil. Yet it is they themselves in their blindness, madness, or folly who are responsible for giving themselves up and rendering themselves deserving of God's judgment.[27] Some parallel to this can be observed in David's household. Following his heinous acts of committing adultery with Bathsheba and orchestrating the murder of Uriah, David was told: "the sword will never depart from your house, because you despised me and took the wife of Uriah the Hittite to be your own." Yahweh added, "Out of your own household I am going to bring calamity upon you."[28] Yahweh sovereignly effects this through the actions of Amnon and Absalom and yet in both instances these men are fully responsible and accountable for their own evil deeds.

In 2 Kings 14 we learn that King Amaziah, when he ordered the execution of those responsible for his father's assassination, refused to kill the assassin's sons in obedience to this very law.[29] This same principle is insisted upon in Ezekiel where God declares, with clear allusion to Deuteronomy 24:16: "The soul who sins is the one who will die. The son will not share the guilt of the father, nor will the father share the guilt of the son."[30] We find the same expressed at Jeremiah 31:30: "everyone will die for his own sin." In the New Testament we are informed: "God 'will give to each person according to what he has done.'"[31]

If space allowed we might give further attention to other points. For example, biblical notions of corporate responsibility; God's judgment only falling on "those who hate me"; and the immense socio-cultural pressure for children to imitate their parents in evil.[32]

---

27. As John Piper puts it, "The sins of the fathers are punished in the children through becoming the sins of the children," since they are "those who hate me." Piper, "How God Visits Sins."

28. 2 Samuel 12:10, 11.

29. 2 Kings 14:6 = 2 Chronicles 25:4.

30. Ezekiel 18:20.

31. Romans 2:6.

32. Exodus 20:6; Deuteronomy 5:9; cf. 7:9–10. As Priest et al. comment: "If we wonder how it is that children often end up with the same sins as their parents, we need not resort to undisciplined speculations. The Bible itself points to the role of parents in teaching and modelling and carries solemn warnings to those who lead children astray or cause them to stumble. Direct parental influence, then, is what is key. Such influence is a moral influence, not a magical one." Priest et al., Missiological Syncretism," 67.

Using such passages to support a doctrine of generational sins and curses is not only a flagrant mishandling of Scripture. There is also a fundamental logical flaw involved in this view. Most people have not only bad but also good ancestors. Now we have seen that God judges idolatrous Israelites to the third and fourth generation. But he also expresses his love to a thousand generations—a round about way of saying "forever." Think about it. If a person is subject to God's judgment because of sins committed four generations ago, then isn't he also the beneficiary of God's love as enjoyed by an ancestor who lived 1000 generations before? It follows from this that the idea of generational curse presupposes that a sin committed before one is born cancels out any and all blessings that would otherwise flow from generation to generation. The doctrine of generational curses implicitly teaches that God's judgment exceeds his mercy, which is to turn Exodus 20:4–6 on its head.

There are people living in animistic societies who believe, completely independently of the Bible, that there are curses which can blight families from generation to generation. Clearly great wisdom is required in knowing how to communicate the gospel to such people, given that the Bible does not directly address this issue. We must start by recognizing that the doctrine of generational curses is not taught in the Old Testament. The other fact is that not a single passage in the New Testament even remotely teaches the idea of a generational curse.[33] It should come as no surprise to find that nowhere in Scripture is there to be found any direct basis for recommending diagnostic tests, rituals, and prayers to deal with supposed generational curses.

Demons and Generational Curses

It is one thing to confront the demonic in the pagan world and the phenomenon of generational curses in animistic societies, but it is very disturbing when those who are "in Christ" are encouraged to see themselves as subject to demonic activity through no direct fault of their own. Anderson declares: "Demonic or familiar spirits can be passed on from

---

33. In Matthew 23:29–31 Jesus pronounces a woe or curse on contemporary scribes and Pharisees who by their actions demonstrate that they "are the descendants of those who murdered the prophets." But this is not a generational curse. It is just that these religious leaders are deceiving themselves when they think they are honoring the prophets, because their opposition to Jesus demonstrates that they are behaving in the same way as their ancestors.

one generation to the next if you don't renounce the sins of your ancestors and claim your new spiritual heritage in Christ. You are not guilty for the sin of any ancestor, but because of their sin, Satan may have gained access to your family."[34]

Anderson seeks to help Christians discover the demonic strongholds in their lives due to generational sins. He counsels them to perform deliverance ceremonies to break such strongholds. But he also teaches that there are cases where the demonic foothold is so strong that counselors with special knowledge of demonic strongholds are needed to assist them. Like Anderson, as can be readily seen from glancing at a vast number of websites, those who hold this view typically provide readers with techniques,[35] elaborate diagnostic tests and checklists, and recommend the words to use during the deliverance ceremony.

Joyce Meyer openly claims that a demon of lust has tormented her family:

> I told you that there was a spirit of incest in my family bloodline . . . And the thing that I want you to understand today is when there's a spirit like that in a bloodline, until some person believes on Jesus and takes the blood of Jesus and draws it across that natural bloodline, that devastation goes on for generations and generations . . . Well see, my father's grandfather had problems and so his father had problems and so my dad had problems and so I had problems and so if I wouldn't have stood and believed Jesus, my kids would have had problems and their kids would have had problems and so on and so on."

In her book *Prepare for War*, Rebecca Brown teaches that even after a person accepts Christ it is possible for demons to continue to remain

---

34. Anderson, *Freedom From Fear*, 332. Anderson recommends praying: "Dear heavenly Father, I ask You to reveal to my mind now all the sins of my ancestors that are being passed down through family lines. I want to be free from those influences and walk in my new identity as a child of God. In Jesus's name, amen" (p.333). He then encourages his reader to utter a wordy declaration Anderson has composed in which the reader cancels out all demonic working and "every curse that Satan and his workers have put on me." This declaration includes the words: "I reject all blood sacrifices whereby Satan may claim ownership of me" (p.334).

35. On the Vann Hutchinson ministries webpage we are informed: "Our advanced Deliverance School includes a new model for advanced deliverance which will unveil a revolutionary technique to deal with the following: 1. How to identify and break witchcraft curses. 2. How to identify and cast out the strongman. 3. How to break bondages from New Age, Eastern religion, and occult activities." Hutchinson, "Warriors for Christ."

in that person's life because demons still have the legal ground to do so through sin and / or ignorance.³⁶ Indeed, many who see generational curses as demonic believe that "Satan has the right to continue to hold legal claim against Christians who have not effectively dealt with their generational curses." So experiences of "failure, violence, impotence, profanity, obesity, poverty, shame, sickness, grief, fear, and even physical death" are seen as consequences of this unresolved issue.³⁷

It is highly ironic that this false teaching concerning generational sins and curses is aimed at combatting demonic forces. This teaching itself is demonic, precisely because it undermines gospel truth. While we find ourselves speaking out against the peddlers of such wrong and injurious doctrine, our real struggle here "is not against flesh and blood, but against the rulers, against the authorities, against the powers of this dark world and against the spiritual forces of evil in the heavenly realms" (Ephesians 6:12). Consequently, following what Paul urges us to do in this very context, the Christian needs to don the gospel armor to combat such false and psychologically damaging teaching.

Fullness in Christ and Generational Curses

In Colossians Paul sets himself against all that implies Christ is not enough. He states, "For in Christ all the fullness of the Deity lives in bodily form, and you have been given fullness in Christ, who is the head of every power and authority" (Colossians 2:9–10).

There is no power, no authority that can prevent any believer from possessing fullness in Christ. Yet, in clear rejection of such teaching, Derek Prince states:

> Before we can enjoy true liberty and the fullness of the new creation in Christ, this weed must be completely pulled out, with all its roots. The most important root, and the one hardest to deal with, is the tap root that links him to many generations who have worshiped false gods. Nothing but the supernatural grace and power of God can effectively remove all these roots. But thank God, there is hope in the promise of Jesus in Matthew 15:13: "every plant which my heavenly Father has not planted will be uprooted."³⁸

36. See Nunnally, "The Sins of Generational Curse."
37. Nunnally, "The Sins of Generational Curse."
38. Cited by Brooks, "Generational Curses. Part 1."

Notice that telling word "before." The person who has chosen to follow Christ but has not yet pulled out this "tap root" will not be able to enjoy "true liberty and the fullness of the new creation in Christ." Hence, this is a gospel of Christ PLUS. Similarly, it is a contravention of Colossians 2 to teach that demons have strongholds in the lives of Christians until they acquire necessary knowledge and command them to depart. As DeWaay rightly observes, this is a revival of the Colossian heresy: "We supposedly need Christ plus knowledge and some religious process to gain victory over the forces that are deemed to stand between us and 'completeness' in Christ."[39]

Many who adhere to the doctrine of generational sins and curses also sabotage the sufficiency of Christ's sacrifice for sins. So, as Nunnally points out, many who take this view of generational curse believe that while "Jesus's blood was shed for the sins of the individual . . . an additional step must be taken to remove the guilt a person inherited from his ancestors."[40]

An elaborate ceremony is required if a person is to be delivered from the bondage that holds him or her captive to ancestral sins. Commonly, the person concerned lists the sins of his or her ancestors up to four generations, confesses sins on their behalf, recites recommended prayers and declarations, and personally breaks the supposed curses. In his book *Blessing or Curse. You Can Choose* Prince teaches that the root cause can actually go back even thousands of years.[41]

Every person who becomes a follower of Jesus immediately becomes a son or daughter of Abraham. The New Testament is emphatic that this is not a matter of physical descent. Indeed, whatever one's ancestry might be, the one who owns Jesus as Lord immediately inherits all that Christ died to achieve on the cross for his people. As DeWaay comments, "Even if our parents, grandparents, and great-grandparents were atheists, occultists and blasphemers, God will pour out the full blessings of the New Covenant upon us if we truly come to Him through the cross."[42]

Those who teach that there need to be special ceremonies and prayers to deal with supposed generational sins and curses are doing the very thing the book of Galatians inveighs against: they are bringing people back under the curse of the law, under a system of works.

39. DeWaay, *Generational Curses*.
40. "The Sins of Generational Curse."
41. Cited by Nunnally, "The Sins of Generational Curse."
42. *Generational Curses*.

THE DECEITFULNESS OF THE HUMAN HEART

A psychologist was treating a woman with psychodynamic psychotherapy, a psychological approach which focuses on unconscious processes. He was exploring the woman's unconscious, or "implicit" mental processes as specialists might term it.

Paula (name changed) had a very negative view of her sister. She saw her as a spiteful person who said mean things about their father to embarrass him. By contrast, she saw her father as a kind and caring man. To her mind, their father had done nothing to deserve her sister's hostility and ingratitude.

After much questioning, Paula finally gave an example from her early years that she felt demonstrated this. Ironically, her father nearly drowned her sister, who was seven at the time, by holding her underwater. But Paula seemed incapable of understanding that she was describing child abuse. She saw this as evidence of her sister's bitchiness and provocativeness, which could even make a loving and caring father lose his temper in this way. Even as she recalled other instances in the past where her father had acted violently against her sister, this remained her constant opinion.

There was no evidence on Paula's part of any attempt to mislead or hide the truth. Further, she did not have a "repressed memory," but, in fact, a very lucid one. But she had fixated on one interpretation of her experiences and had not allowed herself to consider other ways of interpreting those same events. The psychologist, Jonathan Shedler, commented, "Most psychological difficulties were once adaptive solutions to life challenges. They may have been costly solutions, but they were solutions nevertheless."[43]

But then our circumstances change and we find ourselves applying the same old solutions, which no longer work and may well be self-defeating. To explore our hearts is to enter a labyrinth of unknown, convoluted, and sometimes dead-end pathways. There is no one who can truly understand our hearts, not us, not even a skilled and highly trained professional analyst. Well, there is one exception: "Nothing in all creation is hidden from God's sight. Everything is uncovered and laid bare before the eyes of him to whom we must give account" (Hebrews 4:13).

Consider the ways in which we hide from ourselves and others. Take Paula who hid from herself and others the true nature of her father's

---

43. Shedler, "That Was Then."

treatment of her sister. Shedler speculates that as a small child she clung to her interpretation of her father as being kind and caring, because of her desperate need to feel safe and secure in such a terrifyingly unsafe environment. But there is a danger here of merely thinking of this woman as employing "defence mechanisms" or "self-exonerating mechanisms."[44] A biblically informed psychology will not be satisfied if this is the only language used to describe what she was doing and continued to do.

I have compared the human heart with a labyrinth. In Greek mythology a half bull, half human monster, the Minotaur, at the very center of the Labyrinth created by Daedalus and Icarus, waited to devour the seven Athenian youths and seven maidens periodically sent into the labyrinth. There are monsters, enemies within the human heart, often well-concealed, that threaten to seriously wound or destroy us.

"The purpose in a man's heart is like deep water, but a man of understanding will draw it out." So reads the Proverb.[45] As the story of the woman above indicates, there is the potential for much good to eventuate when a skilled person draws hidden purposes and motives out of the dark depths of the human heart. Having served as a leader in a mission organization I am glad when I see mission agencies require candidates to meet with experienced and competent psychologists.

Our sovereign God may use those who approach psychology without gospel presuppositions to improve the psychological health of people in certain key respects. However, notwithstanding the positive benefits they may bring, when psychologists fail to see the deceitfulness of the human heart as moral corruption, they are thickening the layer of deceit that is already shutting God out of the solution.

Jeremiah said, "The heart is deceitful above all things, and desperately sick; who can understand it?"[46] We may feel very compassionate towards Paula. But the bottom line is that, like each one of us, she has a deceitful, desperately sick heart. Like each one of us she was born with a heart that is not merely faulty but has a default. In our fallen condition we have hearts that are pre-set to reject God's authority, that are ignorant of his power and lack consciousness of his presence.

Our hearts go out to Paula, but however much we understand the psychological processes involved, at the end of the day her heart is calling evil good when she thinks of her child-abusing father as kind and caring.

44. See Powlison, "Human Defensiveness, 40–55.
45. Proverbs 20:5.
46. Jeremiah 17:9.

Like all of us Paula needs to hear God speak with authority into her life. She needs to submit her life to his control. She needs to learn to live in the presence of God.

Think about "defence mechanisms" a bit more deeply. What is happening when secular psychologists become the authority speaking into troubled hearts, the ones to whom the heart yields control and the ones whose presence becomes vital to psychological health? The heart is effectively defending itself against any attempt of God to intervene in any significant manner. To do this it does what it always does. It constructs an idol. In this case secular psychology becomes the idol that replaces God.

"The hearts of men . . . are full of evil and there is madness in their hearts while they live, and afterward they join the dead."[47] Biblically controlled Christian psychologists begin with this knowledge. Of course, it helps to identify the profound impact of Paula's childhood experiences upon her life and to highlight deep-seated unmet needs. But Christian psychologists must never believe inner evil is the product of unmet needs or the result of crushing external experiences. True psychological health presupposes repentance and forgiveness. It presupposes the innermost workings of the Holy Spirit, transforming us into the image of Christ as we appropriate the means of grace—feeding on God's Word, relating to the Lord in prayer, and fellowshipping with his people.

Idols of the Heart

We have seen that there is an unhealthy tendency to give Satan far more attention than he receives in the Bible itself. The fact of the matter is that Satan and demons receive scant mention in the Old Testament. The bulk of references occur in the Synoptic Gospels concerning Jesus's confrontation with Satan and the demonic. But them, as Bolt puts it, "there is a tiny demonic dribble into the period of history recorded by the Acts, and only an occasional drip elsewhere in the New Testament."[48]

When it comes to spiritual warfare it is human evil rather than Satan that takes center stage. Jesus made it clear that "out of the heart come evil thoughts, murder, adultery, sexual immorality, theft, false testimony,

---

47. Ecclesiastes 9:3.
48. Peter Bolt cited by Ferdinando, *Message of Spiritual Warfare*, 6.

slander."⁴⁹ In his book *The Peacemaker*,⁵⁰ Ken Sande looks at a passage which effectively applies what Jesus said, namely James 4:1–3: "What causes quarrels and what causes fights among you? Is it not this, that your passions are at war within you? You desire and do not have, so you murder. You covet and cannot obtain, so you fight and quarrel. You do not have, because you do not ask. You ask and do not receive, because you ask wrongly, to spend it on your passions."

The link between our own inner moral corruption and ungodly conflict is highlighted by James. James immediately follows this up with this indictment: "You adulterous people! Do you not know that friendship with the world is enmity with God? Therefore whoever wishes to be a friend of the world makes himself an enemy of God" (James 4:4).

That word "adulterous" is a common biblical metaphorical synonym for "idolatrous." It is therefore appropriate that in his consideration of verses 1–3 Sande traces "the progression of an idol." Sande identifies four stages in this process:

- I Desire ("I wish I could have this")
- I Demand ("I must have this!")
- I Judge (because others are not meeting the desires I demand must be met)
- I Punish (others should suffer for failing to meet our desires)

Sande proposes some "X-ray" questions to help us discern when a good desire might be turning into a sinful demand:

- What am I preoccupied with? What is the first thing on my mind in the morning and the last thing on my mind at night?
- How would I answer the question: "If only . . . , then I would be happy, fulfilled, and secure"?
- What do I want to preserve or to avoid at all costs?
- Where do I put my trust?
- What do I fear?
- When a certain desire is not met, do I feel frustration, anxiety, resentment, bitterness, anger, or depression?

---

49. Matthew 15:19.
50. Sande, *The Peacemaker*, 104.

- Is there something I desire so much that I am willing to disappoint or hurt others in order to have it?

It is a great error to think that the Old Testament view of idolatry is all about making and bowing down before physical images of gods or objects like sacred stones, trees, and other observable natural phenomena such as the sun, moon, and stars. At one point the word of God comes to Ezekiel concerning the elders of Israel:

> Son of man, these men have set up idols in their hearts and put wicked stumbling blocks before their faces. Should I let them inquire of me at all? Therefore speak to them and tell them, "This is what the Sovereign LORD says: When any Israelite sets up idols in his heart and puts a wicked stumbling block before his face and then goes to a prophet, I the LORD will answer him myself in keeping with his great idolatry. I will do this to recapture the hearts of the people of Israel, who have all deserted me for their idols" (Ezekiel 14:1–5).

"Idols of the heart." This is also what we implicitly find described at three key points in Deuteronomy 6–9. In those chapters recurs the telling phrase: "to say in your hearts." In each instance God's people are warned not to deceive themselves in the depths of their psyche in certain particular ways. Failure to heed these warnings will result in their hearts wandering away from the Lord. As in Ezekiel 14, outward and observable manifestations of idolatry are but the expression of heart-idolatry.

The Idol of Worldly Power

The first warning goes like this: "If you say in your heart, 'These nations are greater than I. How can I dispossess them?' you shall not be afraid of them but you shall remember what the Lord your God did to Pharaoh and to all Egypt" (Deuteronomy 7:17; ESV).

As the surrounding context makes clear, the fundamental mission God gives to his people is to clear the land of all idolatry by clearing the land of all idolaters; and to live lives of total devotion and obedience to God alone in an idolatry-free land.

We must remember that Israel was never commanded to do to other nations what God commanded it to do in Canaan. Israel had no mandate to clear the world of idolatry in the same way. God's purpose for Israel was that other nations look at Israel as a secure and richly blessed nation and join the dots. That is, the nations would see that this was no accident, but due to the fact that here were a people who exclusively worshiped and obeyed God and therefore were blessed and protected by him. The plan was that, seeing this, the nations would themselves be drawn to worship God and seek his favor in like fashion.

God's people today are not called to establish a theocracy like Israel was. But we are called to be church communities that shine like lights in a dark world. We are called to disciple the nations in the knowledge that Jesus holds all authority in heaven and on earth and that his divine power and presence is ever with us. Yet the social pressures and resistance we encounter seem so overwhelming that we often shrink back from doing what we have been so clearly commissioned to do. We speak with bravado within the walls of our church buildings, but, like Peter by the courtyard fire, our voices fall silent when we are in the presence of those whom we do not dare to offend.

So, there's the first of those three Deuteronomic idols of the heart—the idol of worldly power. If only we were the social power brokers and we were the ones calling the shots, then it would be different. Then people would have to sit up and take us seriously.

When we think like this, we are being conformed to the world. Michel Foucault said, "We cannot exercise power except through the production of truth." Foucault denied that there is any such thing as real, objective truth. To the postmodern, pluralistic mind any claim to possess the truth necessarily does violence because by treating other worldviews as invalid, it shuts out the voices of others. All truth claims are really power plays which marginalize the vulnerable by scripting them out of the story. Truth claims are merely tools to legitimate power.

But Foucault himself and such postmodern thinkers can't themselves avoid making truth claims and therefore making their own power play. So what? After all, it's a dog-eat-dog world, isn't it?

Because we say in our hearts that the dice are loaded against us, that we can't win, we withdraw from the public space. We behave as though we should only voice our truth claims if we are in a position to use them to give us greater social power and prestige.

Do our professed beliefs wade or at best swim in shallow waters? Or down in the depths of our psyche is there a bedrock of unshakeable conviction that the Lord will fulfill his great purposes through us as we live for him, refusing to be intimidated by the world around us?

The Idol of Worldly Pride

The second warning in Deuteronomy 6–9 concerning an idol of the heart reads like this: "Beware lest you say in your heart, 'My power and the might of my hand have gotten me this wealth'" (Deuteronomy 8:17; ESV).

The first of these Deuteronomic idols of the heart was that of worldly power. Now we are confronted with the idol of worldly pride.

As God's people, we must take to heart our total reliance on God, as this warning's immediate context teaches. God severely tested his people through the hardships they experienced during the wilderness wanderings. But he did not do this because he is a sadist or spoilsport. He did it to teach them that their utter dependence on him is sober reality. This is what humility is, according to this chapter. Humility is recognizing that I, that we, are always, at every moment, totally and completely dependent on God for every blessing.

We give thanks for our food. Why? Well, as Deuteronomy 8 teaches, God is well able to provide food miraculously, just as he provided that super-food manna for his people during their wilderness journeys. When Jesus, by the way, miraculously fed the 5000 and then the 4000 with just a little bit of bread and fish, he was pointing people back to this wilderness provision. Ah, here's a question for you: Who then should we compare Jesus with? Well, read John 6 and you will see that the wrong answer is "Moses." Think again. Who was it that miraculously provided sufficient food to feed all his people?

But, of course, I certainly don't think the food I eat each day just suddenly materializes on my plate. But I still thank my good and gracious God because I know that he created the sources from which my food came, the people involved in getting the food from its source to me, along with the human creativity exercised in whatever processes were involved. The money with which I purchase such food also ultimately comes from him. He created the taste buds which enable me to savor the food I eat. And we could go on and on in the same vein.

But I know what the cynic will say. What about all the countless millions of people in this world who right now are suffering in abject poverty? What about all those innocent children dying of malnutrition? God isn't doing very well at feeding them.

Given this, if I thank God for my life and health and food and all the myriad blessings I enjoy, am I not being narcissistic? Am I not viewing God as if he treats me with a special favor he denies to others? Is not the humility I've just spoken of, this so-called dependence on God, in reality an expression of deplorable pride and egoism?

We shouldn't be too hasty to protest against such insinuations. Our cynical friend may have a point. After all, think of Jesus's parable about the Pharisee and the tax collector.[51] We see the Pharisee thanking God and as Jesus himself said he "prayed about himself." So, it is indeed very possible for pride and narcissism to lie under the surface of our show of gratitude to God.

So, the cynic's comments do have some bite—excuse the pun. But is he right to think that any expression of thanks to God must necessarily be selfish and egotistic?

Well, he would be correct if the reason I enjoy such plenty is because God regards me as more deserving than those who are dying of malnutrition. But I most certainly am not. The central point is that I thank God not because of who I am—*contra* the Pharisee—but because of who God is. My thanks expresses an understanding I share with billions (when you consider all who have lived and died throughout history) who have been impacted by the gospel. We invite our cynical friend to share this same understanding that God is good and generous.

The problem our cynical friend has is ultimately not with you or me or with Christians in general. His problem is with God. He sees the problem of evil and simplistically draws the conclusion that if God allows innocent children to die of malnutrition—and there is no end of other evils and horrors to cite—then God himself must necessarily be evil.

Humanist philosopher Mary Midgley has little patience with this all-too-common practice of making "God" the scapegoat for evils for which people are ultimately responsible. Nobody, including the humanist, has anything that approaches a complete answer to the problem of evil. The Bible was not written to satisfy all of our intellectual hang-ups. But there is a good deal Christians can say about the problem of evil, though, sorry to disappoint you, this is not the book in which that's going to happen. Again, the gospel, that is, Jesus, lies at the center when addressing this issue. Jesus is God and all the synoptic gospels present him as the object of evil and the one who voluntarily suffers gross injustice for our sake. And he did it all with total unwavering dependence on his Father. The cross lies at the heart of God's way of addressing the problem of human evil in this fallen and doomed world.

---

51. Luke 18:9–14.

So, it is with eyes fixed on Christ crucified that we acknowledge our complete indebtedness to God for all things that life brings our way, whether it be good or ill. Indeed, we are exhorted, "Give thanks in all circumstances, for this is God's will for you in Christ Jesus."[52]

In this spirit George Herbert prayed, "You have given me so much. Give me one more thing—a grateful heart." Ironically, when we have such a heart our God-centeredness does not result in a dilution of wholesome pleasure, but in its intensification. So, David Broughton Knox observes: "Thanksgiving cannot find any place on humanistic principles and this impoverishes life, and, indeed, impoverishes enjoyment, which is the humanists' objective in life, for it is a matter of experience that heartfelt thanksgiving increases the enjoyment of things for which you are giving thanks while you are experiencing them, whether it is sex or surfing or only sitting in the sun."[53]

The Idol of Worldly Piety

We come now to the third Deuteronomic idol of the heart: "Do not say in your heart, after the LORD your God has thrust them out before you, 'It is because of my righteousness that the LORD has brought me in to possess this land,' whereas it is because of the wickedness of these nations that the LORD is driving them out before you" (Deuteronomy 9:4; ESV).

To the idols of worldly power and worldly pride we can now add the idol of worldly piety.

There is a form of spirituality that is self-exalting rather than God-exalting. But we are easily self-deceived. After all, for the Israelites faith and obedience were pre-requisite for entrance into the land. However, as Moses states so emphatically here this does not justify the conclusion that God brought them into the land because of their faith and obedience. Indeed, as Moses goes on to highlight, they would be deluding themselves to think they were righteous. For their track record clearly reveals them to be "a stiff-necked people."

A similar instance of self-deceiving spiritual pride is confronted by Paul in the Corinthian church. At one point Paul bluntly tells them that, "I, brothers, could not address you as spiritual people, but as people of the flesh, as infants in Christ" (1 Corinthians 3:1; ESV.)

---

52. 1 Thessalonians 5:18.
53. Knox, *Not By Bread Alone*.

What we have here is a case of "worldly piety," Christians who actually do consider themselves to be "spiritual people"—the very thing Paul now repudiates. They had deluded themselves into thinking that God had given them certain spiritual gifts because he was impressed with their spirituality, especially their spiritual knowledge.[54]

Self-righteousness carries with it the sense of a right to be treated in a privileged manner. For this reason it easily transmutes into self-pity.

When, after missionary service, we returned to Sydney I came back as a man in his forties who was not well known in Christian circles. As a leader I liked to think I had a lot to offer. It was hard to accept knockbacks, especially when I felt that I was the most experienced or qualified candidate for various ministry positions. I was sorely tempted in such situations to compare myself with others, persuade myself that I was the better man, and then feel sorry for myself.

I think of another man who was sent back home by his mission agency after conflict on the field. Years later he was still filled with bitterness and resentment because he felt he was the victim of a great injustice. I know next to nothing about what happened on the field. But whatever transpired such self-pity covers a self-righteousness that is poles apart from the unfailing godliness of Joseph, notwithstanding the terrible injustices he suffered. It also flies in the face of the piety displayed by our Lord: "When they hurled their insults at him, he did not retaliate; when he suffered, he made no threats. Instead, he entrusted himself to him who judges justly" (1 Peter 2:23).

It is often in conflict situations that the ugliness of self-righteousness becomes especially evident. Many of us have come across the person who refuses to accept that he or she has contributed to the problem, despite this being apparent to others. But it is also in conflict situations that we can frequently see what the other party has done wrong while being blind as to how we have contributed to the problem. With this in mind Jesus warned his disciples:

> Do not judge, or you too will be judged. For in the same way you judge others, you will be judged, and with the measure you use, it will be measured to you. Why do you look at the speck of sawdust in your brother's eye and pay no attention to the plank in your own eye? How can you say to your brother, "Let me take

---

54. 1 Corinthians 8:1. Read also 1 Corinthians 14:37–39 in the context of chapters 12–14. Note too Paul's critique of the Corinthians syncretistic adoption of worldly wisdom (1 Corinthians 1–2).

the speck out of your eye," when all the time there is a plank in your own eye? You hypocrite, first take the plank out of your own eye, and then you will see clearly to remove the speck from your brother's eye (Matthew 7:1–5).

Jesus is not saying that it is wrong to help one's fellow believer to get the sawdust out of his or her eye—to deal with the problem you can see all too clearly. But, before we do any such thing, we need to take a good look at ourselves in the mirror and come to terms with our own sin. Here and elsewhere in the context Jesus particularly attacks hypocrisy, that is, play-acting. We must never behave like an actor on the stage, as if we were other than the sinner we really are. We are succumbing to the same self-righteousness that Jesus so chastized in the Pharisees and teachers of the law when we think we are better than other people, either spiritually or morally. By contrast, Jesus's higher righteousness[55] roots out the idols of the heart.

The Inner Battle

In James 4, James traces the fighting and quarreling that occurs among Christians back to evil desires. In spiritual warfare terms he says such desires do battle within the hearts and minds of believers.[56] He challenges the way in which Christians allow the things they crave for, yet can't have, to cause friction and conflict. Paul speaks of covetousness or greed as idolatry[57] and in similar vein James takes these cravings and wrong motives as justifying his description of such Christians as being "adulterous,"[58] that is, a people who violate their "marriage" relationship with God through illicit self-indulgence. He goes on to make the point that when Christians give free rein to such evil desires they are showing themselves to be friends with the world, while simultaneously making themselves enemies of God.

Such idolatrous cravings involve the attitude "I must have what I want." At the heart of this mentality lies pride. In order to resist the devil it is therefore essential that Christians humble themselves and submit to

---

55. Matthew 7:20.
56. James 4:1–2.
57. Colossians 3:5.
58. James 4:4.

God.[59] When we resist the devil in this way, coming near to God and having him come near to us, then the devil will most certainly flee. Humility and purity of heart and a commitment to right relationships with other believers are preconditions for being able to resist the devil and keep clear of his evil influence. Pride, corrupted desires, and unresolved, conflicted relationships are all indicative of the devil having his way in the church.

Peter also talks about the evil desires that wage war against our souls.[60] Significantly, he reminds Christians that we are to think of ourselves as being aliens and strangers in the world in order to abstain from such hostile sinful desires. This exhortation, then, is very much in sync with the tenor of James's own rebuke. Peter too implies that it is when we feel too much at home in this world that we are susceptible to these sinful desires.

As Paul points out, "the mind governed by the flesh is hostile to God. It does not submit to God's law, nor can it do so. Those controlled by the flesh cannot please God" (Romans 8:6–7).

Christians must not use their freedom to indulge the desires of the old nature, the nature that belonged to our lives before we came to know the Lord, that is, "the flesh." It is when Christians do this and fail to serve one another in love that they "keep on biting and devouring each other" and are in danger of being destroyed by each other.[61]

John too warns against loving the world or anything in the world, declaring, "If anyone loves the world, the love of the Father is not in him. For everything in the world—the cravings of sinful man, the lust of his eyes and the boasting of what he has and does—comes not from the Father but from the world. The world and its desires pass away, but the man who does the will of God lives forever."[62]

We have already considered the destructive role played by worldly cravings and pride. But the world and its desires also includes "the lust of the eyes." Genesis 3 emphasizes the role played by Eve's eyes in the Fall: "When the woman saw that the fruit of the tree was good for food and pleasing to the eye, and also desirable for gaining wisdom, she took some and ate it."

There was that time when David was walking on the roof of his palace. From that privileged vantage point he was able to see that a woman

59. James 4:7.
60. 1 Peter 2:11.
61. Galatians 5:15.
62. 1 John 2:15–17.

was bathing. Instead of averting his eyes he allowed them to take in her beauty and lust after her, with all the disastrous consequences that flowed from this.[63]

SIN IS PREDATORY

It is fascinating to see how sin is treated in Genesis 4. Cain becomes very angry when God looks with favor on Abel's offering but rejects Cain's. God tells him that he too will be accepted if he does right. Then God warns him that "sin is crouching at your door; it desires to have you, but you must master it." Remember that prior to the Fall human beings, as those created in God's image, have a mandate to master all created beasts. Now following the Fall sin itself is treated as though it is another beast to be mastered. Living in a manner consistent with one's constitution as one created in God's image involves mastery over the beast Sin.

Paul evidently had in mind this very portrayal of sin when he said:

> What shall we say, then? Is the law sinful? Certainly not! Nevertheless, I would not have known what sin was had it not been for the law. For I would not have known what coveting really was if the law had not said, "You shall not covet." But sin, seizing the opportunity afforded by the commandment, produced in me every kind of coveting. For apart from the law, sin was dead. Once I was alive apart from the law; but when the commandment came, sin sprang to life and I died. I found that the very commandment that was intended to bring life actually brought death. For sin, seizing the opportunity afforded by the commandment, deceived me, and through the commandment put me to death (Romans 7:7–11).

Paul personalizes sin, such is its power and force. Sin produces in us "every kind of covetous desire." Sin "sprang to life," like a predatory beast, and "I died." Sin deceived me and put me to death.[64]

Such is the power of sin that God's law, far from being able to contain and restrain sin, is actually used by sin as its weapon in bringing about my death. The law, though perfectly good in and of itself, becomes "the law of sin" which makes my body a "body of death."

---

63. 2 Samuel 11:2.
64. Romans 7:7–11.

IS ADAM DEAD YET?

In 1501 Erasmus wrote *The Manual of a Christian Knight* (*Enchiridion Militis Christiani*). In speaking of the "Christian Knight" Erasmus has in mind Paul's description of Christian soldiers in Ephesians 6. In chapter 1 of this book he has this to say:

> And furthermore as though it were but a trifle that so great a company of enemies should assault us on every side, we bear about with us wheresoever we go in the very secret parts of the mind an enemy nearer than one of acquaintance, or one of household. And as nothing is more inward, so nothing is more perilous. This is the old and earthly Adam, which, by acquaintance and customary familiarity, is more near to us than a citizen, and is in all manner studies and pastimes to us more contrary than any mortal enemy, whom thou canst keep off with no bulwark, neither is it lawful to expel him out of thy pavilion. This fellow must be watched with an hundred eyes, lest peradventure he setteth open the castle or city of God for devils to enter in.

Think of the movies and countless TV shows that involve someone being followed by one intent on doing harm. You sense there is something wrong and suddenly wheel around. But you can't see anyone. This foe is an expert at making it seem as though he's not really there, as though it is all in our mind.

Well, as Erasmus recognizes, this enemy really is there and his name is Adam. And Adam is an expert at making sure he sticks with us wherever we go. This is an adversary skilled at hiding in the deepest shadows. In movies spycraft might enable someone to "shake their tail," to adopt a ruse which throws their pursuer off the scent. But this side of glory no amount of cunning will rid us of this foe. For, truth be told, we have been in bed with this old enemy and we find ourselves still strongly attracted by his lures.

Erasmus also points out that no amount of military defence structures—he calls them "bulwarks"—are effective against this enemy. Legislation won't work either. We need a hundred eyes to watch out for this enemy. Give him an inch and he will take a mile. Let Adam loose in our house and he will open up that locked back door and usher demonic villains in. Adam. Why would Erasmus call this innermost enemy by this name?

Remember how all people on earth belong to one of two groups. Either they are "the offspring of the snake" or "the offspring of the woman."

Paul had another complementary way of dividing humanity into two groups and he too goes back to our origins to do this. Paul teaches that people are either "in Adam" or "in Christ" and that these two groups are diametrically opposed to each other. In particular, Paul associates death and condemnation with Adam and life and being declared right with God (justification) with Jesus. Paul reminds us that "just as sin entered the world though one man, and death through sin" so "in this way death came to all men, because all sinned."[65] Paul declares that "in Adam all die," whereas "in Christ all will be made alive."[66]

In confronting this innermost and most intimate of enemies, Adam, we must come to terms with sober reality. Let Adam have his way in our lives and he will be the death of us. Think Adam, think death.

Paul's association of Adam with death is especially traceable back to Genesis 5. "What?" you say. "This is just a genealogy." Well, wait on, there is no such thing as "just a genealogy" in the Bible. Arguably, every biblical genealogy is profoundly theological. They all have essential truths they are designed to communicate.

Look at Genesis 5. It starts with "When God created man, he made him in the likeness of God." That's God's original intent for people, that we image him and be like him. But, Genesis 5 presupposes Genesis 3 and 4. We need to bear this in mind as we continue reading Genesis 5 and come across the early words: "When Adam had lived 130 years, he had a son in his own likeness, in his own image; and he named him Seth."

What a statement! It's a double-banger. Yes, the image of God has not been obliterated. Adam still bears the likeness of God, though it has now been seriously damaged. The car is close to being a write-off but it's still on the road. But can you see the parody? To say Adam had a son in his own likeness, in his own image, is almost to treat Adam as though he now stood in God's shoes. Which, of course, is precisely where Adam and Eve put themselves.

Being "like God" does not mean being the same as God. Indeed, there is even a likeness to God that is improper and evil. Only God is able to ultimately discriminate between good and evil, right and wrong. That's why he banned our first parents from arrogating this for themselves—symbolized by forbidding the eating of the fruit of the knowledge of good and evil. I won't go into a long explanation of why this is so. But

---

65. Romans 5:12.
66. 1 Corinthians 15:22.

at the heart of any adequate answer lies the plain fact that God is perfectly good and is the only source of all goodness. So, for people to assume the authority to determine for themselves what is good and evil is itself necessarily evil, because this is a denial of God as the source of all goodness and a denial that he is perfectly good. Just look back at Genesis 3 and you can see for yourself that this is precisely the deceiver's implication. He insinuates that God does not have the best interests of Adam and Eve at heart; that he has a sinister reason for denying them enjoyment of the fruit of the knowledge of good and evil.

Anyway, to be born in Adam's image is both a blessing and a curse. I still, through Adam, can look back to the time when I as "man," a human being, was created in God's image. But as one "in Adam," the offspring of Adam who cannot shake off his legacy, I am also a deeply marred individual.

Look back at Genesis 5 and observe what happens to everyone, with one significant exception, who is "in Adam." Can you see the repeated pattern?: "When A had lived B years, he became the father of C. And after he became the father of C, A lived D years and had other sons and daughters. Altogether, A lived B + D years, *and then he died*."

You can see I have italicized those words "and then he died" because that's one of the main truths being hammered in this genealogy. God told the man and the woman that they would die if they disobeyed him. They did and now humanity, all of us, suffer the consequence. We live our lives. We have children. We live more years. But every single one of us has to face reality. We will die.

THE LAST ADAM

But, and, yes, it is a big "but," there is actually one notable exception in this genealogy. We are told that Enoch did not die. Instead we are informed, "Enoch walked with God; then he was no more, because God took him away" (Genesis 5:25).

As is so often the case with Old Testament material this statement looks back and looks forward at the same time. It looks back to the time when people experienced the heavens and the earth as a single, integrated reality. This was the time before the Fall when God walked in the garden and Adam and Eve did not hide behind trees but walked with him.[67] Enoch

---

67. Genesis 3:8.

enjoyed a quality of relationship with God that had been lost since the Fall. He too, like our first parents before that tragic turn, "walked with God."

The writer to the Hebrews reflects on Enoch and comments: "By faith Enoch was taken from this life, so that he did not experience death: 'He could not be found, because God had taken him away.' For before he was taken, he was commended as one who pleased God" (Hebrews 11:5).

Nowhere in the Bible is Enoch presented as a super-saint. He is just one among many exemplars of faith. He was not more holy that Abraham or Moses, both of whom died. But God in his grace spared Enoch from experiencing death.

This exception within the genealogy points forward to God's ultimate purpose for humanity. Although we are all "in Adam" it does not necessarily follow that we must all die. Indeed, in his great chapter on the doctrine of resurrection, 1 Corinthians 15, Paul contrasts Adam and Christ in a particularly significant manner. He says, "Thus it is written, 'The first man Adam became a living being'; the last Adam became a life-giving spirit."[68]

See how Jesus is described: "the last Adam." Jesus is the source of a new humanity, but it is not "new" in the sense that it completely replaces the old humanity. We are still talking about humanity that is Adamic.

Something happened to both Adam and to Christ that caused them to "become" something. Again, remember that 1 Corinthians 15 is all about resurrection. So, it was God's act of creation that caused Adam to become a living being. But it was the resurrection—glorious new creation—that resulted in Jesus becoming a life-giving spirit.

Paul goes on to say that "flesh and blood cannot inherit the kingdom of God, nor does the perishable inherit the imperishable."[69] All "in Adam" are living beings like him and as such have merely earthly bodies which are perishable "flesh and blood." Nobody who is in Adam will inherit the kingdom of God. All who are in Adam will be excluded from the new creation over which God will rule completely unopposed. But Jesus brings in a new age and all who are "in the last Adam" share his humanity which involves having a Spirit-created resurrected body which is imperishable and breathtakingly glorious.

Adam versus Last Adam. Death versus life.

---

68. 1 Corinthians 15:45. I have chosen the ESV translation instead of the NIV because it rightly emphasizes the theologically significant word "became" for both Adam and Christ.

69. 1 Corinthians 15:50.

WHAT WILL I WEAR TODAY?

Paul also likes to call Adam "the old man." In our own culture it is often a term of affection used by children to refer to their father. There is not one ounce of endearment in Paul's tone when he calls Adam the old man.

Christians need to be quite clear where they stand with respect to "the old man." Paul teaches us "that our old self ['man'] was crucified with him so that the body ruled by sin might be done away with, that we should no longer be slaves to sin—because anyone who has died has been set free from sin."[70]

Western sensitivities to gender issues don't encourage the rendering "old man." But Paul's use of this term is not anti-woman but simply drawing on the idea of Adam representing a particular type of humanity. Paul makes the key point that it was the crucifixion of Jesus that dealt the death blow to Adamic humanity. Adamic humanity is humanity ruled by sin and Jesus died to end that and give us a new humanity which is no longer enslaved by sin. But these two humanities are incompatible.[71] Adamic humanity must die if the new humanity is to find expression in our lives.

Paul makes this very clear: "You were taught, with regard to your former way of life, to put off your old self ('man'), which is being corrupted by its deceitful desires; to be made new in the attitude of your minds; and to put on the new self ('man'), created to be like God in true righteousness and holiness" (Ephesians 4:22–24).[72]

Christians are to turn their backs on the way of life that belongs to a pre-Christian state. This involves "putting off" the old man, Adamic humanity, and "putting on" the new man, the new humanity which Jesus gave us.

Think of getting up in the morning. You take off your pyjamas or nightie, clothes that belong to the darkness, and you put on your day clothes that belong to the light. In fact, there is another passage where Paul uses much the same imagery:

---

70. Romans 6:6–7.

71. "[T]hese two realms have different rulers—the Old Humanity is that realm over which the powers have ultimate influence and in which they hold humanity captive to death through their influencing people to indulge in transgressions and sins. The New Humanity, on the other hand, is that realm that is united to Christ and receives its life from Christ—it is the new creation and those in it share in the resurrection life of Christ himself." Gombis, "Triumph of God in Christ," 137.

72. Compare this passage with Colossians 3:5–10.

And do this, understanding the present time: The hour has already come for you to wake up from your slumber, because our salvation is nearer now than when we first believed. The night is nearly over; the day is almost here. So let us put aside the deeds of darkness and put on the armor of light. Let us behave decently, as in the daytime, not in carousing and drunkenness, not in sexual immorality and debauchery, not in dissension and jealousy. Rather, clothe yourselves with the Lord Jesus Christ, and do not think about how to gratify the desires of the flesh" (Romans 13:11–14).

When Paul says "And do this" he means commit yourselves to loving one another.[73] Christians are to live as though the end is near, the time when their salvation will be fully realized. That is, "the night is nearly over; the day is almost here." The history of sin and death is drawing to a close. Soon it will give way to endless day, when the light of life in God's glorious kingdom will shine forevermore.

There is a real sense in which we Christians are still living in the night. However, we have woken up before daybreak, while it is still dark, because we want to be ready to meet the day. But having woken up we need to get ourselves dressed in readiness for the day. That means, if I may be allowed a little crudity, taking off soiled nightclothes, "the deeds of darkness," and clothing ourselves with "the armor of light."

The shining armor of light. That's significant, isn't it? After all, Paul is talking about something that will involve great conflict. We can expect that being still in the thick darkness of night we will feel a longing to put our night clothes back on and slither back into bed. Did you notice how Paul continues? To put on the armor of light means behaving in a way that is consistent with living in the light: that is, behaving decently so as to please and honor God.[74] But it means refusing to engage in the deeds of darkness. The list of sins that follows deliberately conjures up images of behavior people typically engage in at night time—orgies, drunkenness, sexual immorality, debauchery, fighting in pubs and on the street, expressions of hateful jealousy.

Then we come to the grand summary, and what a climax it is! "Rather, clothe yourselves with the Lord Jesus Christ, and do not think how to gratify the desires of the sinful nature ('flesh')" (Romans 13:14).

---

73. Romans 13:8–10.

74. Apropos is Pytches's statement, cited by Smith, "Church Militant, 98: "the answer to darkness is to switch on the light."

We are at the heart of the struggle here. This is why we need to put on armor. The desires of the flesh, our evil desires, are very strong. If we allow our minds to think about how to gratify those desires then we will find ourselves slipping back on those soiled nightclothes, getting back into bed, and closing our drooping eyes, totally unprepared for the coming of the Day when the Lord will return to judge us all. What we must do instead, and this parallels putting on the armor of light, is to clothe ourselves with the Lord Jesus Christ. That's what we must set our hearts on. Becoming more and more like Jesus. Being part of a new humanity that is made to be like God.

Paul has a lot to say about what he calls "the flesh," which many translators render as "the sinful nature." I guess that's a pretty accurate translation. It captures much of Paul's basic thrust. But if you've ever tried to learn another language you know it is often not possible to just substitute a word or phrase from your own language for the word in the other language and keep the same meaning. Indeed, "sinful nature" as a translation does miss something that is very much part of Paul's idea of "the flesh" and which that very word naturally brings to our mind. I mean the human body, the flesh in which we live.

Think back to the distinction Paul makes between Adam and the Last Adam. The humanity belonging to Adam has to do with an earthly body and the humanity belonging to the Last Adam with a heavenly body. Those strong desires that push us towards evil are desires that result from being in bodies which somehow are wrongly wired. To be "in the flesh" is to be in a physical order of existence that is Adamic, involving slavery to sin. Hence "sinful nature." To be "in the Spirit" is not to be in a non-bodily state. On the contrary, this is a different physical order of existence that involves a new Christlike humanity possessed of resurrection life and Spirit-created desires.

It would be possible to misunderstand this emphasis on the physical. To develop one of Tom Wright's images, when we think of life in the flesh and life in the Spirit we should not be comparing, as it were, a wooden ship and an iron ship, as if the stress was on the difference between what the flesh and the Spirit are composed of. Rather, this is more a matter of the difference between a sailing ship and a nuclear-powered ship. That is, "a difference between one of two principles that energizes the life we live in our physical bodies and in the flesh and blood reality of our everyday world."[75]

The old man, Adam, is supposed to have been left on the cross with Jesus. But the exhortation to put off the old man is one Christians need to hear over and over again. Because the reality is that "the flesh desires what is contrary to the Spirit, and the Spirit what is contrary to the sinful nature." As Paul says, "They are in conflict with each other, so that you do not do what you want."[76]

Now where else have we heard Paul say something very much like this? Yes, I'm thinking of some very famous, often quoted words of Paul, written in a passage which is remarkably parallel to the context of the verse above:

> We know that the law is spiritual; but I am unspiritual, sold as a slave to sin. I do not understand what I do. For what I want to do I do not do, but what I hate I do. And if I do what I do not want to do, I agree that the law is good. As it is, it is no longer I myself who do it, but it is sin living in me. For I know that good itself does not dwell in me, that is, in my sinful nature. For I have the desire to do what is good, but I cannot carry it out. For I do not do the good I want to do, but the evil I do not want to do—this I keep on doing. Now if I do what I do not want to do, it is no longer I who do it, but it is sin living in me that does it.
>
> So I find this law at work: Although I want to do good, evil is right there with me. For in my inner being I delight in God's law; but I see another law at work in me, waging war against the law of my mind and making me a prisoner of the law of sin at work within me. What a wretched man I am! Who will rescue me from this body that is subject to death? Thanks be to God, who delivers me through Jesus Christ our Lord!
>
> So then, I myself in my mind am a slave to God's law, but in my sinful nature a slave to the law of sin (Romans 7:14–25).

Christians experience conflict and tension in their lives because the desires of the flesh and the desires of the Spirit are ever fighting against each other. That is indeed our Christian experience. I know not everyone agrees, but I take Paul to be speaking about the very same reality in these famous words above. I do not find it easy to live a life that always honors and pleases God. This does not come naturally. Why is it so hard? Because

---

75. Derek Tidball makes use of Wright's metaphor and makes this key point. Tidball, *Message of Holiness*, 255.

76. Galatians 5:17.

there is a "law at work in me" which is "waging war against the law of my mind," the mind associated with my inner being which delights in and desires to do God's will. I am being pulled in two directions and this tussle will continue until the Lord returns. We are more than conquerors through him who loved us. Jesus has delivered us. So, I do not have to live as a slave of sin and the Lord is to be thanked for that. But if I step back into the old clothes of fleshly Adamic humanity then I place myself under the tyranny of sin yet again. The reality is that all Christians do precisely this over and over again and therefore need constant cleansing and to make regular confession of our sins.[77]

MISSION DEBRIEF

- **Falsity of Generational Sins.** The perpetuation of the error of generational sins and curses, based on a distorted reading of Scripture, is a species of animism which denies the sufficiency of Christ and has the potential to cause considerable psychological damage.
- **Psychology and Sinful Deceit.** Sound psychology, consistent with the biblical understanding of the deceitfulness of the human heart, will not treat inner evil as merely the product of unmet needs or the result of crushing external experiences.
- **Psychology and Transformation.** True psychological health presupposes repentance and forgiveness and the transforming work of the Holy Spirit.
- **Idolatry and the Human Heart.** The Bible does not treat idolatry as merely concerned with externalities (e.g. bowing down before idol-images) but sees this as deeply rooted in our hearts. For example, Ezekiel speaks of "idols of the heart" and, in like vein, the book of Deuteronomy exposes the heart-sourced idolatries of worldly power, worldly pride, and worldly piety.
- **The Inner Battlefield.** A spiritual war is raging within our own persons as we do battle against evil, idolatrous cravings, conscious that sin is a dangerous predator that deceitfully uses even God's law to bring about our undoing.

---

77. 1 John 1:5–10.

- **The Corrupted State of Unsaved People.** Fallen Adamic humanity does not constitute the loss of God's image, but it is in a state of ruination and headed for destruction.
- **The New Humanity.** By virtue of their union with Jesus, the Image of God (perfect man), Christians are part of the new humanity which possesses eternal life.
- **Christian Experience of the Old and New Humanity.** Until Jesus returns Christians face a continuing struggle within themselves as the old humanity seeks to reassert itself. Against this, believers must ever choose to live according to the new humanity, living as conquerors as they experience the reality of Christ's love and deliverance and draw on the transforming power of God's Spirit.

GATHERING INTELLIGENCE

Read Galatians 5:16–26

1. What are the two ways of life depicted in this passage and what makes them so very different?
2. How does Adamic humanity ("the flesh"; "sinful nature") express itself? See especially verses 19–21.
3. How does the new humanity (living by the Spirit) express itself? See especially verses 22–23.
4. If verse 24 is true how are we to explain the continued expressions of sin in the lives of God's people?
5. What does it mean to "keep in step with the Spirit" (verse 25)

Chapter Six

Facing Fabricated Enemies

"There can never be a culture-free gospel. Yet the gospel, which is from the beginning to the end embodied in culturally conditioned forms, calls into question all cultures, including the one in which it originally was embodied."

LESSLIE NEWBIGIN, *FOOLISHNESS TO THE GREEKS*

IN THE MOST HORRIFIC of wars, where the stakes could be no higher, we fight with the immense power of divine words against both inhuman and human foes. Defeated demonic forces are filled with malicious intent to sabotage God's plan to create a new humanity in a new creation. We discriminate between such foes and the human agents often conscripted into the service of the evil one. God's justice demands the ultimate removal of evil and this will inevitably involve violence. However, in Christlike fashion we are committed to love, bless, and pray for those people who make themselves our enemies, ever conscious of the power of the gospel to save and transform lives. But the most insidious level of conflict is the one that rages in the very depths of our own selves, with evil desires belonging to our old Adamic humanity waging war against the God-honoring desires belonging to the new humanity that is ours by virtue of our union with Christ. And the intensity of this inner battle is exacerbated by the fact that we live in a world which has been fashioned by sinful people, a social environment that panders not only to our base lusts but also to the feeling that the true and living God has no right to tell us how to live our lives.

> Richard Bauckham hits the nail on the head in his description of society: Society is more than the sum of individuals. It is a school of evil in which we are all educated, a reservoir of evil to which we all contribute, a web of evil in which we are all entangled. Of course, it is no more wholly evil than is the individual. But just as society can nourish the good in an individual and make more of it than it could be in itself, so society can recruit people for atrocities of which the mere individual would not have been capable.[1]

Every year people are drowned because they fail to swim between the flags. God's Word warns against friendship with "the world." Sometimes Christians swim outside the flags. They flirt with danger. For some the consequences are disastrous. They are sucked under by the undercurrents of worldly thought in all its cultural, ethical and religious expressions.[2]

THE BIAS OF CULTURE

Inhuman, human, and inner foes. Isn't that quite enough to contend with? Tragically, these three foes together have fashioned a world, an environment that is sometimes as hostile to the new humanity as living on dry land is to a fish.

Cultures Are Expressive of Worldviews

Think of all the humanly developed institutions and structures that are so integral to our lives—political, legal, educational, economic, religious, and so on. As we seek to live for Christ in this fallen world we find time and time again that there are points at which our values and beliefs fundamentally diverge from those expressed and often instutionalized in such social and cultural systems. There are competing philosophies and moralities, a pressure to conform to societal norms and political correctness,

---

1. Bauckham, "Nature of Evil," 16.
2. I'm grateful to Derek Tidball for this helpful image. Tidball, *Message of Holiness*, 254.

dubious and downright immoral modes of entertainment, media that at times resemble a pack of wolves with the scent of blood in their nostrils.

Many have taken on board James Davison Hunter's contention that at the heart of culture lies not so much worldview involving beliefs, values, and ideas, but the strength of cultural institutions controlled by an elite.³ It is this reality that often especially makes culture so intimidating for Christians. However, Hunter's view of worldview is purely cognitive and therefore excludes consideration of the force of deep-seated human feelings such as fear of the spirit world, the longing for honor and the dread of being shamed, and the emotional weight of guilt.⁴ Such feelings, which are integral to cultural worldviews, also often create barriers to the gospel.

Some time back I was asked to take up a collection on my street for the National Heart Foundation. There were many neighbors on my street that gave to this charity. But there were a number of houses I came to which had clear notices saying they didn't welcome any door-knockers, which is what I was. Having been on the receiving end of some nuisance callers I quite understand why people might do this. My illustration here is not critical of such people. But it does show how the world in which we live is one in which people feel the need to put up such notices, have locks on their doors, develop child-protection policies, pass endless laws to defend our freedoms and rights, and develop all manner of structures aimed at preventing the bad stuff we fear from spoiling the quality of life we want.

So much of the world in which we live is a fabricated reality. And a great deal of that manufactured world will have no place in the new heavens and earth. Of course, there are some things that are perfectly fine but are provisional, like marriage for example. There won't be marriage in that new creation but something far more intimate and wonderful. Good and fulfilling marriages should whet our appetites for that.

---

3. See Bjoraker, "How Do Cultures Really Change?" Bjoraker takes on board Andy Crouch's counter-emphasis on culture making "at local scales" which are "out of reach of 'cultural elites.'" However, he recognizes that "Hunter provides a necessary corrective to the popular view that 'grassroots' movements are *the key* to culture change." As he adds, "Such small-scale change in a cultural enclave or sub-system can bring good, but is subject to the larger nation-state's hegemony." Bjoraker, "How Do Cultures Really Change?" 78.

4. See Bjoraker, "How Do Cultures Really Change?" 17.

Confronting Clashing Cultural Values

But there is also a great deal which would have no place in this world, if it weren't for the presence of evil. So it is that Christians find there is much in this world which is not conducive to living a godly life and a great deal that is either deeply disturbing or poses an immediate threat. Fabricated foes: that's what I'm calling such aspects of culture and society that are to a lesser or greater degree at odds with the lives God's people are seeking to live.

Think of the training program Nebuchadnezzar had developed to prepare specially selected young men for royal service.[5] Some might, but I wouldn't call this system of indoctrination especially evil. I'm not sure it's all that different from many of the training programs companies may run for their employees. But Nebuchadnezzar's program threatened to erase the self-identity of Daniel and his friends as God's chosen people. Daniel found a way of drawing a line in the sand and securing his core identity. However, from a human standpoint it involved taking a huge risk which, if it had backfired, would have had extremely dire consequences.[6]

Strangely enough, or so it may seem to us, Daniel and his friends did not refuse to study "the literature of the Babylonians."[7] Given their own faith we might well have understood if they had taken such a stand, though to do so would certainly have cost them their lives. The fact is that Chaldean literature was suffused with magical formulae and idolatrous content.[8] Yet we are told that at the end of their training, when the king tested them, they were "ten times better than all the magicians and enchanters in his whole kingdom."[9] These men mastered this literature and yet managed to preserve their core identity and moral integrity. Just as Meshech, Shadrach, and Abednego emerged from the blazing furnace without a hair singed or their clothing scorched,[10] and as Daniel

---

5. Daniel 1:3–5.
6. See Daniel 1:8–10.
7. Daniel 1:4, 17.
8. Baldwin observes that such literature included omen texts with some concerning "devils and evil spirits," magic incantations, copied sign lists, prayers, hymns, word lists, paradigms, myths, legends, "scientific" formulae for skills such as glass-making, economic data, historical texts, mathematics, and astrology, to which can be added law codes and much else. See Baldwin, *Daniel*, 80; Miller, *Daniel*, 62.
9. Daniel 1:20.
10. Daniel 3:26–27.

came out of the lion's den unscathed,[11] so Daniel and his friends waded through the filth of Babylonian thought and remained clean.

Many Christians face similar challenges today. There are, for example, in many Muslim countries, millions upon millions of Christians who are forced to study Islam and are not permitted to have Christian studies. Even in our Western schools and universities there are arts courses that require exposure to material that involves explicit immoral content. It is not that these courses are deliberately set up to cause problems for Christians, but they are part of a culture that often doesn't sit well with Christian beliefs and values.

Culture, of course, is necessarily a fabricated reality. I'm assuming here a basic difference between cultural behavior and purely biological behavior.[12] Actually, the word "purely" only applies to an extremely limited range of observable biological behavior. For example, the natural blinking of the eyes as opposed to using a blinking of the eyes to deliberately convey a message. It's very hard to think of any other observable behaviors that are purely biological. The reality is that most of our behavior is cultural, that is, learned behavior.

Biased People, Biased Culture

We are not clones. Each one of us has a unique individual persona. We live in different places at different times in different climates mixing with different people and subject to many external factors over which we have no control. It follows that there will necessarily be endless variants on the ways we learn to live life. There is no such thing as an all-encompassing culture, but rather a vast array of differing cultures. But even though cultures are very varied one thing remains constant. Every person on earth is biased against knowing and honoring the true and living God.

---

11. Daniel 6:23.

12. So Kraft describes culture as "the total non-biologically transmitted heritage" of people. Kraft, *Christianity in Culture*, 45–46. In a broad sense culture is often thought of as involving the passing on of knowledge and values from generation to generation. Culture has an effect on the way people think and therefore often influences behavior. However, unlike the genetic characteristics of humankind, it is passed on through social rather than biological means. For example, for the Dinka tribe of the southern Sudan, spearing fish is a traditional fishing technique which fathers teach their sons. From an early age boys practice to acquire the speed and balance fish spearing requires. See Coleman and Watson, *An Introduction to Anthropology*, 13.

It therefore follows, as surely as night follows day, that all cultures are necessarily biased against God.[13]

As we will shortly see, this does not mean that such cultures are irreligious. Indeed, throughout history the cultural bias of which I speak has often been demonstrably true of highly religious cultures in which lip-service has been given to the knowledge of the God of the Bible. It has been acknowledged by some leading American Christian voices that American Christian culture, though characterized by relatively high rates of church attendance, gives scant evidence of true devotion to the Lord.[14]

H. Richard Niebuhr proposed a number of possible relationships Christians may assume with respect to culture. One of them was a Christ against culture stance, though we might also include the "defensive against" and "purity from" paradigms proposed by Hunter.[15] It is certainly the case that whenever people submit their lives to the Lord there will be aspects of culture they discover to be completely incompatible with their newfound allegiance.

As I have indicated earlier, people are not merely sinners. They remain people created in God's image and as such may exhibit very noble and laudable traits and behavior. I am by no means dissing culture. I fully recognize that there is much in culture that is praiseworthy, serving necessary and helpful purposes. What I am saying is that over time sinful people develop cultures that rationalize the way of life they want to live

---

13. Lingenfelter remarks: "I reject the notion that culture or worldview is neutral. Analogies such as Kraft's 'map' or 'a tool for communication and interaction' . . . are inadequate to capture the pervasive presence of sin in the lives and thoughts of human beings. Using the tool analogy, culture is more like a 'slot machine' found in Las Vegas's gambling casinos than a wrench or screw driver. Culture, like a slot machine, is programmed to be sure that those who hold power 'win' and the common players 'lose'; when or if the organized agenda is violated, people frequently resort to violence to reestablish their 'programmed' advantage. Every cultural system brokers power to its members, although the 'power' advantage may be held by either individuals or groups. The structures and organizations of cultures are not neutral; people define and structure their relationships with others to protect their personal or group interests, and to sustain or gain advantage over others with whom they compete. Video games provide better analogies to culture than Kraft's 'map,' because they reflect the various power advantages, access to survival resources, and hostile opposition that typify cultural systems. Culture then is created and contaminated by human beings; culture is the penitentiary of disobedience from which freedom is possible only through the gospel." Lingenfelter, *Transforming Culture*, 18.

14. Read, for example, Wells, *God in the Wasteland*.

15. But see Smith's stated reservations to the way in which these differing paradigms have been applied by both Niebuhr and Hunter. Smith, "How (Not) To Change the World."

and that it is not natural for people to develop ways of life that express a genuine seeking after God and a desire to glorify him.

The Counter-Cultural Dimension of Christian Values

All cultures then are fabricated and all cultures and sub-cultures involve processes of enculturation and socialization that embed certain aesthetic and moral values. Conflict between societies, people groups, and nations often involve clashing value systems and, of course, the Christian value system, when the rubber hits the road, will often be perceived by people in virtually all societies as counter-cultural.

For example, in the West many think the Christian value of forgiveness sounds so noble and nice until they come up against Christians talking of forgiveness for child sex offenders and rapists. A news bulletin tells of a Catholic family in which the father, with the mother's knowledge, sexually abused all of his daughters. The mother would tell a deeply distressed daughter that as Christians we must forgive and so she had a duty to forgive her father and just learn to live with this sordid reality. This is deplorable and a complete misunderstanding of what the Bible teaches about justice and forgiveness. Yet, tragically, it is precisely stories like this that lead people to believe deep down that Christian morality is at best sentimental niceness that has no real relevance to the cat-and-dog, rat-race world in which we live.

THE BIAS OF ETHICS

Culture Conflict and Ethical Behavior

Some popular definitions of culture think of it as a kind of organism, a united entity where, like a body, every part is inter-related. While there is an important element of inter-connection in culture, this is pure fantasy. Conflict is far more integral to cultural life than harmony. Conflict occurs not merely between cultures but within cultures. This is to be expected because culture is just human nature writ large. As Eliphaz correctly observed, "Man is born to trouble as surely as sparks fly upward."[16] There are many aspects of culture that express human nobility. But every culture papers over the ugly cracks of human evil. If we look behind closed doors,

16. Job 5:7.

in how many cultures would we find high incidences of wife-beating and various forms of child-abuse, which cultural norms prevent from ever being properly addressed? The value of male honor, so intrinsic to many cultures, serves to sanction great injustices, just as the value of individual freedom sanctions gross and open moral perversion.

So when we talk about cultures, or ways of life, we are inevitably caught up in questions of ethics and morality, in conflicting views as to what is acceptable and what is not, what is right and what is wrong and, indeed, for some, whether there is any such thing as evil at all.

Authority and Ethics

Back to Genesis 3 we go. I have already stressed that though people are created to be like God in many respects there is one major point of difference, a difference symbolized by the tree of the knowledge of good and evil.

In the ancient world the king was typically the supreme court of appeal. God is the absolute ruler—there is no higher authority. Therefore, as such God is the ultimate judge. He is the only one with the authority to determine what is good and what is evil, what is right and what is wrong. For any other being to presume to make such determinations is to claim an authority which that being simply does not have. Further, such an attempt effectively seeks to dethrone God, to deny his right to be the absolute ruler, the one who should call the shots. On top of that, to restate an earlier point, such presumption effectively denies that God himself is good, for it fundamentally calls into question his distinctions between good and evil, which are rooted in God's own character.

There are many other aspects to such monstrous presumption that we might draw out if we were to linger. But for now, simply note that after each day of creation God as the ultimate authority judges his work and evaluates it to be "good" and, indeed, "very good." When God tells people that death will follow eating fruit from the tree of the knowledge of good and evil he is only stating what should make perfect sense to each of us. If God's good purposes for creation are to be realized, then we can't have others second-guessing God or making their own decisions as to what they think should be treated as good and what should be regarded as evil. For people to arrogate this right to themselves is to put themselves in the place of God, to give themselves the authority to make such decisions— an authority that they plainly do not have.

Human Autonomy and Ethics

Satan's first success was to seduce our first parents into assuming such authority. Ever since, the default mode for all human thought and conduct is to work out and decide for ourselves how to live our lives, which includes deciding to let other people do this for us. It is unnatural for any of us to seek God's will for our lives, which is why the psalmist, as cited in Paul's indictment of human evil in Romans, bemoans the fact that nobody seeks God, not one.[17]

Some years back a popular book was written by Frank Peretti called *The Hidden Darkness*. In a highly unbiblical manner Peretti invites us to adopt a paranoid worldview, imagining that every unliberated person in the world has a demon clinging to his or her back, whispering in their ears.[18] To understand how Satan's hidden power actually operates we simply need to recognize that following the Fall of our first parents, it is not natural for any person, no matter how religious they may be, to genuinely seek to know the true and living God.

For Satan keeping people blinded to the truth about God is not high maintenance. It is very low maintenance. There is no need for demons to cling to people's backs in order for Satan to wield control. We have all played into his hands and we do this as we continue to think we can live our lives without reference to God.

If it is true, as the psalmist and Paul declare, that nobody seeks God and his will, and that people live their lives as though they are not really accountable to him, then it follows that the arenas of ethics and religion are the devil's playgrounds.

THE BIAS OF RELIGION

Religion and Human Corruption

Religion is poison. So say the New Atheists. And, as shocking as this may sound to many Christian ears, there is much to be said for this. Indeed,

---

17. Romans 3:10–11. Here Paul is citing words found at both Psalm 14:1–3 and 53:1–3.

18. "The result of Peretti's success is that a host of similar books have followed in its wake, many of those less than sound in content. Cumulatively, that has produced a new generation of Christians who are beginning to see the world through a grid that has more in common with Greek and Persian mystery religions than with Christianity." Riddlebarger, "This Present Paranoia," 278.

to a substantial degree this is precisely what the Bible teaches. As Paul explains in Romans 1, the suppression of truth by all people is the repudiation of the knowledge of God as self-revealed by our creator.[19] But, Paul goes on to point out, this rejection of truth doesn't take place in a vacuum. It always involves replacing the truth with a lie: that is, idolatry.[20] The human heart is the factory floor for the never-ceasing manufacture of idols. The darkening of our ignorant hearts always finds its essential expression in exchanging the (revealed) glory of the incorruptible God for our own idols.[21] Yes, as Paul indicates, people have prostrated themselves before idol-figurines resembling birds, animals and reptiles—the categories of creatures laid out in Genesis 1 as those over which humans should rule, not serve in worship.[22] But the central exchange is that of displacing the incorruptible, immortal God in all his glory with the essential corruption of the image of God, with corruptible, mortal "man": that is, people.

Religion and Humanism

There is then a very real sense in which the default setting of every human heart is humanistic. God's self-revelation as our glorious and good creator, one who is truly to be honored and thanked, constitutes "truth," reality. From birth all people are predisposed to live a lie, to see the world in the way they are taught to by their parents, peers, and culture. Idolatry should not be treated in a simplistic fashion, as though it can be reduced down to the things we spend our time and money upon. Such things are signs pointing to a deeper level, a worldview, a social imaginary, a lifeworld—call it what you will—that etches into the human mind and heart a divergent and ultimately false understanding of reality and how we should live our lives in the light of this distorted understanding. The psalmist speaks of a voice sounding out the glory of God to the whole creation.[23] But this voice is drowned out by the other voices we listen to, our own voices and the voices of others—all telling us to live life as they direct.

---

19. Romans 1:18.
20. Romans 1:23, 25.
21. Romans 1:23.
22. Genesis 1:28.
23. Psalm 19:1–4.

Religion and Moral Decency

It would be tempting to think that all of these idolatrous voices are calling upon us to engage in gross evils, such as theft, adultery, kidnapping, and murder. But, of course, normally this is not at all the case. The counterfeit reality they present is usually one that promotes what people consider to be moral, decent behavior. Jesus lampooned the Pharisees of his day seeing them as the prime evidence that his generation was "wicked and adulterous,"[24] with the word "adulterous" being another term for "idolatrous." The reason Jesus's sustained attack on the Pharisees had such shock value in his day was because these religious leaders were actually regarded by many of their contemporaries as models of moral decency. They were not people associated with vices and gross moral evils. Jesus was friends with many such people, while he castigated the moral Pharisees and told parables that completely up-ended the cultural value system of his day.

Religion and Idolatry

As modern Western societies indicate, idolatry can have a secular rather than a religious face. At one level we can argue that atheistic and materialistic constructions of reality and values are just as religious as any other fabricated reality. But for now let's think more narrowly of religion as an institutional reality involving such things as rituals, officiants, and beliefs about ultimate reality that go beyond that which can be strictly observed according to the scientific method.

All ancient societies and almost every person on the face of the earth believed in deities and supernatural powers. In the Old Testament idolatry was particularly, though not exclusively, associated with the observable cultic worship of gods other than the true and living God who had especially revealed himself to the people of Israel as "I am who I am" (Yahweh).

Idolatry was the most serious sin God's people could commit. It constituted the most fundamental breach of the covenant between God and his people. The Ten Words, often called the Ten Commandments, begin with God, self-revealed as the great "I AM," insisting that his people, the Israelites, have nothing whatsoever to do with anything else

---

24. Matthew 16:4.

that is purported to be a god or is in any way invested with divinity. So implacable is God in his opposition to idolatry that he demands that his people, upon entering Canaan, totally destroy all the accoutrements of idolatrous religious expression.[25] Indeed, God is utterly ruthless when he sets himself to deal conclusively with idolatry, requiring the removal of everyone living in the land, given the reality that all were thoroughly enculturated and socialized idolaters.

Religion and Holy War

It is precisely in this context of opposing idolatry that the Old Testament presents a doctrine of holy war. Recall when God parts the waters of the sea to deliver his people from the pursuing Egyptian forces, only then to close those waters so as to drown the Egyptians.[26] Moses sings a song in celebration of this which declares God to be "a warrior."[27] In this case God did not call upon his people to engage in battle with the Egyptians. He himself engaged them in battle on Israel's behalf and utterly destroyed them.

The book of Numbers shows that during their wilderness journeys God was toughening and preparing his people for the war they would have to conduct when the time came for them to invade Canaan as God intended. So it was that the entire camp of Israel was organized in military formation with the tabernacle occupying a role and place akin to the Pharaoh's tent in an Egyptian military camp. The book of Deuteronomy repeatedly reminded God's people that when they entered Canaan God would fight for them, that he would instill a holy terror in the hearts of the people in the land, causing Israel's foes to scatter before them. The conquest of Canaan is effectively God waging total war on the Canaanites so as to extirpate idolatry from the land and enable his people to live lives of pure devotion to himself, free of temptation.[28]

Religion and Worship

In the ancient world idolatry was very much associated with worship of deity. God commanded his people to perform sacrificial and other rituals

25. For example, Deuteronomy 7:5, 25–26; 12:2–4.
26. Exodus 14:21–28.
27. Exodus 15:3.
28. Deuteronomy 7:2–4.

and set in place a dedicated priesthood and ordered the making of a sanctuary for worship and meeting with him. There was an institutionalized worship system the Israelites were expected to honor by eradicating all other worship systems in the land of Canaan. There must be only one people in the land practicing one true worship system, faithful to God's self-revelation.

What are the implications of this? What difference if any did the coming of Christ make? Are Christians to treat all other religions with utter contempt and, if circumstances permit, seek their destruction? How are Christians to relate to people with different religious faiths? These are particularly pressing questions for both missionaries and Christians living in religiously pluralistic societies. Is God at war with these religions and are Christians called to fight against them and destroy them?

Before we address these questions we need to take a second look at the conquest of Canaan.

First, we need to recognize that it was not an attack on religion as such. As we previously observed in chapter 4 (Facing Human Enemies), the conquest occurred when moral depravity in Canaan reached the tipping point. The conquest was God's attack on evil, not religion as such.

Secondly, although all ancient societies had their organized and institutionalized places of worship, and officiants, and rituals there was no dividing line between "religion" and everyday life. People had no concept of a separate entity for which they used a word corresponding to our modern term "religion." The conquest of Canaan concerned God's opposition to an entire evil way of life, not religions as we conceive of them in the modern Western world.

Religion and Animism

Most of the world's religionists belong to tribal and folk religions, even if they fall under the ambit of such major religions as Islam, Buddhism, or Hinduism. The vast majority of people believe and practice many things which they would not do if they adhered strictly to the teaching of their scriptures. So, for example, commonly found is belief in the evil eye and in the magical properties of charms and curses, and spells and sacred words, along with many other superstitions.[29]

---

29. Of similar ilk is the use of the phrase "the blood of the Lamb" by Christians as a ritualistic phrase that can ward off evil powers. Moreau, *Essentials*, 166–67.

Religion and Ethical Relativism

The social mindset or understanding of reality held by religionists certainly bears an intimate relationship with their way of life. Ethical relativists may regard all ways of life or cultures as equally valid, but this is plain nonsense once the existence of objective, creation-grounded moral values is accepted. All ways of understanding reality and all ways of life that involve the suppression of the knowledge of the true and living God, the Father of our Lord Jesus Christ, are necessarily deviant to some degree or other. But, to echo C. S. Lewis, just as some wrong answers to a mathematical problem are closer to the right answer than others, so too some worldviews and ways of life are less deviant than others.

Religion and Divine Judgment

God held back his judgment on the Canaanites for over 400 years until their evil had become so horrendous that the cup of his wrath boiled over and could no longer be restrained. However much people may decry the massacre of Canaanites during this limited time frame in a limited geographical zone, we need to recognize that this is minor compared to the immensity of the eternal slaughter that will take place on the Day of Judgment. Contrary to the New Atheists, the horror of ultimate divine judgment does not show God to be a monster, but rather underscores the uncompromising nature of his blazing holiness and the immensity of human evil.

On the Day of Judgment God will not judge Islam or Buddhism or Hinduism or Sikhism or Mormonism or Confucianism. He will judge people according to their deeds, words, and innermost thoughts and attitudes which only he can see. In the same way, the missionary and the Christian living in a religiously pluralistic society treats people as people, not as religionists. We give priority to building personal relationships and seek to lead God-treasured people to the only one who can save and rescue them from the great plight they are in. This does involve using non-worldly weapons, namely gospel words, to demolish the arguments and strongholds of thought that prevent people from having a saving knowledge of God and of the glory of Christ's lordship. So to the extent that Buddhist, Hindu, Sikh, Islamic, or "religious" teachings are bricks in the stronghold then we do need to confront them, albeit in culturally appropriate ways that do not compromise the integrity of the gospel.

Religion and Human Nobility

But do recognize that we have been talking about total ways of life. People are created in the image of God and James warns us most severely against speaking in a way that expresses dishonor towards other human beings.[30] The image of God has certainly been seriously damaged but it has not been destroyed. There is still a great deal of nobility to be seen in the lives of those who don't know the Lord, sometimes of such a scale that it puts God's own people to shame. Culture, people's way of life, which includes "religion"—a conceptual entity to Western minds—is just an expression and working out of what people are. Therefore, we expect to find in culture, and even "religion," not merely shameful aspects which betray human rebellion against God, but also glorious expressions of human nobility as those who remain created in God's image.

We must remember this when we interact with people we might think of as Buddhists or Hindus or Muslims, whatever. It is common in the West to make a sharp division between the sacred and the secular, accompanied by an attempt to jettison religion from the public arena. This is not replicated in the vast majority of non-Western societies. So we can expect that in the way of life we think of as Buddhist or Hindu or Muslim or Sikh or whatever, there will be not merely that which distresses us, but also that which is to be commended. Our doctrine of total depravity reminds us that even as God's people, until Christ returns and our transformation is complete, we remain as those who are tainted by sin in all areas of our lives. This should temper an otherwise over-critical spirit. So, while we might still see a gap between the best in other religious ways of life and biblical truth, this should not stop us from respecting that which approaches truth and rightness.

Religion and Truth

We have just touched on something we need to take very much to heart. The danger of having a concept of truth and of our own relationship to it that leads us to be self-righteous and to look down on those who as yet do not share in this. One of the most sobering aspects of the Old Testament depiction of God as the divine warrior is that God not only fights for Israel against their enemies, but he also fights against his own people

---

30. James 3:9–10.

when they became his enemy. We see a parallel to this in the risen Christ's letter to the church at Pergamum. Observing that some church members are following false teaching, Jesus commands the church to repent, warning that if they don't he will soon come and "fight against them with the sword of [his] mouth" (Revelation 2:16).

Religion and Judgment of God's People

In the Old Testament what was true of all ancient people was also true for Israel. They too were called to live a total way of life consistent with their God-ordered social mindset or understanding of reality. However, one of the major themes of Old Testament historical narrative is the incorrigibly idolatrous nature of God's people. Indeed, the Bible is far more severe in its critique of the "religious" life of God's own people than it ever is of others.

CULTURE, ETHICS, RELIGION, AND THE OCCULT

The Reality of the Excluded Middle

Especially in Western societies there are many Christians who live with a worldview which involves "the flaw of the excluded middle," to use Paul Hiebert's phrase. Such Christians believe in God, the upper level, and what their physical senses encounter each day, the lower level. But there is a whole spirit world in the middle that they either deny or, more commonly, only recognize in a formal manner.[31] This is all the stranger because, as Peter Jones makes all too clear in his book *Spirit Wars*, American culture is in the process of being profoundly reshaped by an experiential approach to spirituality that smacks of pagan revival, especially reminiscent of ancient Gnosticism.[32]

In Australia, as in many Western societies, there are many people who engage in various forms of divination including astrology, palmistry, divining rods and pendulums, psychometry, and dreams and visions. Fertility charms, amulets, incantations, spells, and spiritism are also much more in vogue.[33]

---

31. Lane, *The Unseen World*, ix.
32. See Jones, *Spirit Wars*.
33. See the chapter "Distractions by Demons—The Occult" in Dickason, *Angels,*

The TV and movie industries constantly pump out programs and films of an occult nature. It is increasingly difficult to rationalize many of these as being but harmless entertainment. C. S. Lewis's *Narnia* tales create a fantasy world that incorporates witchcraft and magic and yet do this in a way that positively and constructively engages with truth. Programs and movies that center on vampires, witches, werewolves, demons, and zombies are not new. It does not necessarily follow that programs and movies that involve such themes are pernicious. But the fact is that many modern productions go beyond entertainment, reflecting the dangerous worldviews of their writers and producers. Such is the changed climate that it became acceptable to have a prime-time show, *Lucifer*, that has Satan incarnated and living in Los Angeles and using his powers to solve murders and help people.[34]

The Misrepresentation of the Excluded Middle

Boyd observes that in the Old Testament we find none of the obsession with evil spirits that was to be found in the surrounding cultures: "The fear and superstition, as well as the preoccupation with methods of protection and exorcism, that characterize these other Near Eastern cultures are altogether absent from the Old Testament."[35]

Significantly, and in sharp contrast with other literature in the ancient world, there are only two angels who are given names in the entirety of the Bible.[36] Unfortunately, there are many Christian writers whose treatment of spiritual warfare not only seems to major on the occult, but also misrepresents it. David Powlison wisely observed, "A great deal of fiction, superstition, fantasy, nonsense, nuttiness, and downright heresy flourishes in the church under the guise of 'spiritual warfare' in our time ... But the warfare we need to wage engages and implicates our humanity, rather than bypassing it for a superspiritual, demonic realm."[37]

As Powlison rightly recognizes, spiritual warfare is first and foremost about what and who controls the human heart and mind. To portray

---

Elect and Evil, 196–209.

34. The TV show is based on the character developed in the comic book series, *The Sandman*. It is imagined that Satan becomes bored with being the Lord of Hell, so he abandons his throne and becomes incarnate as Lucifer Morningstar.

35. Boyd, *God at War*, 80.

36. Boyd, *God at War*, 165.

37. Cited by Justin Taylor, "Spiritual Warfare 101."

spiritual warfare as something that takes place on a super-spiritual plane is to distract Christians from engaging with that which is of central importance, having a gospel-grounded right relationship with our Lord.

Powlison observes that the popular wrong-headed approach to spiritual warfare conceives of a demon as an alien intelligence and will that is able to infiltrate one's personality and take control over it. It is like a virus on the hard disk of the soul that is able to execute commands. Along these lines Neil Anderson thinks of demons as being like bats in a cave that have to be eliminated. The "computer virus" needs to be scrubbed.

The Bible and the Occult

There are Christian leaders and writers who have developed an occult theology which is shaped by their understanding of typically extreme experience and is then read back into the Bible.[38] Their own encounters with the occult and animism, and exposure to bizarre behaviors, including extreme personality disorders, may play a part. Also of importance to this theology are such things as extreme sins against persons, such as rape and incest, tantrums or bouts of rage, instances of people doing the same evil things over and over again, and examples of evil behavior that appears to be intergenerational.

Once such a theology is developed on the basis of seeing such experiences as occult, then eisegesis (reading meaning into the Bible) trumps exegesis (reading meaning out of the Bible). So, for example, biblical exorcisms performed by Jesus and the apostles have frequently been misconstrued as confirming what has already been concluded on the basis of an interpretation of experience, not biblical revelation.

It is important to realize that when exorcisms are described in the Bible they never involve deliverance from sin as such.[39] Ferdinando

---

38. There is much to be said for Smith's view that "the popularity of the praxis model in theology is partly due to the cultural shift towards postmodernity, where experience as the prime mediator of truth and reality is preferred." Smith, "Church Militant," 24. Smith's personal conviction "shares with many Christians a high regard for the inspiration of Scripture, but also recognizes that particular interpretations should always be open to re-examination, and tested against our experience and those of others in the Christian community, both now and in the tradition," (p.25–26).

39. "Exorcism" is not a word used in the Bible and is not an ideal word to use given that it often seems to presuppose use of a ritual. As Moreau points out, in the New Testament the casting out of demons is rather a pure exercise of authority. Moreau, *Essentials*, 62.

states this simple, basic fact: "Nowhere does the Bible explain human sin in terms of demonic possession."[40] The deliverance is always from suffering, misery, and torment. This is in contrast to popular deliverance ministries that involve deliverance from moral evil. Further, as Ferdinando points out, "the way in which Jesus drove out demons was quite different from the more or less magical techniques employed by contemporary exorcists."[41]

Contemporary exorcists typically try to force a demon to speak and reveal its name and then seek to bind it, employing a special vocabulary, incantations, and rituals "followed to the letter." In contrast, "Jesus did none of this. There is no evidence in the Gospels, including the expulsion of the demons from the Gerasene man, that Jesus even prayed when he drove out spirits."[42]

Demonization is indeed a very real phenomenon, strongly recognized in the Bible.[43] This is often referred to as demon possession, though the idea is not of ownership but of control.[44] As Ferdinando recognizes, it is not presented as a consequence of sin, it can be continuous or intermittent, more or less severe, and usually involuntary.[45] Most Western Christians have never had any direct experience of this. People may be "taken over" by something that grips and controls them which is not spirit-related such as an illness, fever, an epileptic fit, or an asthma attack, hysteria (personal or mob), hypnotism, intoxication and drug addiction, extreme trauma, and so on.[46] Given our socialization and enculturation in Western culture, it is tempting for Western Christians to view biblical descriptions of demon "possession" as but the cultural way of the time for understanding certain forms of extreme mental illness.

Here we need to remember that Satan is first and foremost the master of deceit, the one who leads the whole world astray. Given the Western tendency towards secular materialism and the disavowal of the

40. Ferdinando, *Message of Spiritual Warfare*, 95.
41. Ferdinando, *Message of Spiritual Warfare*, 89.
42. Ferdinando, *Message of Spiritual Warfare*, 89.
43. Notably, as Smith observes, "by the mid-1990s the Church of England had appointed at least one official exorcist in each diocese, and bishops liked to be kept informed about exorcism matters." Smith, "Church Militant," 60.
44. Moreau, *Essentials*, 62.
45. Ferdinando, *Message of Spiritual Warfare*, 87–88.
46. I'm indebted to Scott Moreau for a presentation he gave me on "Supernatural Experience" which includes a slide on "Possessive States," discriminating between physiological, psychosocial, spirit-related, and other forms of possession.

supernatural, it does not suit Satan's purposes to parade his power to demonically possess people. Satan wants Westerners who don't believe in the supernatural to continue to think this way. So, the predominance of demon possession in some cultural contexts rather than others should not surprise us. As real as this phenomenon is, there is no doubt that it also belongs to particular social and cultural contexts.

There would appear to be no New Testament example of a Christian being demon possessed. However, Satan does succeed in filling the heart of Ananias and Sapphira causing them to engage in a level of deceit that causes God to strike them down dead. And we do have examples of some who once belonged to the Christian community now choosing to follow Satan.

Animism and the Occult

There is a strong tendency among many Christians to assume that when we move into a third world setting where occult practices are much more embedded in culture that it now becomes okay to interpret this experientially rather than through the lens of biblical revelation.[47] This is precisely at odds with the way in which the Israelites were prepared for their entrance into a land where this was very much the case. They were told quite plainly that the gods worshiped by the Canaanites were not to be treated as having any essential reality. Prophetically anticipating the time when the Israelites would adopt the same animistic worldview as the Canaanites, Moses says, as though he is now looking back, "They sacrificed to demons, which are not God—gods they had not known, gods that recently appeared, gods your fathers did not fear" (Deuteronomy 32:17). God's verdict is stated: "They made me jealous by what is no god and angered me with worthless idols" (verse 21a). God declares, "See now that I myself am he! There is no god besides me" (verse 39a).[48]

---

47. Gardner observes, "Much spiritual warfare teaching is similar to charismatic teaching. In fact, charismatics would feel at home in the spiritual warfare movement since both groups allow for extra-biblical revelation. He cites Wagner's remark in *The Third Wave of the Holy Spirit*: "I still study the Bible, of course, but I find this other dimension of personal intimacy equally important. Then I ask God to give me the ability to obey both the Scriptures and his direct word to me." Gardner, *Spiritual Warfare*, 4. Vann Hutchinson states, "Most deliverance ministers, *through experience*, know that demons can indwell Christians" (my emphasis). Hutchinson, "Warriors for Christ."

48. As Greenlee comments, "[T]he Old Testament does not ascribe ontological reality to the gods worshiped by the Canaanites, gods to whom they granted

There are many Christians who show themselves to be the descendants of idolatrous Israel when they too fly in the face of divine revelation to justify what is essentially an animistic approach to spiritual warfare. Those engaged in cross-cultural communication and ministry would do well to recognize that Satan is a master at adapting his own mission enterprise to differing cultural contexts and he has complete fluency in all of the world's languages.

Think of some of the ways in which Satan has developed cultural modes of deception. Take, for example, the widespread cultural construct of the evil eye, which is to be found in varying forms in many Middle Eastern, Asian, Latin American, and African contexts.

Many Ethiopians believe that there are Buda people who are enabled by evil spirits to harm others merely by glancing at them in a malevolent way, especially when those at whom they look are experiencing feelings of fear or anxiety. In many cultures precious persons or things are constantly vulnerable to hurt or destruction caused by other people's envy. In many traditions it is especially strangers, malformed individuals, and old women who are most often accused of casting the evil eye. Such people may do so involuntarily. For example, it will be taken for granted by many that the childless woman can cause harm because she cannot help herself from looking upon mothers with envy.

We should not think that any of these phenomena are merely cultural constructs only having power in people's imaginations. After all, behind such modes of deceit is to be found one who is extremely powerful and keen to exploit such superstitions to achieve his evil ends. Demons are for real and the Bible is under no illusions as to what they are able to accomplish.

Magic and the Occult

In the Western world we are familiar with a number of great magicians who astound their audiences with what they are able to do. They often leave us scratching our heads. Yet for all our puzzlement we know that what we have witnessed (or, more accurately in many cases, failed to witness) is a great trick or illusion. However, the Bible makes it clear that there is such a thing as real magic, the production of phenomena by supernatural means.

---

phenomenological reality." Greenlee, *Territorial Spirits Reconsidered*, 509.

Consider the war between God and the gods of Egypt spoken of in Exodus 12 and portrayed from the moment Moses and Aaron relayed God's demand to the Pharaoh to let his people go. Moses throws down his shepherd's staff and it becomes a snake. Yet the Egyptian magicians, when summoned by Pharaoh, "also did the same things by their secret arts." Significantly, their power, as real as it is, is trumped by God's infinitely greater power, with the snakes they cause their staffs to turn into being devoured by Moses's snake.

Similarly, Aaron stretches out the staff over the waters of Egypt and they all turn into blood. But again we read that the Egyptian magicians did the same things by their secret arts. Aaron strikes the dust of the ground with his staff and the dust becomes gnats, something that lies beyond the ability of the Egyptian sorcerers to replicate. Still, throughout this narrative there is no doubt that there is such a thing as "the secret arts," with Egyptian magicians able to appropriate supernatural forces to produce extraordinary phenomena.

In Acts 8 we find that a man named Simon was renowned for the magic he performed, though he himself was staggered by the far greater acts of power that accompanied Philip's ministry of preaching the gospel of the kingdom of God.

In Acts 19 "God did extraordinary miracles through Paul." In one instance it became widely known that a demon overpowered seven Jewish would-be exorcists, declaring, "Jesus I know, and I know about Paul, but who are you?" Many became believers as a result of this. Further, a "number who had practiced sorcery brought their scrolls together and burned them publicly." Imagine the following in order to gain some appreciation of how profoundly accepted and extensive the practice of magic was in the Greco-Roman world. Let's say a man of the time is earning an average daily wage but never spending any of it. It has been estimated that it would take him around 140 years to earn enough to buy these scrolls.

In the biblical world magic involved genuine acts of supernatural power. Since God is not the source of such power it follows that evil forces are involved. It is notable that in Ephesus the burning of magic scrolls by new converts followed on from their confession of evil deeds.[49]

---

49. A study of the collection termed the "magical papyri" shows that in the first century AD there was a very close relationship between the almost universal use of ritual magic and the "principalities and powers," supernatural powers and demons. See Gombis, "Triumph of God in Christ," 37–42; Arnold, *Powers of Darkness*, 21–30.

MISSION DEBRIEF

- **Socio-Cultural Threats to Godly Living.** There are aspects of culture and society, developed by a fallen humanity, which are not conducive to the living of godly lives.

- **Cultural Bias.** There is much in culture to be lauded. Nevertheless, all cultures, insofar as they are an expression of fallen humanity, are necessarily biased against God.

- **Cultural Bias and Religion.** Cultural bias against God is also demonstrably true of highly religious cultures.

- **Cultural Bias and Anti-God Ethics.** Fallen human cultures undermine God's own standards of good and evil and their own ethical systems reinforce human suppression of the knowledge of God.

- **Religion and Idolatry.** To a large extent the Bible concurs with the New Atheist depiction of religion as poison, because idolatry, typically, though not exclusively expressed in religion, is the default setting of a heart which substitutes "man" (ourselves and others) for God.

- **Idolatry: The Greatest Sin.** In the Old Testament holy war is especially set in the context of opposing idolatry, the most serious of all sins and the most radical form of covenant breach by God's people.

- **Holy War Opposing Idolatry.** The ancient world did not discriminate between the sacred and the secular. Holy war was not therefore an attack on what modern Westerners now dub "religion," but on a total way of life and worldview deemed to be idolatrous.

- **Culture, Religion, and the Image of God.** Because people remain in God's image not only culture but also human religions, as an expression of culture, do involve expressions of human wisdom and nobility.

- **The Reality of the Spirit World.** It is a misrepresentation of the excluded middle to treat spiritual warfare as something that takes place on a super-spiritual plane. Some Christian leaders effectively promote a species of animism, reading their own experiences of the occult into the Bible, and treating such phenomena as exorcism and demon possession and evil spirits in a manner never sanctioned in Scripture.

- **Culture and the Demonic.** The power of evil spirits lies behind cultural constructs which involve such phenomena as the evil eye and real magic.

GATHERING INTELLIGENCE

Read Daniel 3

1. In this chapter what are the various humanly manufactured systems and institutions which served to shape and express human behavior and thought? To what extent were these conducive to living God-fearing lives?

2. What competing systems of ethics and morality are illustrated by this series of events?

3. To what extent is it valid to see this chapter as dealing with a threat posed by false religion? What lies at the heart of the idolatry depicted in Daniel 3?

4. In what way does this chapter serve as a corrective to the fallacy of the excluded middle?

Chapter Seven

Facing the Last Enemy

"Thou thy worldly task hast done,
Home art gone, and ta'en thy wages.
Golden lads and girls all must,
As chimney-sweepers, come to dust."

WILLIAM SHAKESPEARE, *CYMBELINE*.

MANY WILL BE VERY much aware of human enmity. But their antipathy towards knowing the true and living God means that they are following Satan's lead, not opposing him. As moral and decent as such people may be, they are enslaved to sin, especially the evil of continuing to spurn their good and faithful creator. But there is one harsh reality that everyone knows they must face. We will all die. Paul calls death "the last enemy."

Satan is a defeated foe. We love, pray for, and bless those humans who make themselves our foes. The work of Christ, our union with him and the indwelling presence of the Holy Spirit mean that we no longer live as the slaves of that most insidious of foes, sin. But even Christians die. Have all other foes been sent reeling except for death?

DEATH WISH? THE DEATH OF CHRIST AND GOD'S PEOPLE AS OVERCOMERS

In the book of Revelation we come to terms with what true followers of Christ will do if faced with the choice of whether to remain true to their Lord or die. In that book God's people are called to be "overcomers." John has a vision of the immense glory of our risen and exalted Lord. In this vision the Lord Jesus tells him to write letters to seven churches, Ephesus, Smyrna, Pergamum, Thyatira, Sardis, Philadelphia, and Laodicea. While these letters do address issues particular to those churches, use of the symbolic number seven indicates that they are designed, as a set, to have representative significance for all churches in all ages. It is striking to see that each of these seven letters ends with Jesus promising rewards to the one "who overcomes."

Later in the book this overcoming is described as an overcoming of the dragon, that is, Satan. He is described as the one who accuses Christians, "before our God day and night."[1] In portraying Satan in this way, John is taking us back to Zechariah 3. There Zechariah has a visionary experience in which he sees "Joshua the high priest standing before the angel of the LORD." But he also sees Satan standing at Joshua's right side to accuse him. God responds, "The LORD rebuke you, Satan! The LORD, who has chosen Jerusalem, rebuke you! Is not this man a burning stick snatched from the fire"? (Zechariah 3:2). The narrative goes on to describe the Lord ordering that Joshua's filthy clothes be removed. This has symbolic significance, as the Lord himself explains, "See, I have taken away your sin, and I will put rich garments on you."

In Revelation 12 we see Satan launching the same accusatory attack on every believer. When we sin he is quick to draw this to God's attention. He does this because he knows that God is perfectly just and that his justice demands that no one who commits evil be admitted into his kingdom. Paul teaches that "the wages of sin is death,"[2] and this is what Satan is demanding. Every time a Christian sins he is demanding that he or she pay the ultimate price for such treachery.

But every true believer prevails against such accusations. However, they do not overcome the evil one by appealing to a sinless life. The whole point is that they have sinned, which is why Satan is launching his accusation in the first place. If they have indeed sinned and if God's justice

---

1. See Revelation 12:10.
2. Romans 6:23.

demands that the sinner experience eternal death then how is it possible for Christians to overcome Satan? We are told: "They overcame him by the blood of the Lamb and by the word of their testimony; they did not love their lives so much as to shrink from death" (Revelation 12:11).

Here the effect of "the blood of the Lamb" parallels the removal of Joshua's filthy clothes which enabled him, as high priest, to enter God's presence. True disciples are those "who have come out of the great tribulation" and "have washed their robes and made them white in the blood of the Lamb" (Revelation 7:14).

The point is that in this closing chapter of history in which we are now living, God's people suffer greatly. Yet when our sufferings are over and we join the angelic hosts in worshiping our wonderful Lord, it will be because Jesus's death on the cross satisfied God's justice and washed us clean in God's sight.

FACING DEATH, AND GOD'S PEOPLE AS OVERCOMERS

But this conquest is not based on some mere legal fiction. I might claim to be forgiven and therefore secure. However, Satan's accusations have real bite if I do not back up my confession with a life lived for the Lord. So, our "word of testimony," the fact that we are able to refer to solid evidence of devotion to Christ, also plays a key role. And do note that this word of testimony is expressive of another reality: "they did not love their lives so much as to shrink from death." True disciples are not the recipients of cheap grace. John's words especially presuppose life-threatening persecution. But for true disciples, when it comes to the crunch, their devotion to Christ is such that they are prepared to lay down their lives for him. There is doubtless also the thought contained here that their fear of death is removed by their assurance of eternal salvation.

It has been recognized by many commentators that symbolism used in the book of Revelation points to terrible persecution against Christians perpetrated by the Roman empire. The reality of martyrdom is recognized in a number of passages. For example, in the letter to the church in Smyrna, Christians are told: "Do not be afraid of what you are about to suffer. I tell you, the devil will put some of you in prison to test you, and you will suffer persecution for ten days. Be faithful, even to the point of death, and I will give you life as your victor's crown" (Revelation 2:10).

At another point in the book of Revelation the symbolism of the opening of seven seals expresses the reality that Jesus, "the Lamb," is the one who controls the entire course of history. In this context too we read: "When he opened the fifth seal, I saw under the altar the souls of those who had been slain because of the word of God and the testimony they had maintained" (Revelation 6:9).

Towards the end of the book, John sees:

> the souls of those who had been beheaded because of their testimony for Jesus and because of the word of God. They had not worshiped the beast or his image and had not received his mark on their foreheads or their hands. They came to life and reigned with Christ a thousand years. (The rest of the dead did not come to life until the thousand years were ended.) This is the first resurrection. Blessed and holy are those who share in the first resurrection. The second death has no power over them, but they will be priests of God and of Christ and will reign with him for a thousand years (Revelation 20:4–6).

There is some tantalizing symbolism here which has been subject to various interpretations and applications. This is not the place to conduct a rigorous exegesis. Some of the basic questions concern whether the thousand years (millennium) is to be understood literalistically or metaphorically; whether Christ returns after the millennium (post-millennialism) or before it (pre-millennialism); or whether the age in which we are now living is the millennium (a-millennialism); and whether the reign takes place in heaven or on earth. Whatever one might decide on these matters it is clear that for God's people death is not the end and that beyond death lies the prospect of being the royal priests we were created to be. But it is apparent from the texts we have considered in Revelation that by the end of the first century martyrdom on a significant scale was very much a part of Christian experience.

Throughout history there have been those who have deliberately placed themselves in the jaws of death in order to win honor and glory for themselves and perhaps their family and community. Throughout church history we see not only Christians who are made martyrs but also Christians who seek martyrdom. But there is something unhealthy about the mind that seeks death. Jesus deliberately laid down his life for us. But, as his prayer in the Garden of Gethsemane reveals, Jesus was not seeking death.[3] Yes, to follow Jesus involves taking up our own cross, losing our

---

3. Matthew 26:39, 43.

lives as those who live no longer for ourselves[4] but for the one who died for us and was raised again.[5] Like Shadrach, Meshech, Abednego, and Daniel many Christians have found that their commitment to follow Christ has put them in harm's way. Sometimes this involves, as the Apostle Peter well knew, being pressured by others as to whether we will deny Christ to preserve our lives, or confess Christ and lose them.

THE FEAR OF DEATH

The writer to the Hebrews describes all people outside of Christ as "held in slavery by their fear of death."[6] Death, Paul tells us, is "the last enemy to be destroyed." Christ's own resurrection in history is the essential and only foundation of our own hope of resurrection and it is because of this reality that we can claim "victory through our Lord Jesus Christ." The hope of resurrection assures us that "death has been swallowed up in victory," so that as we face death we can mock it: "Where, O death, is your victory? Where, O death, is your sting?"[7]

But is it true that all who do not know our Lord are "held in slavery by their fear of death"? Atheists, for example, may appeal to the supposedly peaceful death of David Hume. But this misses the point. The default position of every human heart is to fear death. Inevitably, people have developed their own strategies for dealing with this and some work better than others in overcoming that fear. Suicide bombers may reassure themselves that their despicable action will please their false god and guarantee their entrance into paradise. Because they think their karma has been sufficiently good, some Buddhists and Hindus may convince themselves that they are likely to have a favorable rebirth. An atheist may convince himself or herself that death is the absolute end and accept this.

Just before the writer to the Hebrews speaks of people being held in slavery by their fear of death, he speaks of the devil as the one who holds the power of death. It is the devil who effectively keeps people in a state of slavery. The coping mechanisms and strategies people adopt in dealing with the natural fear of death are themselves pointers to their enslavement. People are trapped by their delusions and false ways of thinking about life and death. Only Jesus can free those who are held in slavery by

---

4. Matthew 16:24–25.
5. 2 Corinthians 5:15.
6. Hebrews 2:14.
7. 1 Corinthians 15:55.

their fear of death. Only in Jesus is it possible to stare death in the face with fully warranted confidence that it is a defeated foe.

Missionaries and Christians living in religiously pluralistic societies need to make much of the fact that all people fear death. We do have the answer here. We do have the authority and the right to press people on this issue and to ask them what they expect will happen to them after they die. It is precisely with respect to this matter of life after death that opportunity is provided to speak not only about the resurrection of Christ but also the significance and meaning of his death, for, we are informed, it is by his death that Jesus will bring about the destruction of the one who holds the power of death, the devil.

Victory over death belongs to a much broader understanding of Christian conquest, as indicated in Romans 8 where Paul exults in the wonder of God's love by saying: "No, in all these things we are more than conquerors through him who loved us. For I am convinced that neither death nor life, neither angels nor demons, neither the present nor the future, nor any powers, neither height nor depth, nor anything else in all creation, will be able to separate us from the love of God that is in Christ Jesus our Lord" (Romans 8:37–39).

A more in-depth study of Romans 8 would reveal that the entire chapter is concerned with the doctrine of the image of God. Indeed, this motif is much more integral to the book of Romans than is commonly recognized. At any rate, this marvellous ending to Romans 8, with those telling words "nor anything else in all creation," points to the fact that in Christ the image of God is completely restored so that, as God purposed when he created us, we now enjoy dominion as conquerors over all of God's creation. Death was the punishment decreed for Adam and Eve should they disobey God. When our first parents were created in God's image there was no prospect of dying. So human conquest over death is essential to the restoration of our true humanity.

MISSION DEBRIEF

- **Satan's Demand.** Satan appeals to God's justice, demanding that eternal death be the fate of all sinners. But Christians overcome Satan by appealing to Jesus's death and the lived-out reality that he means more to them than life itself.

- **Fear of Death & Enslavement.** The fear of death enslaves all unbelievers, with many adopting false worldviews in their attempt to quell or dismiss such fears.
- **Fear of Death & Gospel Opportunity.** Encouraging unbelievers to face such natural fear without prevarication opens opportunities to explain the wonderful significance of Christ's death and resurrection.
- **Image-Restoration & Conquest Over Death.** Our union with Christ involves such a complete restoration of the image of God that Christian emerge as "more than conquerors" over everything in creation, including even death.

GATHERING INTELLIGENCE

Read 1 Corinthians 15:12–28

1. If the bodily resurrection of Jesus from the dead is a fiction where would this leave us as Christians in the face of death?
2. What fate awaits (a) all who are outside of Christ and (b) all those who are in Christ?
3. Why is Jesus's conquest of death so foundational to the fulfillment of God's ultimate purpose?

Chapter Eight

Facing Enemies Together

"Be sure you stand in close order amongst yourselves; these times give us too many sad examples of such, who first fell from communion with their brethren, and then into the devourer's hands; stragglers are soon snapped, you will find you are safest in a body."

WILLIAM GURNALL, *THE CHRISTIAN IN COMPLETE ARMOUR*.

WE HAVE CONSIDERED A variety of foes that confront us as we commit ourselves to obeying our Lord. Whether we think of opposition emanating from inhuman, human, fabricated, or inner sources, the New Testament is adamant that we should not be facing these foes alone.

THE ARMORED CHURCH

In this respect it is important to grasp the force of what Paul is urging in perhaps his most famous passage on spiritual warfare:

> Finally, be strong in the Lord and in his mighty power. Put on the full armor of God, so that you can take your stand against the devil's schemes. For our struggle is not against flesh and

blood, but against the rulers, against the authorities, against the powers of this dark world and against the spiritual forces of evil in the heavenly realms. Therefore put on the full armor of God, so that when the day of evil comes, you may be able to stand your ground, and after you have done everything, to stand. Stand firm then, with the belt of truth buckled around your waist, with the breastplate of righteousness in place, and with your feet fitted with the readiness that comes from the gospel of peace. In addition to all this, take up the shield of faith, with which you can extinguish all the flaming arrows of the evil one. Take the helmet of salvation and the sword of the Spirit, which is the word of God (Ephesians 6:10–17).

I must confess that so imbued am I with a Western individualist mindset that I have read this passage for most of my Christian life as though it were addressed to me as an individual Christian. This misses the point entirely. Earlier in this same letter, Paul has given a clear example of the devil's "schemes" (*methodeia*). For he uses the very same word when he sets before the church, as the body of Christ, the goal of being built up "until we all reach unity in the faith and in the knowledge of the Son of God and become mature, attaining to the whole measure of the fullness of Christ" (Ephesians 4:13).

Paul immediately observes, "Then we will no longer be infants, tossed back and forth by the waves, and blown here and there by every wind of teaching and by the cunning and craftiness of men in their deceitful scheming [*methodeia*]. Instead, speaking the truth in love, we will in all things grow up into him who is the Head, that is, Christ. From him the whole body, joined and held together by every supporting ligament, grows and builds itself up in love, as each part does its work" (Ephesians 4:14–16).

Isn't this fascinating? At one level the "deceitful scheming" is experienced as people, using their "cunning and craftiness," teach things that sway and destabilize Christians. But, as Paul is now making clear at the end of the book, in reality our struggle is not so much against false teachers and those who unsettle believers with wrong thinking. We must see that the real enemy is Satan and his forces. It is actually the schemes of the devil that lie behind the deceitful scheming of people.

But the parallel in chapter 4 is instructive for other reasons. It indicates to us what Paul means when he asks us to be strong in the Lord and in his mighty power. Christians are strong when they are fully-fledged members of the body of Christ, a church community that is united "in the faith and in the knowledge of the Son of God." Christians are strong when together, as the body of Christ, they are mature and seeking to enjoy together "the whole measure of the fullness of Christ."

See how important it has been to track back Paul's thought! It is a great error, as Western Christians are only too prone to do, to read Ephesians 6 in an individualistic fashion. Paul is not so much requiring each individual Christian to don the armor of God, but the entire body of Christ. It is when we all put on God's armor and fight in company, as a regiment, that we are able to stand against the devil's attempts to move us away from our firm position in Christ.[1]

Ephesians 4, by the way, begins by urging Christians "to keep the unity of the Spirit through the bond of peace." Paul continues: "There is one body and one Spirit—just as you were called to one hope when you were called—one Lord, one faith, one baptism; one God and Father of all, who is over all and through all and in all" (Ephesians 4:4–6).

A united stand then is what Paul is calling for and, indeed, it is most significant that every verb and every noun that refers to disciples of Jesus in Ephesians 6:10–17 is plural.

Here's one example of how we let Satan get the better of us. Someone in the Corinthian church had sinned badly and had been disciplined accordingly. But now Paul urges them to forgive this person "in order that Satan might not outwit us. For we are not unaware of his schemes."[2] One of Satan's schemes, then, is to introduce modes of thought into the minds of Christians that lead them to justify and rationalize what in reality are unforgiving, unloving responses to regrettable behavior by other Christians.

The Ephesians 4 parallel to Ephesians 6 is significant for another reason. A church that stands strong, united, and mature is a church that has been "equipped" to do this, by those with word gifts—the apostles, prophets, evangelists, and pastor-teachers the Lord has given to the church. So, the church grows in maturity and strength as it is shaped by the gospel, the teaching of God's Word.

---

1. Gombis, following Neufeld, comments, "Here, the divine warrior is no longer God, but the church, which is engaged in warfare with the powers ruling the present evil age. The call to 'be strong in the Lord and in the power of his strength' (6:10) is an exhortation to the corporate church to take up God's power in order to engage the conflict." Gombis, "Triumph of God in Christ," 3.

2. 2 Corinthians 2:10–11.

As we continue to read this great passage from Ephesians 6, let's do so as a church, as churches, as Christians in community who are committed to combining our strength to face our foes.

"PUT ON THE GOSPEL ARMOR"

Look at the different components to "the armor of God." The hymn writer gets us to sing "Put on the gospel armor" and he is dead right. That's precisely what every piece of our armor is about. Every piece is just another aspect or dimension of the gospel. Truth, righteousness, peace, faith, salvation, "the Word of God"—these are all just different ways of speaking about what the gospel means for us as Christians.

It has often been thought that Paul's description of "the armor of God" is based on his observation of the Roman armor he was seeing at close quarters every day. But, of course, almost everything Paul says would be applicable to a soldier in almost any army in the ancient world. It was standard to wear helmets, breastplates, and so on.

In addition, do recognize that Paul's language deliberately adopts Old Testament phrases. Think here of "the breastplate of righteousness," "the helmet of salvation," "belt of truth," "the sword of the Spirit." Consider the following Old Testament sources on which Paul is drawing:

- "Truth is nowhere to be found, and whoever shuns evil becomes a prey. The LORD looked and was displeased that there was no justice. He saw that there was no one, he was appalled that there was no one to intervene; so his own arm achieved salvation for him, and his own righteousness sustained him. He put on righteousness as his breastplate, and the helmet of salvation on his head; he put on the garments of vengeance and wrapped himself in zeal as in a cloak. According to what they have done, so will he repay wrath to his enemies and retribution to his foes; he will repay the islands their due" (Isaiah 59:15b–17).

- "[B]ut with righteousness he will judge the needy, with justice he will give decisions for the poor of the earth. He will strike the earth with the rod of his mouth; with the breath of his lips he will slay the wicked. Righteousness will be his belt and faithfulness the sash around his waist" (Isaiah 11:4–5).

- "Listen to me, you islands; hear this, you distant nations: Before I was born the LORD called me; from my mother's womb he has spoken my name. He made my mouth like a sharpened sword, in the shadow of his hand he hid me; he made me into a polished arrow and concealed me in his quiver. He said to me, 'You are my servant, Israel, in whom I will display my splendor'" (Isaiah 49:1–3).
- "How beautiful on the mountains are the feet of those who bring good news, who proclaim peace, who bring good tidings, who proclaim salvation, who say to Zion, 'Your God reigns!'" (Isaiah 52:7).
- "As for God, his way is perfect: The LORD's word is flawless; he shields all who take refuge in him. For who is God besides the LORD? And who is the Rock except our God? It is God who arms me with strength and keeps my way secure. He makes my feet like the feet of a deer; he causes me to stand on the heights. He trains my hands for battle; my arms can bend a bow of bronze. You make your saving help my shield, and your right hand sustains me; your help has made me great" (Psalm 18:30–35).

Paul draws on Old Testament imagery and thought, especially from the book of Isaiah, in describing every part of the soldier's armor in Ephesians 6. God himself is the warrior who dons the breastplate of righteousness and the helmet of salvation.[3] Another text presents the promised Davidic king, the Messiah, going to war, belted with righteousness and faithfulness, to bring true justice to the world. Similarly, we see David himself being armed by God for battle and holding the shield of victory or God's "saving help." Then there is the Suffering Servant, the encapsulation of all that Israel was intended to be, portrayed as a prophet-like figure, with the words that proceed from his mouth being God's sword—the likely inspiration for Paul's image of the word of God being "the sword of the Spirit." When Paul speaks of footwear associated with the gospel of peace he has in mind that great image of beautiful feet running to announce the peace that has been brought in by the coming of God's reign.

All in all, there is a sense that to put on "the armor of God" is to don the same armor God himself or Jesus, as the Messiah or Suffering

---

3. As Gombis, summarizing Neufeld states, "In Isaiah 59 Yahweh appears as the Divine Warrior who is preparing to judge his apostate people and warns them to repent. In preparation for coming in his awesome judgment to wage war, he puts on his armor, which consists of his own righteousness, salvation, vengeance, and zeal (Isaiah 59:16–17)." Gombis, "Triumph of God in Christ," 3.

Servant, would wear. No wonder that when we don this armor we are "strong in the Lord and in his mighty power"![4]

Linger on this thought. We have here the very opposite of what we encounter on the battlefields of this world. There we find that the strength of a general lies in his troops. To use one of Gurnall's images, like a bird that cannot fly if its wings are clipped, so the general is impotent if the power of his army is smashed. But, by contrast, the strength of every Christian and, indeed, the entire Christian army lies in its general, the Lord.[5] If he so chose the Lord could defeat all opposing forces single-handedly, but in his wisdom and grace he has chosen instead to accomplish this through us, his people.

Yet, for many Christians who are overpowered by sin, this truth concerning God's absolute might and power—to adapt another image used by Gurnall—is like an unfired, unoiled revolver that is left to rust in a moldy room.[6] May God grant such Christians a fresh and liberating understanding of the gospel of grace!

When Paul describes the armor of God that Christians as a church must wear he is not merely alluding to this rich Old Testament background. He is also gathering up some of the important themes he has been developing in this letter to the Ephesians.

Think of the belt of truth. Paul has had some significant things to say about truth in this epistle. He teaches that it was when the Ephesians heard the message of truth, the gospel of their salvation, that they were included in Christ.[7] Later he reiterates that it was after being taught about Jesus through the truth of the gospel that they came to know Christ. Further, through gospel truth they were taught to put off "the old man" with all its corruption and put on "the new man, created to be like God in true righteousness and holiness."[8] As Moreau says, "Knowing truth is not the final goal; believing and acting on that truth is."[9] Christians now have passed from living a life in darkness to living a life in the light, characterized by "goodness, righteousness, and truth."[10] It is

---

4. Ephesians 6:10.
5. See Gurnall, *Christian in Complete Armour*, 18.
6. Gurnall's image is of a rusty sword hardly drawn out of the scabbard. Gurnall, *Christian in Complete Armour*, 26.
7. Ephesians 1:13.
8. Ephesians 4:20–24.
9. Moreau, *Essentials*, 25.
10. Ephesians 5:9.

when the Ephesians lovingly speak sound gospel doctrine ("the truth") to each other that they become a mature church community.[11] Moreau hits the mark in his identification of four key ways of equipping ourselves for spiritual warfare, namely engaging the truth, putting off sin, putting on righteousness, and exercising our authority in Christ.[12]

Read Ephesians and see how Paul in similar vein develops the themes of righteousness, peace, faith, salvation, and the Word of God. You will discover that the book of Ephesians is very much about the church. Of course, individual Christians have to take seriously truth, righteousness, peace, and so on. But in this letter Paul is especially addressing Christians as church. Take that word "peace," for example. Here Paul's major teaching in the second chapter looms large, where he describes how Jesus as "our peace," having made Jews and Gentiles one new humanity ("man"). Jesus "came and preached peace to you who were far away (Gentiles) and peace to those who were near (Jews)."[13] It is as a church community that we wear God's very own armor, the gospel armor, and stand strong against a much weaker, though diabolical foe.

Consider now how Paul portrays Satan in this great passage. God's armored people are to take their stand "against the devil's schemes." They are to ready themselves for the coming of "the day of evil." The shield of faith is needed to "extinguish the flaming arrows of the evil one."

One of the striking implications of Paul's teaching in this passage is that the "rulers," "authorities," "powers of this dark world," and "the spiritual forces of evil in the heavenly realms" are not able to match the strength of God's people when we stand as a united armored military force. That's why Satan has to resort to trickery and firing missiles from a distance.

Paul makes it quite clear that if we put on the full armor of God and take our stand together in the gospel and all it implies then Satan's trickery and missile-firing will fail. Warfare has changed enormously since Paul's day. But the basic principle remains the same. Provided we as God's people fully avail ourselves of what God supplies for our protection, and stand shoulder to shoulder, then no cunning ploy on Satan's part and no dishonorable mode of attack will defeat or destroy us.

---

11. Ephesians 4:15.

12. Moreau, *Essentials*, 15–18. Moreau develops each of these themes in the course of his book.

13. Ephesians 2:14–17.

JOINT PROTECTION

It is not only when contending against inhuman foes that we need to do so as a church community. This also applies to our individual struggles with sin. We are out of line with New Testament teaching if we suppose that it is simply up to each and every one of us to manage our own personal struggle with sin.

Especially in the Western world, many professing Christians treat churches as if they were spiritual shops or supermarkets. This week they shop at Coles. Next week maybe at Woolworths. Oh, we are pretty well stocked up at present. So, no need to shop this week. And so you have Christians who church hop or attend church maybe once a month. Involvement in the church is pretty light on too. They come to the service and maybe even enjoy the groovy music—what a cool band! But they don't hang around long before heading home and that's church for the week.

Even to describe some Christians in this way is to indicate that indeed they have a major spiritual problem in their life. After all I have just described sinful behavior. Listen to this: "And let us consider how we may spur one another on toward love and good deeds, not giving up meeting together, as some are in the habit of doing, but encouraging one another—and all the more as you see the Day approaching" (Hebrews 10:24–25).

Even in the early church there were those who had largely given up meeting with other Christians. But don't be too quick to draw analogies with our modern Western experience. This biblical exhortation presupposes that fear of persecution is the major reason why some had developed a habit of not meeting with other Christians. Here is rich irony! For in so many parts of the globe Christians place themselves in danger if they meet together and yet do so, so great is the value they place on this.

Professing Christians who treat being members of a church as a light matter reveal by this alone that they have succumbed to the deceitfulness of sin. Further, it is only when we are in healthy relationships with other Christians in a church context that we are able to help each other in our individual struggles with sin. We were never intended to shoulder these burdens alone.[14]

We need to take to heart the following warning: "See to it, brothers and sisters, that none of you has a sinful, unbelieving heart that turns away from the living God. But encourage one another daily, as long as it is

---

14. Galatians 6:1–2.

called 'Today,' so that none of you may be hardened by sin's deceitfulness" (Hebrews 3:12–13).

The church community needs to be a context in which we take responsibility for each other's spiritual wellbeing and not simply leave it up to each individual to manage this themselves. A healthy church will be one in which there are high participation rates, not just in church services but in small group meetings devoted to prayer, Bible study, and building relationships.

CHURCH DISCIPLINE

In dealing with sin there is also a need for churches to exercise appropriate discipline. Jesus himself insists on this, when he gave instructions on how a Christian should act when sinned against by another believer. In the first instance he encouraged the one who has been offended to seek to "win over" the offender in a private conversation. The offended believer does not enter such a private meeting in an aggressive, domineering manner because the goal is reconciliation. Still, Jesus knows full well how hard it is for us to admit that we have done wrong. So, Jesus sets out a second measure to take if the offender will not accept that he or she has done anything that needs to be put right. This involves having yet another meeting with the offender but this time involving one or two other believers as witnesses to what is being discussed. Here Jesus assumes a situation where one believer has clearly wronged another. The church as a whole must address this issue if the offender still refuses to acknowledge sin and put things right. Now what could have been handled more sensitively and discreetly by a private conversation or just among a few has exploded into something that is right out there, in the open. But do observe that any private sin has ramifications for the spiritual health of the entire body of Christ. My sin is never just "my" problem. It is the church's problem, though this does not mean that the church as a whole has to deal with every instance of individual Christian sin. Some naïve Christians talk of being transparent in a way that is not biblical and, as we see, Jesus was not encouraging that.

If the private sin of an individual Christian does become a problem that the whole church is faced with then what happens if the individual will not confess sin or seek to put things right when even the church requires this? Then, Jesus says, the church is to treat the offender as they would a pagan or tax collector. This means, on the one hand, not treating the offender as a member of the church community: that is, excommunication. But, remembering that Jesus himself partied with tax collectors and sinners, this does not necessarily mean that the church cuts off all future relationships with the excommunicated person.

In the second of Paul's recorded letters to the Corinthians, he speaks of the grief caused to the entire church by the sinful actions of one of their church members. In this case church discipline had been exercised by the church and Paul comments, "The punishment inflicted on him by the majority is sufficient for him." Accordingly, he urges the church to forgive him and restore him to the fellowship of the church and all of this presupposes that the offender has come to terms with the wrong he had done. But forgiveness is urged "in order that Satan may not outwit us" because, as Paul adds, "we are not unaware of his schemes."

There is that word "schemes" again. From time to time church discipline will be necessary, but unforgiving harshness plays into the hands of Satan. Here it is also important to recall the context of Jesus's own words on church discipline, which we considered above. These are bracketed by the Parable of the Lost Sheep and the Parable of the Unmerciful Servant, with the latter pointedly concluding, "This is how my heavenly Father will treat each of you unless you forgive your brother from your heart."[15] Consequently, all of Jesus's teaching on how to respond when a believer sins is concerned with seeking to find this lost sheep and bring him back to the fold.

So, it's very important to get the balance right. Forgiveness should never be used as a reason for not exercising church discipline when it is needed. But church discipline should never be used as an excuse for a harshness which excludes the possibility of forgiveness when confession and repentance do take place.

MISSION DEBRIEF

- **Anti-Church Deceit.** Satan's schemes lie behind the deceitful scheming of people who threaten the destabilize the church.
- **Strength in Unity.** Such Satanic attacks via human deception fail to unsettle God's people when they are united together as part of a well-taught, mature, united, loving, and Christ-dependent community.

15. Matthew 18:35.

- **The Gospel and Protective Divine Power.** The power of God completely protects Christians against Satan and his forces when together with fellow believers, as members of a church, their lives are thoroughly shaped by the gospel.

- **The Lord Himself Is Our Strength.** Unlike human armies where a general's strength lies in his troops, the strength of God's people is vested in the Lord, the ultimate warrior.

- **Satan's Devious Tactics.** Satan is not able to match the strength of the gospel-armored Christian church and is therefore forced to resort to more devious tactics in seeking to wreak damage.

- **Vulnerable Believers.** Those Christians are especially vulnerable to Satan's attacks who trivialize meeting together with other believers and participating in church life.

- **Restorative Discipline.** Churches must exercise appropriate discipline in dealing with relationship-breaking sin in their midst. This does not legitimate heavy-handedness but presupposes that at every level the primary concern is that of restoring the recalcitrant one.

GATHERING INTELLIGENCE

Read Hebrews 3

1. Why was it that the generation of Israelites which exited Egypt were refused entry into the promised inheritance, God's rest?
2. What is the danger that each believer must confront?
3. How might such a threat develop? See too 2:1–4; 6:11–12; and especially 10:19–25.
4. What role is played by the house of God, the church, in countering this threat?

Chapter Nine

"More Than Conquerors"

"This is the victory that has overcome the world, even our faith."

1 John 5:4

The enemies we face are formidable, whether human or inhuman, whether external or internal, whether in life or in death. But they have all been defeated and are hopelessly outmatched. Yet, when we are engaged in battle, there can be severe consequences if we get our timing wrong. To overemphasize that which is "already" leads us to unbiblical notions that encroach on perfectionism. There are those who exaggerate the fruits of victory that Christians can enjoy in the here and now. We are saints who have experienced the transforming work of the Spirit in shaping our characters to become increasingly more like that of the Lord Jesus himself. But we deceive ourselves, make a liar out of our Lord, and fail to grasp biblical truth, if we downplay the sin that still dogs our steps.[1] There is much that still awaits the consummation of the victory already won.

But, at the other extreme, we must be careful not to overemphasize that which is "not yet." To do so is to become defeatist and succumb to

---

1. 1 John 1:8–10.

evil instead of being the salt and light we already are by virtue of our union with Christ and the empowering of the indwelling Spirit of God.[2]

THE CONQUEST OF CHAOS

The Bible begins with the subduing of the forces of chaos. Plainly, Genesis 1 is very different from all other creation accounts we find in the ancient world. There is no mention of other gods, just one God, the true and living God. Creation is not the result of conflict and sexual activity between gods. There is no mention of sea monsters being slaughtered and carved up.

With these qualifications in place, recognize that "the earth was formless and empty" and that "darkness was over the deep." These are all familiar images describing what we might describe as "uncreation" forces, which scholars denote as "chaos." But it's nothing like the chaos other ancient people had in mind when they thought about such forces.

Genesis 1 is polemical. What I mean is that it doesn't simply ignore other ancient ways of thinking about creation. It is plainly written in awareness of other ancient creation accounts and critiques them at various points. So, for example, Genesis 1 sets itself against the common ancient view that reality is fundamentally dualistic. Ancients thought of cosmic order and chaos as eternal polar opposites of commensurate power. We see a similarly unbiblical notion of essential reality in the Daoist Yin-Yang dualism so integral to much of Chinese thought.

By contrast, in Genesis 1 we see a God-purposed chaos over which he has absolute control. The chaos conditions themselves are part and parcel of the creation process.[3] In his work of creation God demonstrates that such forces are completely at his command. There is not so much as a whisper that these forces pose any threat to the realization of God's great creation purposes. There is not even a suggestion that these "uncreation" forces are evil or sinister.[4]

---

2. Compare the above with Stott's contrast between the "already" and "not yet" of eschatological reality. Stott, *The Cross of Christ*, 280.

3. This is not the chaos which results from some previous conflict, as Boyd mistakenly supposes as per "the gap theory," which Boyd prefers to call "the restoration theory." Boyd, *God at War*, 104.

4. Going well beyond the biblical text, Moltmann, influenced by Barth, supposes that in order to create the world it was first necessary for God to create an empty space or *nihil* outside of himself, which involved God withdrawing his presence and restricting his power. It is from this "God-forsaken space" that Nothingness emerges,

This foundational truth that God, as creator, has absolute and total control over all forces of chaos is placed beyond all doubt at the cross. Satan discovers that, far from having succeeded, his evil has been fully incorporated into God's plan of salvation.

Gregory Boyd refuses to accept that God does indeed have total control over all forces of chaos. He is well known for his championing of "open theism" and rejecting the classical view of divine foreknowledge and predestination.[5] He believes, for example, that God took a risk when, as a loving God inviting created agents to share in his love, he gave them freedom.[6]

In keeping with his theological *cum* philosophical assumptions, Boyd has led a recent charge which questions what he dubs the "blueprint worldview," the view that "assumes that everything somehow fits into 'God's secret plan.'"[7] On this front Boyd takes issue with Augustine and Calvin. To his mind the horrific things that happen to children cast significant doubt on the idea that a "higher reason" of God is involved. Indeed, he contends that while God sometimes allows or ordains suffering for a particular higher purpose, Scripture itself "does not support the view that there must be a specific divine reason behind all events."[8] Boyd contends that a more biblical view of the matter is to say that God is "warring against human and angelic opponents who are able in some measure to thwart his will." Therefore, God is to be seen as "striving to establish his will 'on earth as it is in heaven' (Mt 6:10)."[9] It is this which Boyd calls the "warfare worldview" of the Bible.[10]

---

the demonic negation of God that constantly opposes creation. See Smith, "Church Militant," 185–86.

5. Boyd, *Satan*: see chapter 3, "A Risky Creation," 85–115, and chapter 4, "A Question of Balance," 116–44.

6. Boyd, *Satan*, 86.

7. Boyd, *Satan*, 11–14.

8. Boyd, *Satan*, 14, 19.

9. Boyd, *Satan*, 15.

10. Boyd, *Satan*, 15. Smith remarks, "The relative lack of other references [sc. apart from Eph 6:10–12] to the demonic realm in Paul is . . . a reminder that the warfare motif is not quite as 'center stage' as Boyd maintains." Indeed, Smith notes Guelich's observation that as but one of several biblical metaphors for the Christian life, spiritual warfare "does not appear at all in the Gospels and in only one passage in the Pauline corpus with reference to Satan and the evil forces," with Jesus identifying the primary source of evil in the vices arising from the human heart (Mark 7:21–22) and Paul in the sins of the flesh that are opposed to the Spirit (Gal 5:19–21). Smith, "Church Militant," 248–49.

In promoting this view, and seeking to defend God as all-good and all-powerful, Boyd contends that horrific and evil things happen not because God chooses not to intervene but because he is unable to prevent them.[11] As he puts it: "in this present fallen world order God does not always get his way."[12] This is so because God's invitation to contingent creatures to share in his triune love necessarily allows for war, the rejection of his love.[13] Angelic and human agents are not merely responsible for the particular evil deeds they commit but they, not God (against the blueprint worldview) are the ultimate reason for such acts.[14]

Indeed, Boyd extensively argues that evil agents—Satan and demons—are the ultimate reason for "natural" evils, including the suffering of animals, as something which was going on for aeons before the emergence of human beings.[15] This, however, plainly clashes with the unavoidable fact that following the creation of humans God declares that everything he has made is very good.[16] Boyd's deviant theology involves distorted understandings, not only of God's sovereignty but indeed of God's Word, God's glory, and God's love, which he tragically evacuates of any association with violence. Here he fails to understand that evil can only be removed from the universe by divine violence and that this is in fact the very expression of genuine and ultimate love, God's love, which not only clings to the good but also therefore necessarily hates evil.

---

11. Boyd, *Satan*, 16.

12. Boyd, *Satan*, 39. His emphasis.

13. Boyd, *Satan*, 16–17. Boyd devotes a chapter to what he calls "the first thesis of the Trinitarian warfare theodicy," namely that "love must be chosen." See chapter 2, 50–84.

14. Boyd, *Satan*, 19. Boyd argues that prior to Augustine, the promulgator of "blueprint theology," the church fathers were heading in the right direction given their emphasis on evil being caused by free agents. See Boyd, *Satan*, 39–49.

15. Boyd, *Satan*, 242–318; see too Boyd, *God at War*, 109. Smith questions Boyd's view that the Bible has demons involved in all the battles on earth involving both natural and moral evil, noting "in reality specific references are decidedly sparse." Smith, "Church Militant," 260. Smith also comments: "if earthquakes and tsunamis from a geological perspective are caused by slow movement of tectonic plates over millennia, it is difficult to imagine (though not impossible) how fallen angels could in any way be responsible for causing such natural disasters." But he adds, "one conclusion seems well-founded—there is a category of natural causation of suffering and pain with an element of randomness, as Jesus clearly taught (Luke 13:4, the tower of Siloam), which is neither attributed directly to God's judgment (potentially tarnishing his goodness), nor directly to the devil, avoiding an exaggerated dualism." Smith, "Church Militant," 312.

16. Genesis 1:31.

IMAGE-BEARERS, CONQUEST, AND CHAOS

It is important to recognize that when God creates people in his image and likeness that a great deal of what this entails has already been disclosed in the way God himself has been revealed. Scholars have observed how some ancient kings would place an image-statue of themselves in conquered territory by way of saying that this land is now subject to their reign. Further, Genesis 1 has stressed God's character and role as the creator-king whose royal fiat ("Let there be . . .") must be obeyed. For the man and the woman to be created in God's image means that they too, like God, are rulers both in character and function and are commissioned to rule. Similarly, just as God subdued or "conquered" chaos in his work of creation so the man and the woman are also commissioned to subdue or "conquer" the earth.

At one point the prophet Jeremiah deliberately uses the phrase "formless and empty" at a time when he looks into the future and sees the devastation that lies ahead for the promised land God gave to the people of Israel. That land was intended to serve as a symbol of new creation populated by an exalted new humanity. But, tragically, Jeremiah sees that the land will revert to a state of uncreation: "My people are fools; they do not know me. They are senseless children; they have no understanding. They are skilled in doing evil; they know not how to do good. I looked at the earth, and it was formless and empty; and at the heavens, and their light was gone. I looked at the mountains, and they were quaking; all the hills were swaying. I looked, and there were no people; every bird in the sky had flown away. I looked, and the fruitful land was a desert; all its towns lay in ruins before the Lord, before his fierce anger."[17]

What was the initial cause of the Fall of our first parents? Their arrogation of a right that properly belongs to God alone—autonomous discrimination between good and evil. Why, according to Jeremiah, will there be such a reversion to chaos for Israel? Because of the inability of God's people to discriminate between good and evil. So, the land will go back to the chaos-like state described at the very beginning of the book of Genesis. It will be "formless and empty," covered with darkness, without people or fruitful life.

Sin causes chaos, but chaos of a different order from the original chaos described in Genesis. Now darkness and the sea become symbols of evil chaotic forces. For this reason, in a post-Fall world, we find that in

17. Jeremiah 4:22–26.

the Psalms and prophetic literature God comes to be depicted as one who slaughtered the chaos sea-monster.

As Boyd recognizes, Satan plays a relatively minor role in the Old Testament compared to the New. Overlooking God's conflict with evil humanity, Boyd sees the warfare worldview of the Old Testament as "expressed in terms of God's conflict with hostile waters, with cosmic monsters, and with other gods."[18]

In the ancient Near East it was certainly common to depict the story of divine struggle against chaos as a battle between deities.[19] The chaos deity was typically a sea god or goddess, the depiction of whom usually involved a watery abyss and a sea serpent or dragon. The deity who conquers this chaos deity is typically a storm god or at least one with whom storm imagery is associated.[20] Such stories are not unique to the ancient Near East. They have also been found in Anatolia, Greece, Mari, Canaan, Syria, India, Egypt, and Persia.

In the Babylonian creation myth (*Enuma Elish*), the god Marduk, armed with a lightning bolt, slays the goddess of "the deep," the goddess of chaos, Tiamat. Marduk cuts the corpse of this massive sea monster in two, and in this way forms the waters above and the waters below. We don't need to read Genesis 1 as written especially against this Mesopotamian creation account. Indeed, there is a good deal to suggest that Egyptian accounts of creation were much more in the firing line. But *Enuma Elish* does illustrate a common ancient way of thinking about origins which are effectively refuted in the Genesis account of creation.

When the Israelites entered the land of Canaan they were exposed to Baalism with its many local variants. There too we find Baal viewed as a god who conquered a dragon-like sea monster named Yammu.[21]

Daniel 7 exploits ancient mythology, indicating that the chaos waters provide the source for all the monsters who wreak chaos on earth through anti-God, blasphemous human rule.[22] Significantly, the book of Revelation draws on this imagery from the book of Daniel in painting its own picture of chaotic evil. Satan is identified with a dragon which stands

---

18. Boyd, *Satan*, 30.

19. Scholars use the German word *Chaoskampf* to denote the divine contest with chaos.

20. See Mabie, "Chaos and Death," 42.

21. In the *Ugaritic Poem of Baal* (fourteenth century BC) Baal subdues the dragon sea-monster, Yammu = Naharu = Tannin = Bathan, by way of securing his own dominion over gods, men, and earth.

22. See especially verses 2–3.

by the seashore. Next we read of a beast coming out of the sea, as though it had been "created" by Satan, with this beast symbolizing, as in Daniel, anti-God blasphemous human authority.[23]

In one psalm we read: "You rule over the surging sea; when its waves mount up, you still them. You crushed Rahab like one of the slain; with your strong arm you scattered your enemies. The heavens are yours, and yours also the earth; you founded the world and all that is in it" (Psalm 89:9–11). As the psalmist reflects on God's work of creation he stresses God's mastery over the sea which clearly symbolizes chaos. To express this he speaks of God slaying the sea-monster Rahab, by way of stressing that there is no god worshiped by ancient peoples who can compete with the God of Israel. The psalm has another agenda. Because there are no chaotic forces that can undermine God's rule he can be totally relied on to faithfully pursue his regal purposes, at the center of which stands his pledged commitment to "David," that is, a king who is the son of David.[24] As God has crushed Rahab so he will crush the foes of the Davidic king, significantly enabling him too to rule over the forces of chaos symbolized by the sea and rivers.[25]

Psalm 74 speaks of God splitting open the sea by his power, destroying the sea-monster Leviathan.[26] Leviathan is one of the names used for the primeval dragon, the personification of the forces of chaos, the mythological sea deity. This particular psalm was written during the exile when Jerusalem and Temple have been destroyed, that is, at a time of chaos. That's why there is a need to go back to the foundations of creation and recall how God triumphed over the forces of chaos. It is this creator whom the psalmist calls upon to remember his people amidst the chaos they are now experiencing.

Even more pointedly Isaiah sees the day when:

> [T]he LORD will punish with his sword,
> his fierce, great and powerful sword,
> Leviathan the gliding serpent,
> Leviathan the coiling serpent;
> he will slay the monster of the sea (Isaiah 27:1).

---

23. Revelation 13:1–7.

24. Verse 14, 17. These verses deliberately echo the language of 2 Samuel 7, the covenant God made with David.

25. See especially verse 25: "I will set his (David's) hand over the sea, his right hand over the rivers."

26. Psalm 74:13–14.

In Psalm 24 we meet a famous refrain: "Who is this King of glory? The LORD strong and mighty, the LORD mighty in battle."[27] This psalm presupposes that Jerusalem is God the King's capital city from which he rules the created world. The psalm pictures God returning to Jerusalem as the great conquering king. God in battle has conquered the forces of chaos symbolized by the sea, which is why the psalm begins by describing the world as that which God "founded . . . upon the seas."

In Psalm 65 God is remembered as the creator-conqueror "who stilled the roaring of the seas, the roaring of the waves, and the turmoil of the nations." This text is particularly interesting because it associates "the turmoil of the nations" with the forces of chaos overcome by God.

This association of chaos with political threat is more strongly developed in Psalm 46:

> God is our refuge and strength,
> an ever-present help in trouble.
> Therefore we will not fear,
> though the earth give way
> and the mountains fall into the heart of the sea,
> though its waters roar and foam
> and the mountains quake with their surging (Psalm 46:1–3).

This psalm begins with the vision of the chaos waters threatening the security of the world. However, even if the chaos waters could conquer the world they cannot conquer Jerusalem:

> There is a river whose streams make glad the city of God,
> the holy place where the Most High dwells.
> God is within her, she will not fall;
> God will help her at break of day (Psalm 46:4–5).

The threat symbolized by the chaos waters is identified with political threat: "Nations are in uproar, kingdoms fall; he lifts his voice, the earth melts."[28] The remainder of the psalm is devoted to describing God's conquest over the hostile nations—the particular expression of chaos. This illustrates how the Old Testament, as per standard ancient thought, did not sharply discriminate between "spiritual" and "physical" realities. So, God's overcoming of the threat posed by the evil sea monster Rahab concerns God's victory over Egypt.[29]

---

27. Verses 8–10.
28. Verse 6.
29. See Boyd, *Satan*, 32. Note the identification of Egypt with Rahab at Psalm 87:4

The symbolic function of the sea in denoting anti-creation chaos forces is picked up in the book of Revelation. There too there is a particular association of chaos with political threat. John interacts with the language of Genesis 1 when he says, "Then I saw a new heaven and a new earth, for the first heaven and the first earth had passed away, and there was no longer any sea" (Revelation 21:1). We are not to interpret this in a literalistic fashion and think that there will be no going to the beach and swimming in the sea in the new heavens and earth. We have already seen how Revelation 13, following Daniel 7, uses the sea as a symbol of chaos. What John is saying with highly symbolic language is that in the new universe there will no longer be any hostile chaotic forces.

JESUS, THE DIVINE CONQUEROR

It is particularly in the book of Revelation where we see the New Testament picking up the motif of God as divine warrior. There it is applied to none other than our Lord Jesus. Boyd contends, that an apocalyptic assumption underlies almost everything Jesus said and did, namely that "creation has been seized by a cosmic force and that God is now battling this force to rescue it."[30] This is close to the reality but use of the word "seized" overstates the case. It is true that Satan is called "the god of this age"[31] and that Jesus refers to him as "the prince of this world," but this does not mean that he controls creation.

Boyd sees "the kingdom of God," as taught by Jesus, as essentially a warfare concept—Jesus binding the strong man, Satan, to take from him the property over which he had assumed control—the earth and its inhabitants. According to Boyd's skewed understanding of Scripture, Jesus never treated disease and demonization as serving a divine purpose, but only as the work of the enemy, with the victims viewed as casualties of war—all outside of God's so-called "sovereign plan."[32] Boyd erroneously contends that all disease was viewed by Jesus as satanically generated. While correctly observing that the bringing in of God's kingdom involved overthrowing Satan's kingdom, he makes the cardinal error of so

---

and Isaiah 30:7. In Ezekiel 29:3 Pharaoh is addressed as "the great monster" of the Nile (cf. 32:2). This imagery all goes back to the Exodus 15 where Yahweh as "the warrior" (v.3) conquers the chaos waters, and vanquishes Egypt.

30. Boyd, *Satan*, 35.
31. 2 Corinthians 4:4.
32. Boyd, *Satan*, 36.

exaggerating Satan's power as to marginalize the ways in which God's rule is also at loggerheads with human evil in its own right. This leads him to construe Jesus's healing miracles, exorcisms, along with his miracles over nature, in an unbalanced one-dimensional way. He sees them as primarily eschatological acts of war "that accomplished and demonstrated his victory over Satan."[33] In Boyd's wonky reading of Scripture, Jesus and his disciples viewed all evil in the world as ultimately caused (and sometimes directly) by the Satanic kingdom, whether barren trees, threatening storms, or diseases.[34] As Ferdinando observes, Boyd's "ground-level deliverance model" of spiritual warfare "fails to recognize . . . the centrality of human sin as the enemy that Jesus came to battle." And, for all Boyd's attempt to treat the cross as central to his theology, it is ironic that he "accords little place to [Jesus's] death which atones for sin and, in consequence, also brings about Satan's defeat."[35]

Compare the visions of Christ's glory in Revelation 1 and Revelation 19. The former vision speaks of a double-edged sword proceeding from Christ's mouth, while the latter repeats this imagery, but even more explicitly casts Jesus as the ultimate divine warrior:

> I saw heaven standing open and there before me was a white horse, whose rider is called Faithful and True. With justice he judges and wages war. His eyes are like blazing fire, and on his head are many crowns. He has a name written on him that no one knows but he himself. He is dressed in a robe dipped in blood, and his name is the Word of God. The armies of heaven were following him, riding on white horses and dressed in fine linen, white and clean. Coming out of his mouth is a sharp sword with which to strike down the nations. "He will rule them with an iron sceptre." He treads the winepress of the fury of the wrath of God Almighty. On his robe and on his thigh he has this name written: KING OF KINGS AND LORD OF LORDS." Revelation 19:11–16.

Such is the imagery associated with the return of our Lord in judgment. It is the day of God's fury. But it is a day that must eventually come as an expression of divine faithfulness and in the interests of truth. Those familiar with the Old Testament will observe how John's vision brings together language drawn from a number of sources. The Messiah, the

---

33. Boyd, *God at War*, 213.
34. Boyd, *God at War*, 235.
35. Ferdinando, *Message of Spiritual Warfare*, 5.

promised Davidic Messianic king, is depicted in Psalm 2 as one who will rule the nations with an iron sceptre. Similarly, there are images drawn from Isaiah, Ezekiel, and Zechariah. The splicing together of these sources serves to underscore the fact that when Jesus returns it will be to destroy as in war all who rebel against and reject his rule.

Indeed, there is a grisly end for all who fight against King Jesus:

> And I saw an angel standing in the sun, who cried in a loud voice to all the birds flying in midair, "Come, gather together for the great supper of God, so that you may eat the flesh of kings, generals, and the mighty, of horses and their riders, and the flesh of all people, free and slave, great and small." Then I saw the beast, and the kings of the earth and their armies gathered together to wage war against the rider on the horse and his army. But the beast was captured, and with it the false prophet who had performed the signs on its behalf. With these signs he had deluded those who had received the mark of the beast and worshiped its image. The two of them were thrown alive into the fiery lake of burning sulphur. The rest were killed with the sword coming out of the mouth of the rider on the horse, and all the birds gorged themselves on their flesh (Revelation 19:17–21).

Here we have an image of vultures and carrion-eating birds feasting on the flesh of the slaughtered rebellious foes of King Jesus. Not merely the leaders of such rebellion but all rebels regardless of their station in life, whether free or slave. These are all described as those who have been marked as belonging to the beast, as those who worship its image.

John's one beast from the sea corresponds to the four beasts from the sea of Daniel 7. One of those four beasts was like a lion, one like a bear, one resembled a leopard, and the fourth was simply "terrifying and frightening and very powerful." In Daniel these four beasts represent blasphemous, anti-God rule and so too does John's composite beast, which significantly bears the features of a leopard, bear, and lion. In the first instance, John would have been thinking of the Roman empire, with the seven heads of the beast representing its emperors ("seven" being symbolic of all such emperors). Using the opening language of Psalm 2, John envisages a scene where the Roman empire along with all other kings of the earth conspire against God and his Messiah.

As in Daniel, whatever immediate historical reference may have been in mind, John's beast does not merely represent the blasphemous, anti-God human rule and authority of the Roman empire and its emperors.

We are told this beast "was given power to make war against the saints and to conquer them." Certainly, Roman emperors like Nero, Caligula, and Domitian provided immediate historical illustrations of this, given their terrible persecution of Christians. But, as Revelation 19 makes clear, this beast is still alive and active when Christ, the divine warrior, returns to destroy it. So, the beast represents all blasphemous, anti-God human rule that persecutes and seeks to destroy the church wherever and however it finds expression.

Jesus the Messiah's conquest is not merely over the beast but also over "the false prophet." Revelation 13 describes this figure as a second beast who comes out of the earth. We are told: "It exercised all the authority of the first beast on its behalf, and made the earth and its inhabitants worship the first beast, whose fatal wound had been healed" (Revelation 13:12).

Evidently, the false prophet represents the ideology and the ideologues that compel people to submit themselves and align their lives with what is required of them by blasphemous, anti-God human authorities. In the first instance, John was presumably thinking of the priests who served the emperor worship cult of his day, no doubt along with all State officials who used their power and influence to promote this. But again, when Jesus returns to execute final judgment this beast too is still very much alive and active. So, just as with the beast from the sea, this beast too represents all ideologies and all influential promoters of such ideologies which justify the anti-God, blasphemous stance of human authorities and encourage their persecution of God's people.

Christ's conquest over all the anti-God blasphemous human authorities which persecute God's people and all the ideologies which justify this will be consummated when he returns in glory. The vision of these two beasts being cast into the lake of fire, with all other rebels against the Messiah also being slain, is a vision of all threats to Jesus's glorious rule being removed forevermore. The outcome of this spiritual war is certain. There can only be one winner.

THE CORNERED RAT

We are warned to beware of the cornered rat. Satan is already a defeated foe, but until he is destroyed he will continue to cause havoc. Satan is a loser, but he is the poorest loser the universe has ever seen.

"MORE THAN CONQUERORS"

War is a major motif in the book of Revelation and at its most profound level this war is between heavenly and demonic forces. Revelation 12 is the chapter in which the battle lines are first most clearly drawn. It begins with an image of the church, represented by a pregnant woman crying in pain as she is about to give birth. This is followed by the depiction of a terrifying and vastly powerful dragon, Satan. Alluding to Herod's attempt to kill the infant Jesus, John describes this dragon as standing in front of the woman so that he might eat and destroy the baby to whom she would give birth. John's continuing descriptions of the woman make it plain that he is indeed seeing her as representing the entirety of God's people and not merely identifying her with Mary.

Now we come to the heart of the war motif. For John states that "there was war in heaven."[36] With Daniel 10 in mind John speaks of Michael and his angels fighting against the dragon, with the dragon and his angels fighting back. As terrible and powerful as the dragon is, we are not describing a dualistic universe here. We are not to think that Satan's power is almost as great as God's own power. God is totally sovereign and in his sovereign wisdom uses the evil of Satan and his demonic angels to achieve his great and good purposes, even though this involves immense suffering, especially for God's own dearly loved people.

Anyway, we are told that Satan loses his heavenly battle and his place in heaven. He is hurled to the earth. That is, Satan's sole focus becomes that of inflicting as much damage as he can on God's people, seeking to destroy them. We are told, "He is filled with fury, because he knows that his time is short."

Indeed, the New Testament has significant things to say about the way in which the death of Christ ironically deals the death blow to Satan.

The death of Christ brings forgiveness and the effect of this is to disarm Satan's powers, called "the powers and authorities" by Paul. Satan succeeds in bringing about the destruction of people if he keeps them in an unforgiven state. Apart from such forgiveness everybody is condemned by the law and what it requires of us in order to attain the level of moral perfection that alone can satisfy an uncompromisingly holy God. In short, everybody is "a child of wrath," headed for eternal destruction, because nobody can meet the law's demands. But this law, with its demands, has been canceled by God. Using a powerful image, Paul

---

36. Revelation 12:7

describes the law as nailed to the cross.[37] It "dies" with Christ. That is, God's acceptance of people is no longer dependent on the extent to which they are able to do what the law requires, but on what Christ has achieved for them, as their substitute.

The death of Christ delivers such a shattering blow to Satan and his demonic forces that Paul not only speaks of them as being disarmed but also contends that God has "made a public spectacle of them, triumphing over them by the cross." In short, the humiliating death of Christ has humiliated Satan. What Satan thought was his victory over Christ has turned out to be Christ's triumph over him.[38]

Further, precisely because of what Jesus accomplished on the cross, Paul can give thanks to God as the one "who always leads us as captives in Christ's triumphal procession and uses us to spread the aroma of the knowledge of him everywhere" (2 Corinthians 2:14). Satan then is a defeated foe. However, this does not mean that Christians can be blasé. Satan is still extremely powerful and very dangerous. To reiterate: "He is filled with fury, because he knows that his time is short."

The Bible links Satan with the following activities: lies, deception, false teaching, temptation, persecution, and murder. It is Satan who leads the whole world astray. All people outside Christ follow Satan, though, of course, the vast majority are entirely unaware of the extent to which their lives are controlled by this thoroughly evil external agent. Satan is not a micro-manager. Satan is only interested in that level of control and management of people that will secure their destruction. In the case of most people this is low maintenance. People are born with a disposition that is biased against God. People want to be free to live their lives as they choose without divine interference. That is the default state of the human heart. So, Satan is working with very cooperative and pliable material. All he has to do is to encourage people to follow the natural inclination of their wicked hearts.

Peter warns that Satan is a roaring lion who prowls about seeking a prey to devour. In context, Peter has in mind the sufferings experienced by Christians at the hands of persecutors. Persecution of Christians is demonic, though, of course, persecutors are seldom aware that they are being used as the tools of Satan. Amid the danger of experiencing

---

37. Colossians 2:14.

38. Boyd's unbalanced theology subordinates all evil to Satan and therefore it is hardly surprising that he cannot agree with classical theology that treats atonement for sin as primary and the defeat of Satan as secondary. See Boyd, *God at War*, 238–68.

persecution with its associated suffering, Peter exhorts Christians to resist the devil by standing firm in their faith.[39] James says, "Resist the devil and he will flee from you."[40]

Both Peter and James urge Christians to resist the devil. They have different scenarios in mind. While Peter is thinking particularly of how persecution may cause Christians to desert their faith, James is concerned with relational purity. In both cases it remains true that Christians have the upper hand and, ironically, are operating from a position of strength rather than weakness. Of course, in the former case persecution may indeed result in Christians suffering great injustice, physical harm, the anguish of seeing loved ones hurt, and even death. But believers' resistance is successful if, despite whatever befalls, they stand firm in their faith.

Reflecting on the many millions of Christians who have been slaughtered in the twentieth century, John Battle aptly observes, "Compared to this grand, epic struggle, the proud little pronouncements of self-appointed fighters of Satan appear puny and ridiculous. We best fight Satan, not by pronouncing exorcisms or claiming special powers today, but by being loyal to our God. Living a life of simple Christian obedience, witnessing for Christ to those we see day by day, and praying for strength and spiritual growth, are the paths to spiritual victory in our warfare against Satan."[41]

MISSION DEBRIEF

- **No Dualism.** The universe is not subject to the interplay of dualistic forces of cosmic order and chaos that are commensurate in power.
- **God Controls All Chaotic Forces.** Creation reveals God as the ultimate conqueror, revealing his absolute mastery over all chaotic forces.
- **Image of God and Control of Chaos.** Intrinsic to being made in the image of God is that humans were created to exercise Godlike conquest over chaotic forces.
- **The Cause of Chaos in Our World.** The Fall involves human inability to discriminate between good and evil and such sin unleashes forces of chaos at work within the created order.

---

39. 1 Peter 5:9.
40. James 4:7.
41. Battle, "Spiritual Warfare," 17–18.

- **Chaos and Enmity.** Chaotic forces include enemies that pitch themselves against God's people.
- **The Ultimate Removal of Chaos.** Chaos will be eliminated once and for all and will be totally absent from the new heavens and the new earth.
- **Creation Purposes are Certain of Fulfillment.** The consummation of God's creation purposes will occur with the return of the ultimate conquering warrior, the Lord Jesus Christ.
- **Ultimate Destruction of All Enmity.** All of Jesus's enemies, including all expressions of blasphemous, anti-God rule and supportive ideologies will be totally destroyed at this time of final reckoning.
- **Satan's Malice.** While Satan is doomed he is intent, while he can, on wreaking as much damage as he can, with his target-sights locked on God's people.
- **The Doom of the Unforgiven.** Satan is only able to bring about the eternal destruction of people if he keeps them in an unforgiven state.
- **Assurance of Salvation.** Christians are eternally secure as those enjoying the fruits of Christ's conquest over Satan. It is the death of Christ which has disarmed Satan and his forces by bringing about complete forgiveness for believers.
- **Satan's Use of Persecution.** Satan is still extremely powerful and dangerous and will continue to use persecution with its associated suffering in his attempt to force Christians to commit apostasy.

GATHERING INTELLIGENCE

Read Revelation 2:1—3:22 with special attention to the phrase "Him / He who overcomes" (2:7, 11, 17, 26; 3:5, 12, 21).

1. What are the various threats that Christians are encouraged to conquer?
2. What evidence is there of Christians withstanding such threats?
3. What evidence is there of Christians faltering in the face of such threats?
4. What has led to such lamentable failures?

5. What must Christians do if they are to address past failures?
6. What rewards or inducements motivate Christians to conquer such threats?

Chapter Ten

When War is No More

"Peace means the defeat of evil. Peace means breaking down the barrier between man and God. Peace means the presence of God's rich and abundant blessing... Peace is presence, the presence of God. Christ 'is our peace.'"
Leon Morris, *The Atonement: Its Meaning and Significance*.

SPIRITUAL WARFARE HAS BEEN waged for many thousands of years. But the end is in sight. God has not conclusively intervened to put an end to all evil because he is giving people opportunity to repent, to get their lives right with him. But this situation will not last indefinitely. The time will come when God says in effect, "Enough is enough." Then our Lord will return in great glory to judge the world with justice. A new heaven and a new earth will be brought into being in which evil has not a millimetre of room to move in.

A NEW HEAVEN AND A NEW EARTH

Christians laugh at any suggestion that the afterlife involves playing harps while floating on fluffy clouds. Yet there is a prevalent misconception among even many Bible-believing Christians that believers will spend eternity in an otherworldly place they call "heaven."

Go back to the beginning. God created the heavens and the earth. This is all one integrated reality experienced by our first parents when they were created. But then sin entered the world. The man and the woman were cast out of paradise, the Garden of Eden, the place where God walked with them. The attempt to identify a place on the globe where the Garden of Eden was located is misguided. Think about the Great Flood of Noah's time. Are we supposed to believe that the Garden was washed away and the tree of life destroyed? Yes, the early chapters of Genesis do describe what really happened, but they do so in highly symbolic terms. The essential point is that sin separates not only people from God but also creates a gulf between heaven and earth. The creation of the new heavens and earth involves the removal of that chasm.

THE NEW GARDEN OF EDEN AND THE NEW JERUSALEM

Think now of how John envisages this new reality: "Then I saw a new heaven and a new earth, for the first heaven and the first earth had passed away, and there was no longer any sea. I saw the Holy City, the new Jerusalem, coming down out of heaven from God, prepared as a bride beautifully dressed for her husband" (Revelation 21:1–2).

What we have here is the re-integration of heaven and earth. Originally, the Garden of Eden was the place from which God's rule over the world was exercised through his human agents. As history developed, Jerusalem became that center of divine rule exercised through Davidic kingship. John now thinks of life in the new heavens and the new earth as life in a new Jerusalem.

But now see how John goes on to describe what life looks like in this new glorious reality:

> Then the angel showed me the river of the water of life, as clear as crystal, flowing from the throne of God and of the Lamb, down the middle of the great street of the city. On each side of the river stood the tree of life, bearing twelve crops of fruit, yielding its fruit every month. And the leaves of the tree are for the healing of the nations. No longer will there be any curse. The throne of God and of the Lamb will be in the city, and his servants will serve him. They will see his face, and his name will

be on their foreheads. There will be no more night. They will not need the light of a lamp or the light of the sun, for the Lord God will give them light. And they will reign for ever and ever (Revelation 22:1–5).

Jerusalem was the place where the temple was built and the Old Testament speaks of a river of life-giving water flowing out from the presence of God in the Jerusalem temple.[1] This was not an actual river, but pure symbolism which is drawn from the image of rivers of blessing and life flowing out from the Garden of Eden to water the four corners of the earth: that is, symbolically the whole world. The expression "There will be no more night" parallels "and there was no longer any sea." That is, there is no chaos in the new heavens and the new earth, no "darkness upon the face of the deep." The curse of Genesis 3 has now also been removed. The imagery of the tree of life and fruit-bearing trees and leaves that bring healing all confirm that this new Jerusalem is to be identified with the Garden of Eden, with paradise. There will be no temple in this new Jerusalem, however, for God will now rule through his new humanity.

THE NEW TEMPLE

I said there will no temple in the new Jerusalem. John says this explicitly, "I did not see a temple in the city, because the Lord God Almighty and the Lamb [Jesus] are its temple" (Revelation 21:22). This brings to mind what Jesus said about himself when challenged about his authority after driving out traders and moneychangers from the temple: "Destroy this temple, and I will raise it again in three days."[2] As John explains, "But the temple he had spoken of was his body. After he was raised from the dead, his disciples recalled what he had said" (John 2:21–22).

The tabernacle was constructed according to a blueprint revealed by God as a place in which he would dwell among his people.[3] The mobile tabernacle, suitable for a nomadic people, later became a permanent structure, a temple, built for a settled population. We need to use those words "permanent" and "settled" with some sense of pathos. For, though God chose to use the tabernacle and temple as his dwelling place among his people, there was no essential link between these structures and God.

---

1. For example, Psalm 46:4; Ezekiel 47:1–12.
2. John 2:19.
3. Exodus 25:8–9.

Before his martyrdom, Stephen made this very point to his hostile listeners, stating that "the Most High does not live in houses made by men."[4] He then cited from the book where God says, "Heaven is my throne, and the earth is my footstool. Where is the house you will build for me? Where will my resting place be?" (Isaiah 66:1).

God's provisional use of these structures is very much tied to the state of the covenant relationship between God and his people which prophets often likened to a marriage relationship. So in Ezekiel we get to a point where the relationship between God and his "wife," his people, has broken down to such an extent that God's glory actually departs from the temple,[5] as the precursor to the destruction of the temple and the city of Jerusalem at the hands of Nebuchadnezzar's Babylonians.

THE NEW TEMPLE AND ULTIMATE PEACE

Before we continue, we should note that "temple" is just another word for "palace." It's actually the same word in the Hebrew Bible. God's temple is God's palace. Kings don't spend enormous wealth on building an extravagantly glorious palace if they know there is a very real prospect that their land will be overrun by hostile enemies and their palace looted and possibly even destroyed. This is equivalent to building a house on shifting sand. In the same way, the building of a glorious palace for God presupposes solid foundations of peace and security.

David was commended for wanting to build a temple for God. But he was refused because he was associated with war, whereas Solomon, at the time he built the temple, was associated with peace and political stability. This is what Solomon told Hiram, king of Tyre, about his own plans to build a palace for God: "You know that because of the wars waged against my father David from all sides, he could not build a temple for the Name of the LORD his God until the LORD put his enemies under his feet. But now the LORD has given me rest on every side, and there is no adversary or disaster. I intend, therefore, to build a temple for the Name of the LORD my God . . ." (1 Kings 5:3–5a).

The association of God's palace with rest is of crucial importance. When Solomon had completed construction of the temple he prayed publicly and concluded with this prayer: "Now arise, O LORD God, and

---

4. Acts 7:49.
5. Ezekiel 10.

come to your resting place, you and the ark of your might."⁶ This same prayer is incorporated into Psalm 132.⁷ In this psalm we also read: "For the LORD has chosen Zion, he has desired it for his dwelling. 'This is my resting place for ever and ever; here I will sit enthroned, for I have desired it'" (Psalm 132:13–14).

As Solomon made plain, the state of rest prerequisite for temple construction involves the absence of all threats, all wars, and disasters. Indeed, in the ancient world and in various Scriptures we see a familiar sequence of conflict; victory; and the construction of a temple (and perhaps too the celebration of a feast) as symbolic of conquest.⁸ So it is, with enemies under control, that God appropriates the temple as his resting place.

God resting? What does this recall? Think back to the creation account with which the Bible opens.

ULTIMATE SABBATH REST

When ancient people read Genesis 1 they would have readily perceived something which modern readers are likely to miss completely. They would have read this as an account describing God's construction of a cosmic temple, that is, of his resting place. For, let's be frank, the creation of human beings is not the climax of the creation account. We may think of human beings as the most important of all creatures made by God, but

---

6. 2 Chronicles 6:41.

7. See verse 8.

8. See Jung, "Divine Warrior." Chapter 1, "The Divine Warfare Pattern," 11–22 e.g. *Enuma Elish*: Ea defeats Apsu and builds a temple over his corpse; Marduk kills Tiamat and constructs the temple Esharra). Jung applies this motif to John's Gospel: see the temple at John 1:14 and 2:19 as concordant with this. Exodus 15, Isaiah 24–27 and Psalm 24 illustrate this motif. Gombis's analysis reveals the following patterns: (1) *Enuma Elish*: threat, conflict, victory, kingship, house-building (temple), celebration (13); (2) Exodus 15: conflict, theophany, victory, kingship, house-building (18); (3) Psalm 29: conflict–victory, victory shout, kingship, house-building, celebration, blessing (21); (4) Psalm 68:12–14: conflict–victory, kingship, procession, house-building, celebration (25); (5) Psalm 110: kingship, house-building, conflict–victory, celebration (28); (6) Revelation 6:9—7:17: threat, theophany, conflict–victory, victory shout, kingship, resumption of rule on throne (house-building), celebration, blessing (31); (7) Revelation 12:1–12: threat, salvation, conflict, victory, victory shout, kingship, house-building, celebration (32); (8) Revelation 16:12–19: threat, victory shout, theophany, conflict–victory, kingship, house-building (34); (9) The Frieze of the Great Altar of Pergamon: threat, conflict, victory, kingship, house-building, celebration (35). Gombis, "Triumph of God in Christ."

the entire account peaks with God taking rest: "By the seventh day God had finished the work he had been doing; so on the seventh day he rested from all his work" (Genesis 2:2).

God never tires and never sleeps, so he doesn't need to rest in order to recover depleted energy.[9] That's not the picture being painted here. This is temple-rest that is being referred to. The building work has been finished and now the stage is set for God to rule through those created in his image for this very purpose. The rest of God is the center of ultimate peace and security. The writer to the Hebrews teaches us, "There remains . . . a Sabbath-rest for the people of God." He adds, "For anyone who enters God's rest also rests from his own work, just as God did from his. Let us, therefore, make every effort to enter that rest" (Hebrews 4:9–11a). The writer to the Hebrews is referring to the ultimate rest that followers of Christ will enjoy in the new heavens and the new earth.

But Jesus makes it clear that there is an experience of Sabbath-rest we can enjoy in the here and now: "Come to me, all you who are weary and burdened, and I will give you rest. Take my yoke upon you and learn from me, for I am gentle and humble in heart, and you will find rest for your souls. For my yoke is easy and my burden is light" (Matthew 11:28–30).

Matthew has positioned these words from Jesus right before he recounts a particular incident concerning Sabbath observance. We are told Jesus's disciples, being hungry, were picking some heads of grain and eating them while walking through grainfields. Jesus was then criticized by the Pharisees for allowing his disciples to do this. Jesus tells them that "one greater than the temple is here," namely himself. And he also tells them that as the Son of Man he is also "Lord of the Sabbath." Significantly, right before he says this he comments, "if you had known what these words mean, 'I desire mercy, not sacrifice,' you would not have condemned the innocent." Indeed, straight after this we see Jesus extending mercy to a man with a shrivelled hand on the Sabbath, declaring, "it is lawful to do good on the Sabbath."[10]

God instituted the Sabbath as a merciful provision for his people Israel. Each Saturday they were reminded that they had worked as exploited and oppressed slaves in Egypt but had been delivered from this by God's grace.[11] They were now, as God's redeemed people, a new humanity,

---

9. Psalm 121:4.
10. Matthew 12:12.
11. Deuteronomy 5:15.

to "enter God's rest," the very rest God enjoyed following his work of building the cosmic temple.[12] God intended that the land of Canaan, the land promised to Abraham, should be the place where his people would enter his rest. But an entire generation of Israelites perished in the wilderness and did not enter God's rest, the land of Canaan, because of their hard-heartedness.

Indeed, none of the places of rest given to Israel stood the test of time. The Israelites were removed from the land because of their idolatry and rejection of the prophets God sent to them. Both Solomon's temple and the one built by Herod were destroyed.

It is highly significant that the description of the church at Ephesus as "a holy temple in the Lord" presupposes the realization of peace between former "enemies," following Christ's victorious overcoming of the hostility between Jew and Gentile.[13] Which brings us back to the future. In the new heavens and the new earth, we remind ourselves, God and the Lamb are the temple. Here then is ultimate rest and security to be found, for here is a temple that will never be destroyed or even vaguely threatened.

Such complete and total peace is graphically envisaged by Isaiah:

> The wolf will live with the lamb, the leopard will lie down with the goat, the calf and the lion and the yearling together; and a little child will lead them. The cow will feed with the bear, their young will lie down together, and the lion will eat straw like the ox. The infant will play near the hole of the cobra, and the young child will put his hand into the viper's nest. They will neither harm nor destroy on all my holy mountain, for the earth will be full of the knowledge of the LORD as the waters cover the sea" (Isaiah 11:6–9).

Though God dwelt among his people in the tabernacle and temples of old, these structures also served to veil God's glory and create a measure of distance and reserve between God and his people. But the glory of God fills the new Jerusalem with light and all of those whose citizenship is in heaven will see his face. Gone are the curtains and veils. Now all is immediacy,

---

12. Exodus 20:11.

13. Ephesians 2:11–22. See Gombis, "Triumph of God in Christ," 5, 74–85. "Just as triumphant deities in the ANE had temples built in their honor, so here in Ephesians 2, the triumphs of the exalted cosmic Lord Christ are memorialized with the building of his temple, the people of God made up of both Jewish and Gentile believers." Gombis, "Triumph of God in Christ," 84).

direct experience of the living God who "will wipe away every tear from their eyes. There will be no more death or mourning or crying or pain, for the old order of things has passed away" (Revelation 21:4).

And so we cry, "Come, Lord Jesus."[14]

MISSION DEBRIEF

- **The Ultimate Home.** Christians' eternal home is located not in an otherworldly place but in a wonderfully renewed universe devoid of chaos.
- **A New Humanity in a New Universe.** In the new cosmos God's rule will be exercised through the new humanity.
- **God's Palace.** In the Old Testament the tabernacle and temple served as God's palace, the locus of his rule and resting place.
- **God's Rest.** God's temple-rest, the climax of creation, presupposes the conquest of enemies and the security of God's people.
- **The Lord Our Sufficiency.** In the new heavens and earth the unchallenged exercise of God's rule and the perfect enjoyment of rest in God's presence obviates any need for a tabernacle or temple. The Lord himself will be all that his people need.
- **Come to Jesus.** People are invited to come to Jesus to experience this Sabbath-rest in the here and now.
- **Direct Knowledge of God.** The tabernacle and temple veiled God's glory and created distance between God and his people. In the new heavens and earth Christians will know God directly in an unmediated manner.

GATHERING INTELLIGENCE

Read Revelation 21:1—22:6

1. What symbols are used to describe the reality that will be enjoyed in the new heavens and the new earth? What do these various symbols mean? (e.g. "there was no longer any sea," 21:1).

---

14. Revelation 22:20.

2. What is the significance of "the new heavens and the new earth" being described as "the Holy City, the new Jerusalem"?

3. What is the nature of the relationship between God and his people in the new heavens and the new earth?

4. In what different ways does the reality to be experienced in the new heavens and the new earth involve the fulfillment of Old Testament promise and expectation?

Questions and Answers

WHAT IS THE RELATIONSHIP BETWEEN INTERPERSONAL CONFLICT AND SPIRITUAL WARFARE?

(In dealing with interpersonal conflict I recommend the book *The Peacemaker* by Ken Sande)

PAUL EXHORTS, "IF IT is possible, as far as it depends on you, live at peace with everyone."[1] This is helpful. It is not always possible to live at peace with others. It does not always depend on us, since we cannot usually control the way others think and behave.

To the extent that conflict involves sinful attitudes and desires then some degree of spiritual warfare—contending with the world, the flesh, and the devil—is necessarily involved. Take the conflict that occurs between parents and toddlers. All children enter the world not with blank slates, but with sinful orientations. Godly parents are engaged in spiritual warfare as they seek to appropriately discipline their children and help them to place their faith in the Lord. But the demands of child-rearing upon parents also tend to bring out their own sinfulness, uncontrolled outbursts of anger being merely one example of this.

Of course, there is no doubting the reality of spiritual warfare when Christians are treated with hostility for being Christians. This is action on the front line.

---

1. Romans 12:18.

It is not always possible to avoid conflict and sometimes it is even right for us to initiate it. At one point Jesus confronted Peter saying, "Get behind me, Satan!" Nathan was sent by God to courageously confront David following David's sins of adultery and murder. Paul publicly confronted Peter when he compromised the gospel by withdrawing from fellowship with Gentile Christians. The reality of spiritual warfare is palpable in all these instances.

Conflict between Christians is destructive and potentially divisive when it is due to self-seeking motivation. But there are times when Christians simply disagree on how to act as Christians. Paul and Barnabas sharply disagreed with each other over whether to let Mark accompany them or not and ended up going separate ways. But there is no suggestion that their disagreement was sinful.

In short, conflict as such is not necessarily an expression of spiritual warfare. But it will usually accentuate the ongoing spiritual warfare in which we are engaged, as it tests the godliness of our attitudes and our commitment to loving people and seeking to live in harmony with them.

Christians face the same enemies no matter where they are. However, the evils Christians confront do assume different guises. For many centuries in India it was traditional for widows to be burnt on the funeral pyre with their deceased husbands. William Carey did much to see that this practice of *sati* was outlawed. Paedophilia is more openly countenanced in some societies than in others. Honor killings are more characteristic of some cultures than others. There are corrupt police, judges, and politicians in most societies, but in some this problem is extremely pervasive.

Sin is sin but popular perceptions of what constitutes "sin" or "evil" vary from culture to culture and so do people's beliefs as to what are the worst sins. Some cultures regard it as healthy for married couples to vent their anger. Or if anger is viewed as a wrong response it is not considered particularly bad, unless it is the kind of uncontrolled rage that involves violence. But in some cultures almost any expression of anger ranks right up there as one of the most reprehensible modes of behavior. A missionary who loses his temper in his home culture and then seeks forgiveness may feel little enduring damage has been done to relationships. But in many cultures if he loses his temper he may need to consider packing his bags and heading home, such is the permanent damage that can be caused.

In the ancient world the form of idolatry varied from society to society, as God's people well knew. If there is one thing the Old Testament has to teach us it is that the hearts of God's people, and, therefore, of all people, are incorrigibly idolatrous. In the Bible the presence of demons is especially indicative of idolatrous behavior. It is a telling thing that when Jesus lived and ministered in Palestine demons were very active, a sure sign that God's people had allowed demons entrance into their society and into their lives by engaging in idolatry. But how could this be given that since returning from exile in Babylon the Israelites had for centuries refrained from bowing down before idols? Did this not mean that idolatry was a thing of the past for God's people? Not according to Jesus who denounced his generation as being not only "wicked" but also "adulterous," classic Old Testament language for idolatry. In one passage Jesus attacks the Pharisees and teachers of the law for their legalistic views on cleanness and uncleanness. He quotes a passage from Isaiah, castigating them as people whose hearts are far from God and clearly insinuating that right worship of God has been replaced by a worshiping of tradition.

Idolatrous hearts lead inevitably to idolatrous practice in all its diverse manifestations. Demonic activity is as present in Western society as anywhere else, aiming to prevent true knowledge of God, though strategies differ by culture. In some societies, demon possession and black magic are more common, unlike in the West where supernatural events are often downplayed. Missionaries often encounter these overt displays of demonic power in third-world cultures.

IS EVERYTHING THAT GOES WRONG IN OUR LIVES ATTRIBUTABLE TO THE DEVIL?

The Bible has little to say about the operation of Satan in the lives of unbelievers. We know that he blinds their minds and prevents them from having a true knowledge of God. But Satan's works of temptation and seduction through false teaching are particularly directed at God's people. In the same vein, Satan is seen as behind the persecution of God's people.

With respect to unbelievers the Bible indicates that essentially people are left to their own devices. It is not Satan who creates evil desires within people. People naturally do what they think is best and this involves following their own desires. The resultant behavior may actually seem quite moral and decent. What makes such desires and conduct evil is the fact that they confirm a lifestyle of shutting out or marginalizing the true knowledge of God. When people follow their hearts' desires they are therefore doing exactly what Satan wants and so for Satan most people are low maintenance.

Christians are a different story. We are very much in Satan's target-sights. But when we are wearing gospel armor he is unable to match us strength for strength. He is forced to resort to ruses and other ploys in his attempts to undo us. Yet when we fall into sin, we are not thinking straight if we blame Satan for this. As James reminds us, "each one is tempted when, by his own evil desire, he is dragged away and enticed. Then after desire has conceived, it gives birth to sin and sin, when it is full-grown, gives birth to death" (James 1:14–15).

We recognize too that we live in a fallen world. In the original creation, control over forces of chaos was assured because as people ruled over creation it was God's own sovereign rule being worked out through them. But the entrance of sin into the world means that people, being separated from God, are not able to have the degree of control that is an outworking of God's own perfect control. Consequently, tsunamis, floods, tornados, bush fires, volcanic eruptions, Ebola, cancer, and many other plagues and disasters and accidents claim many lives, both non-Christian and Christian.

I recall one Christian family who saw their daughter's learning difficulties as due to Satan's activity, and indeed they viewed much else that went "wrong" in their lives in similar manner. This is most unhealthy and an unhelpful attitude. Further, it does not do justice to the way in which hardship, set-backs, and weaknesses form part of God's great plan for shaping our characters into the likeness of Christ.

WHAT ARE THE PRACTICAL IMPLICATIONS OF SPIRITUAL WARFARE?

Christians are well-equipped to engage in spiritual warfare when they are wearing the armor of God and fighting together, shoulder-to-shoulder. This armor is the gospel in all its dimensions of truth, peace, righteousness, and so on. And the war is one we wage as a company, a regiment which faces an enemy who is not able to match us in strength.

The practical implications of this are as follows:

- We nourish and strengthen ourselves with God's Word, the gospel. Understand here that for Christians the gospel is the whole Bible understood with reference to Jesus and his work. We need to be receiving good Bible teaching and be disciplined in reading and studying God's Word. Many have found it a great help to memorize

God's Word, something no longer strongly encouraged in Western societies that tend to over-react to educational approaches based on rote-learning.

- We must stick close with God's people and be in church communities in which we encourage and build up each other.

Glossary of Names

Who's Who

Althaus, Paul. 1888–1966. German Lutheran theologian who welcomed the rise to power of Adolf Hitler.

Anderson, Neil T. Born 1942. Founder of Freedom in Christ Ministries and formerly chairman of the Practical Theology Department at the Talbot School of Theology.

Antiochus IV Epiphanes. c. 215–164 BC. Ruler of the Seleucid Empire who committed immense atrocities against the Jews.

Arnold, Clinton. Born 1958. New Testament scholar who has served as dean of the Talbot School of Theology and the president of the Evangelical Theological Society.

Athas, George. Director of Research: Old Testament and Hebrew, Moore Theological College.

Augustine of Hippo. AD 354–430. One of Christianity's greatest ever theologians and philosophers who had a massive impact on Western Christian thought.

Barr, James. 1924–2006. Scottish Old Testament scholar who held professorships in biblical interpretation and Hebrew at Oxford University.

Battle, John. Professor of New Testament and Theology, Western Reformed Seminary.

Bauckham, Richard. Born 1946. Senior scholar at Ridley Hall, Cambridge who is making major contributions in the areas of theology, historical theology, and New Testament studies.

GLOSSARY OF NAMES

Blair, Tony. Born 1953. Served as UK Prime Minister from 1997 to 2007.

Boyd, Greg. Born 1957. A leading spokesman in the Neo-Anabaptism movement and a leading advocate of open theism (believing that God's knowledge of, and plans for, the future are conditional upon human actions).

Brown, Rebecca. 1948–2020. A medical doctor who left medicine to teach her views of spiritual warfare.

Calvin, John. 1509–1564. One of the greatest of Protestant theologians who also served as a pastor and reformer in Geneva. He remains one of the giants of Reformed Theology.

Carey, William. 1761–1834. Often called "the father of modern missions." Carey had an extraordinary missionary career in India, making enormous contributions to Bible translation, education, and social reform.

Chance, Linda. Based in Arizona, she is the co-founder of The Apostolic School of Ministry. With her husband Edward she heads up Divine Connection, what they call an apostolic network of churches.

Clark, Jonas. Founder of the Global Cause Network and the Apostolic Equipping Institute.

Collins, John J. Born 1946. Professor of Old Testament Criticism and Interpretation at Yale Divinity School.

Constantine the Great. c. AD 272–337. Roman emperor from 306–37. The first Roman emperor to convert to Christianity. He began the process which led to the Christianization of the Roman Empire.

Copan, Paul. Professor of Philosophy and Ethics, Palm Beach Atlantic University, Florida.

Cromwell, Oliver. 1599–1658. One of Britain's greatest historical figures. He ruled as Lord Protector of the Commonwealth of England, Scotland, and Ireland from 1653–1658.

Davis, Jefferson. 1808–1889. The first and only president of the Confederate States of America from 1861 to 1865.

DeWaay, Bob. American pastor and author.

Erasmus. 1466–1536. One of the most influential thinkers of the Renaissance.

Ferdinand, Franz. 1863–1914. His assassination in Sarajevo in 1914 was the most immediate cause of World War 1.

Ferdinando, Keith. Lecturer and principal at the Faculté de Théologie Evangélique au Rwanda, and theological education consultant with Africa Inland Mission International.

Foucault, Michel. 1926–1984. A major French philosopher very much associated with the rise of postmodernism.

Frame, John. Born 1939. Retired Christian philosopher and one of Reformed Protestantism's greatest contemporary theologians and thinkers.

Greenlee, David. PhD in Intercultural Studies and Director of International Ministry Services for OM.

Greer, Germaine. Born 1939 in Melbourne, Australia and one of the leading voices of so-called "second-wave feminism." She is especially famous for her book *The Female Eunuch*.

Gurnall, William. 1616–1679. Anglican clergyman famous for his three-volume work *The Christian in Complete Armour*.

Hammurabi. c. 1810–1750 BC. An Amorite king in the Old Babylonian Empire who ruled from c. 1792–1750 BC. He is especially famous for producing the Code of Hammurabi, an ancient law code.

Herbert, George. 1593–1633. A Church of England clergyman famous for his poetry.

Hiebert, Paul. 1932–2007. An outstanding missiological anthropologist whose career included serving as Professor of Mission and Anthropology at Trinity Evangelical Divinity School.

Hitchens, Christopher. 1949–2011. A prominent figure in the New Atheism movement, known as one of the "four horsemen," along with Richard Dawkins, Sam Harris, and Daniel Dennett. Also the brother of Peter.

Hitchens, Peter. Born 1951. British academic and journalist who, in contrast to his brother Christopher, moved from atheism to Christianity.

Hoskins, Richard Kelly. Born 1928. He wrote a book called *Vigilantes of Christendom*. It included opposition to interracial relationships, the mixing of races, and anti-Semitism, and inspired terrorist actions.

Howard, John. Born 1939. He served as Australian Prime Minister from 1996 to 2007.

Hunter, James Davison. Born 1955. A prominent American sociologist.

Ibbotson, Don. President of Above & Beyond Counseling Ministries with special stress on deliverance ministry.

Jones, Peter R. Director of truthXchange (www.truthxchange.com), a non-profit organization dedicated to helping Christians understand the rise of neo-pagan spirituality.

Kaufman, Karen. A freelance writer.

Knox, David Broughton. 1916–1994. Principal of Moore Theological College from 1959 to 1985. An outstanding and influential Reformed theologian.

Lactantius. c. AD 250–325. Early Christian author and advisor to Constantine the Great.

Leigh, Samuel. 1785–1852. A Wesleyan Methodist Church missionary who served in early colonial New South Wales and New Zealand.

Lewis, C. S. 1898–1963. An outstanding academic and close friend of J. R. R. Tolkien. He continues to have considerable influence through his justly acclaimed books.

Lowe, Chuck. He has served as English ministry and missions pastor of Chinese Bible Church, Greater Boston, and as a lecturer with OMF in Singapore.

Marcion. c. AD 85–160. Regarded as a heretic in mainstream Christianity. Famous for developing his own canon of sacred Scripture.

Marshall, Peter. 1902–1949. Served as Chaplain of the US Senate.

Mather, Cotton. 1663–1728. A Puritan clergyman who was also a major intellectual in colonial America.

Meyer, Joyce. Born 1943. A very influential American charismatic Christian leader and president of Joyce Meyer Ministries.

Midgley, Mary. 1919–2018. A prominent British humanist philosopher.

Moreau, Scott. Professor Emeritus of Intercultural Studies, Wheaton College, Illinois.

Niebuhr, H. Richard. 1894–1962. An outstanding academic who taught at Yale Divinity School. He is regarded as one of America's most important Christian ethicists.

Nunnally, Wave. Professor Emeritus of Early Judaism and Christian Origins, Evangel University, Springfield, Missouri.

Pawson, David. 1930–2020. Pawson developed an international reputation as a Bible teacher.

Peretti, Frank. Born 1951. He was a New York Times best-selling author of Christian fiction, with special focus on the supernatural and spiritual warfare.

Powlison, David. 1949–2019. He was a visiting professor at Westminster Theological Seminary and also served as executive director of the Christian Counseling & Education Foundation.

Prince, Derek. 1915–2003. He was a highly successful televangelist and his daily radio program, Derek Prince Legacy Radio, was broadcast around the world in various languages.

Rading, Biko Gerro. A multimedia journalist in Kenya.

Rudd, Kevin. Born 1957. He served as Australia's Prime Minister from 2007 to 2010.

Sailhamer, John. 1946–2017. He was professor of Old Testament at Golden Gate Baptist Theological Seminary, California, and also served as president of the Evangelical Theological Society.

Sande, Ken. The founder of Peacemaker Ministries and president of Relational Wisdom 360.

Schleiermacher, Friedrich. 1768–1834. A German theologian and philosopher who is sometimes called the "Father of Modern Liberal Theology."

Shedler, Jonathan. A prominent American psychologist based in San Francisco, California.

Stark, Rodney. 1934–2022. A notable American sociologist of religion who was Distinguished Professor of the Social Sciences at Baylor University, Texas.

Stevens, David E. A pastor, theologian, and missionary.

Strauss, David. 1808–1874. A German liberal theologian.

GLOSSARY OF NAMES

Theodosius I. AD 347–95. Roman emperor from 379–95.

Wagner, Peter. 1930–2016. A key leader of the Church Growth movement and the founder of several independent charismatic Christian organizations.

Walker, William. 1799–1855. At one time the Governor of New South Wales, Thomas Brisbane, declared him "the best educated man in the colony."

Watkin, Christopher. An outstanding academic who lectures at Monash University, Melbourne, Australia. His book *Biblical Critical Theory* was named 2023 Australian Christian Book of the Year.

Wright, N. T. (Tom). Born 1948. An outstanding and highly influential New Testament scholar. He served as Bishop of Durham from 2003 to 2010 and more lately as a senior research fellow at Wycliffe Hall, Oxford University.

Glossary of Terms

Animism. Beliefs and practices which assume that spiritual beings and forces, sometimes highly malevolent and dangerous, are to be found in and expressed through plants, animals, objects such as rivers, springs, rocks, mountains, and phenomena such as storms.

Cleanness and Uncleanness. These terms, as used in the Bible, have little to do with hygiene. These are states of ritual purity and impurity. They are not moral states but rather symbolize such states, intended as powerful reminders that God's people are called to be holy as God himself is holy.

Conquest, The. I take the view, given 1 Kings 6:1, that the Exodus occurred about 1440 BC. If so, the conquest, led by Joshua, began around 1400 BC. Centuries before God had promised the land to Abraham (Genesis 15) and this promise was fulfilled, to the extent that the conquest succeeded in displacing the Canaanites, people under God's judgment.

Crusades, The. Especially between 1095 and 1291, a series of attempts were made, by force of arms, to prevent Jerusalem and surrounding areas from remaining under Muslim control. Some historians argue that the Crusades were sparked by economic factors, political attempts to unite Europe under the papacy, anti-Muslim European religious zeal, etc. Stark is illustrative of those who place greater stress on Islamic provocation, following a long and bloody history of Islamic attempts to bring the West under its control, along with attacks on Christian pilgrims.

Culture. Definitions of this term are multitudinous. No definition will win universal approval. Here is my attempt: Culture is composed of learned, shared, often interconnected, and usually constantly changing structures—behaviors, institutions, values, and beliefs—which give members who are part of a culturally defined group the perception of being distinct from other groups.

Deliverance Ministry. The practices and techniques used by various groups to cleanse and free people from demonic control and influence.

Devil, The (Satan). The implacably evil leader of fallen angels (Revelation 12:7–9).

Dhimmis. Muslims and many secularists commonly define dhimmitude as non-Muslims living under the protection of Muslim law. However, in many Muslim societies, dhimmis have been and continue to be regarded and treated as those in a condition of submission to Islamic dominance.

Divination. This involves a variety of practices and techniques that are used to foretell future events, e.g. omens, astrology, horoscopes, tarot cards, runes, numerology, seances, crystal balls, etc.

Eschatology. "Eschatology deals with the end of things. It includes personal eschatology, what happens to each individual after death, and also historical eschatology, the return of Christ to judge the world" (John Frame).

Enlightenment, The. A tectonic philosophical movement or series of movements, with significant political ramifications, which was driven by various philosophers in the seventeenth and nineteenth centuries. It is especially remembered as a time when human reason was treated as the key to grasping reality.

Excluded Middle. Many in the secular West live as though the spirit world does not exist whereas many in non-Western societies live in animistic cultures, highly conscious of the existence of spiritual beings and forces. The Bible presents a reality which lies between these two extremes.

Fall, The. That time when, instead of trusting in God as the source of all goodness, we humans autonomously arrogated for ourselves the freedom to choose what we consider to be good or evil, regardless of God's will.

GLOSSARY OF TERMS

Flesh, The. When used negatively in the New Testament, this denotes the corrupted condition of human nature after the Fall. Every human being is born with a propensity to suppress the truth about God and sin against him (Romans 1:18).

Generational Curses. The erroneous belief that individuals inherit judgment for sins committed by their ancestors, often resulting in people seeing their suffering and personal problems as God's curse upon them. Rather, God's judgment is a response to personal disobedience.

Holy War. God's use of his people, not to imperialistically expand their wealth and power, but to serve as his instruments through warfare to bring judgment upon a particular people at a particular point in history.

Holiness. God's holiness means that, as the transcendent creator, he is utterly unique and radically different from creatures like us, such that the only appropriate response is one of reverence, awe, fear, and worship.

Humanism. This refers to those cultural and philosophical movements which center upon human nature and concerns. Modern secular humanism effectively decenters God and deifies some expression of human nature.

Idolatry. This is the greatest of all sins and involves a refusal to glorify and give thanks to God as the good and great creator he is and, instead, to give this glory to that which is not God. Since God created humans in his image—to participate in and reflect his glory—it follows that all expressions of idolatry are simultaneously blasphemous and dehumanizing.

Image of God. God created humans in his image with the intent that the entire being of every human, body and soul, would gloriously correspond to what the Triune God is like in certain key respects, especially in relationships with God, other persons, and the created order.

Imprecatory Psalms. This is an artificial but useful category for recognizing that there are many psalms where imprecations or curses occur, with this being especially prominent in certain psalms, e.g. Psalms 12, 35, 52, 69, 70, 83, 109, 129, 137, 140.

Inquisition, The. This denotes the setting up of special ecclesiastical courts to deal with heresy, apostasy, blasphemy, and witchcraft during the medieval period. Penalties varied from confiscation of goods, imprisonment, or even capital punishment.

Justification, Doctrine of. This is an act of God's free grace whereby God legally declares a sinner to be forgiven and in a right covenantal relationship with himself, not because of anything that the sinner can take credit for, but rather appropriated by the sinner's God-glorifying faith in what Jesus has accomplished through his death and resurrection.

Karma. This is a fundamental doctrine in both Buddhism and Hinduism and refers to intentional acts that result in states of being and birth. "I am the owner of my karma. I inherit my karma. I am born of my karma. I am related to my karma. I live supported by my karma. Whatever karma I create, whether good or evil, that I shall inherit." Upajjhatthana Sutta in Anguttara Nikaya V.57 (Buddhist sutra).

Lifeworld. As popularized by the Austrian-German philosopher Edmund Husserl, "lifeworld" refers to the world as people experience it together in a shared consciousness. This world of actual experience, the world we know in everyday life, differs from the world described by science.

Most Holy Place (Holy of Holies). This was the throne-room of God's palace (temple). God was gloriously present here and ruled from here, as symbolized by the fact that in this inner sanctuary were located the Ten Commandments, stored in the Ark of the Covenant.

Open Theism. According to this view, God does not know the future exhaustively and humans are able to make choices that are absolutely undetermined and uncaused.

Pharisees. During the time that the Second Temple stood in Jerusalem (c. 539 BC to AD 136) the Pharisees emerged as a distinct sect within Judaism. They not only treated the Old Testament Scriptures as their authority, especially the law set out in the first five books, but also insisted on the binding force of oral tradition, the origins of which, they believed, went back to Moses himself.

Philistines. A people who inhabited the SW coastal strip of the land that was variously called Canaan, Israel, or Palestine. They were organized into a confederation of five city-states and were possibly of Aegean origin.

Postmodernism. It is difficult to determine precisely what should be included within the parameters of this term and what should be excluded. Much of this highly skeptical and relativistic movement results from negative philosophical treatments of human language which deny essential reference to or connection with reality. Accordingly, there are strong elements of anti-reason, anti-science, and anti-technology. Postmodernism radically critiques and even rejects any story that expresses one's worldview (metanarrative). It is assumed that there is there is no such thing as a unified or objective reality, but rather socially constructed ideologies which represent people's attempts to exercise power.

Qur'an. This is the sacred book of Islam, composed of 114 suras (chapters), which Muslims claim constitutes the word of Allah as dictated to Muhammad by the angel Gabriel and written in Arabic.

Reincarnation (Rebirth). This is a fundamental doctrine in both Hinduism and Buddhism, expressing the belief that sentient beings (not only humans) are doomed to remain trapped in samsara (the endless cycle of birth, death, and rebirth) and to be reborn as some kind of sentient being (not necessarily human) until they escape by attaining an ultimate state (Hinduism: moksha; Buddhism: nirvana / enlightenment).

Righteousness. "The main idea of divine righteousness is that God acts according to a perfect internal standing of right and wrong" (John Frame). Being righteous means acting rightly and especially honoring the obligations and responsibilities that inhere in all relationships.

Sharia Law. Literally, this means "the path leading to the watering place." This is promoted among Muslims as mandatory religious law based on what is taught in the Qur'an and the Hadith (collections claimed to be records of Muhammad's sayings and actions).

GLOSSARY OF TERMS

Social Imaginary. How people, by virtue of belonging to a particular social society and sharing its values, institutions, laws, and symbols, have a common view as to what constitutes valid moral behavior and expectations, along with how people should interact with each other.

Spiritual Warfare. Christians combatting the world, the flesh, and the devil (1 John 2:15; 1 Peter 2:11; Ephesians 6:12).

Synoptic Gospels. Three of the four Gospels bear a strong resemblance to each other with much shared material, namely Matthew, Mark, and Luke. The Gospel of John is very different in style and content.

Temple, The. The temple is God's palace and, like the tabernacle before it, provided the means by which a holy God could dwell among a sinful people, ruling from this center and thus, eventually, from Jerusalem where the temple was situated.

Wars of Religion, The ("Wars of the Reformation"). A series of wars, along with many rebellions and conflicts, occurring in Europe during the sixteenth to early eighteenth centuries including the Knights' War, the Thirty Years War, the Wars of the Three Kingdoms, the Savoyard-Waldensian Wars, the Nine Years' War, the War of the Spanish Succession, and the Toggenburg War. Historians contest to what extent such wars and conflicts were in fact religious in nature and to what extent they were driven by economic and political factors.

World, The. When used negatively in the New Testament, this phrase denotes the corrupted condition of society and culture as shaped by sinful human beings. All socio-cultural systems, at some level, foster ungodly desires, what John summarizes as "the lust of the flesh, the lust of the eyes, and the pride of life" (1 John 2:16).

Worldview (Weltanschauung). A general understanding of the universe and the nature of reality.

Yin and Yang. In Chinese philosophy it was believed that in the beginning there was chaos from which emerged two complementary, interacting and yet also conflicting cyclic forces: form (yin, "dark side") and matter (yang, "light side").

Bibliography

Allison, G. "You Asked: Where Do We Get Our Theology of Satan, Angels, and Demons? September 29." *The Gospel Coalition*, 2011. [Online]. [30 September 2016]. Available from: https://www.thegospelcoalition.org/article/theology-of-satan-angels-demons/

Anderson, N. T. *Freedom From Fear: Overcoming Worry and Anxiety*. Irvine, CA: Harvest House, 1999.

Anderson, N. T. *Helping Others Find Freedom in Christ*. Ventura, CA: Regal, 1995.

———. *Victory Over the Darkness. Realize the Power of Your Identity in Christ, Find Growth, Meaning and Fulfillment as a Christian*. Ventura, California: Regal, 2000.

Arnold, C. *Powers of Darkness: Principalities and Powers in Paul's Letters*. 8th ed. Downers Grove, IL: InterVarsity, 1992.

Athas, George. *Deuteronomy. One Nation under God*. Reading the Bible Today. Edited by Paul Barnett. Sydney South: Aquila, 2016.

Battle, John A. "Spiritual Warfare in Revelation." *Western Reformed Seminary Journal* 5/1 (February 1998) 14–18.

Bauckham, R. "The Nature of Evil: The Unholy Trinity." *Third Way* 17/10 (2017) 16.

Bjoraker, W. "How Do Cultures Really Change? A Challenge to the Conventional Culture Wisdom: Part 1." *International Journal of Frontier Missiology* Spring 28/1 (2011) 13–22. [Online]. [Accessed: 16 August, 2018]. Available from: http://www.ijfm.org/PDFs_IJFM/28_1_PDFs/IJFM%2028%201_Bjoraker.pdf

———. "How Do Cultures Really Change? A Challenge to the Conventional Culture Wisdom: Part 2." *International Journal of Frontier Missiology* Summer 28/2 (2011) 75–88. [Online]. [Accessed: 16 August, 2018]. Available from: http://www.ijfm.org/PDFs_IJFM/28_2_PDFs/IJFM_28_2-BjorakerPt2.pdf

Boyd, G. A. *Cross Vision. How the Crucifixion of Jesus Makes Sense of Old Testament Violence*. Minneapolis, MN: Fortress, 2017.

———. *God at War. The Bible and Spiritual Conflict*. Downers Grove, IL: InterVarsity, 1997.

———. *Satan and the Problem of Evil. Constructing a Trinitarian Warfare Theodicy* Downers Grove, IL: InterVarsity, 2001.

Breshears, G. "The Body of Christ: Prophet, Priest or King." *Journal of the Evangelical Theological Society* 37/13–26.

BIBLIOGRAPHY

Brooks, C. "Generational Curses. Part 1. Refuting False Teachings on Generational Curses." No date. *In Plain Site.* [Online]. [Accessed 29 May, 2016]. Available from: http://www.inplainsite.org/html/generational_curses.html

Calvin, John. *Commentaries on the Four Last Books of Moses Arranged in the Form of a Harmony. Vol 2.* Translated by C.W. Bingham. Christian Classics Ethereal Library. Grand Rapids, MI: Eerdmans, 1989. Available at: https://www.ccel.org/ccel/calvin/calcom04.iii.ii.i.html (Accessed 23/11/17).

Carl, J. L. "An Analysis and Critique of N. T. Anderson's Approach to Spiritual Warfare in Evangelism and Discipleship." PhD dissertation, 2014. Southern Baptist Theological Seminary. Available at: http://digital.library.sbts.edu/handle/10392/4605

Casey, A. "Beware the Animistic Leaven." *Culturnicity.* [Online 2011]. [22 March 2018]. Available from: https://culturnicity.files.wordpress.com/2011/04/animism-paper-final.pdf

Chance, L., and K. Kaufman. *Signs, Wonders and Miracles—What's Blocking Your Miracle?* Maitland, FL: Xulon, 2007.

Clark, J. "Battling Generational Family Curse." No date. *Jonas Clark Holy Spirit Ministry Training* [Online]. [Accessed 29 May, 2016]. Available from: http://www.jonasclark.com/battling-generational-family-curse/

Cole, S. J. "Steak and Arsenic: A Review of Neil Anderson's 'Victory Over the Darkness.'" *Bible.org.* 1998. [Online] [2 October 2013]. Available from: https://bible.org/article/steak-and-arsenic-review-neil-anderson-s-victory-over-darkness

Collins, J. J. "The Zeal of Phinehas: The Bible and the Legitimation of Violence." *Journal of Biblical Literature* 122/1 (2003) 3–21.

Copan, P. *Is God a Moral Monster? Making Sense of the Old Testament God.* Grand Rapids, MI: Baker, 2011.

Dahood, M. *Psalms III, 101–150.* Anchor Bible. New York, NY: Doubleday, 1970.

DeWaay, B. "Generational Curses. Biblical Answers to Questions Raised by the phrase 'visit the iniquities to the third and fourth generation.'" *Critical Issues Commentary,* 2002 [Online] 68. Available at: http://cicministry.org/commentary/issue68.htm [Accessed 31 May 2016].

Dickason, C. Fred. *Angels, Elect and Evil.* Chicago, IL: Moody, 1975.

Doriani, D. "The Speech that Launched the Crusades. 26 November." *The Gospel Coalition,* 2013 [Online]. [31 March 2016]. Available from: https://www.thegospelcoalition.org/article/the-speech-that-launched-the-crusades/

Ferdinando, Keith. *The Message of Spiritual Warfare.* The Bible Speaks Today. Edited by Derek Tidball. London: InterVarsity, 2016.

Firth, D. G. 2015. "Cries of the Oppressed: Prayer and Violence in the Psalms." In *Wrestling with the Violence of God. Soundings in the Old Testament,* edited by M. D. C. Wilgus and J. B. Wilgus, 75–89. Winona Lake, IN: Eisenbrauns, 2015.

Frame, J. M. *Systematic Theology: An Introduction to Christian Belief.* Phillipsburg, NJ: P & R, 2013.

Gardner, J. "Spiritual Warfare: A Study in Contemporary Thought." *Western Reformed Seminary Journal* 5/1 (1998) 2–13.

Goldingay, J. *Psalms 90–150.* Baker Commentary on the Old Testament Wisdom and Psalms. Grand Rapids, MI: Baker Academic, 2008.

Gombis, T. G. " The Triumph of God in Christ: Divine Warfare in the Argument of Ephesians." PhD thesis 2005. University of St. Andrews.

BIBLIOGRAPHY

Gondwe, E. "Breaking Curses, Including Generational Curses. Christian Deliverance and Healing Principles for Overcoming Curses." 2nd ed. Cambridge, MA: JesusWorkMinistry, 2008. Available from: http://livingthetorah.com/wp-content/uploads/2013/12/Breaking-Curses-Including-Generational-Curses-Eric-Gondwe.pdf

Greenlee, D. "Territorial Spirits Reconsidered." *Missiology* 22/4 (1994) 507–14.

Gurnall, W. *The Christian in Complete Armour.* 4th ed. Edinburgh: Banner of Truth Trust, 1983.

Harris, John. *One Blood. 200 Years of Aboriginal Encounter with Christianity: A Story of Hope.* Sutherland, NSW: Albatross, 1990.

Hitchens, C. *God Is Not Great: How Religion Poisons Everything.* 2nd ed. New York, NY: Twelve, 2009.

Hooker, M. *The Message of Mark.* London: Epworth, 1983.

Hunt, K. 2016. "China's Giant Space Telescope Starts Search for Alien Life. 21 September." *CNN: Space and Science.* [Online]. [29 September 2016]. Available from: http://edition.cnn.com/2016/09/21/health/china-fast-telescope-search-for-aliens/

Hutchinson, V., and S. Hutchinson. "Warriors for Christ—Ministering Demonic Deliverance and Inner-Healing to Those who are Bound by Satan." No date. *Vann Hutchinson Ministries.* [Online]. [Accessed 25 August, 2017]. Available from: http://www.vannhutchinsonministries.org/

Ibbitson, D. "Generational Curses and Demonic Oppression." No date. *Above & Beyond Christian Counseling.* [Online]. [Accessed 29 May, 2016]. Available from: https://aandbcounseling.com/generational-curses-demonic-oppression/

Jenkins, P. *The New Faces of Christianity Believing the Bible in the Global South.* Oxford: Oxford University Press, 2006.

Jensen, P. "The Most Dangerous Idea. 17 April." *Phillip Jensen.com.* 2014 [Online]. [8 December 2017]. Available from: http://phillipjensen.com/articles/the-most-dangerous-idea/

Jones, Peter. *Spirit Wars. Pagan Revival in Christian America.* Mukilteo, WA: WinePress, 1997.

Jung, Y. S. "The Divine Warrior Motif in the Fourth Gospel: A Study with a Special Focus on Conflict and Victory." PhD in Divinity and Religious Studies thesis, 2012. University of Aberdeen

Knox, D. B. *Not By Bread Alone: God's Word on Present Issues.* 2nd ed. Edinburgh: Banner of Truth Trust, 1990.

Kraft, Charles. "Allegiance, Truth and Power: Three Crucial Dimensions for Christian Living." *Pneuma Review.* 10 December 2010. [Online] [Accessed 17 August, 2018]. Available from: http://pneumareview.com/allegiance-truth-and-power-three-crucial-dimensions-for-christian-living/

Kreider, A. "Violence and Mission in the Fourth and Fifth Centuries: Lessons for Today." *International Bulletin of Missionary Research* 31/3 (2007) 125–33.

Lane, Anthony N. S., ed. *The Unseen World. Christian Reflections on Angels, Demons and the Heavenly Realm.* Grand Rapids, MI: Paternoster, 1996.

Leaney, A. R. C. *The Gospel According to St Luke.* 2nd ed. Black's New Testament Commentaries. Edited by Henry Chadwick. London: A & C Black, 1985.

BIBLIOGRAPHY

Mabie, F. J. "Chaos and Death." In *Dictionary of the Old Testament. Wisdom, Poetry and Writings*, edited by Tremper Longman III and Peter Enns. Downers Grove, IL: InterVarsity; 2008.

MacDonald, S. D. "Personal or Impersonal? An Analysis of Karl Barth and Merrill Unger's Perspectives on the Personhood of the Demonic." Master of Theology thesis, 2013. Stellenbosch University.

McDonald, M. "*Engaging the Enemy*, by C. Peter Wagner." Reviewed in *Western Reformed Seminary Journal* 5/1 (1998) 43–45.

Miller, E. "Neil Anderson and Freedom in Christ Ministries: A General Critique." Reprint: Christian Research Journal 21/1 (1998). Christian Research Institute. [Online] [30 November 2017]. Available from: http://www.equip.org/article/neil-anderson-and-freedom-in-christ-ministries-a-general-critique/

Moore, D. G., and R. A. Pyne. "Neil Anderson's Approach to the Spiritual Life." *Bibliotheca Sacra* 153/609 (1996) 75–86.

Moreau, A. Scott. *Essentials of Spiritual Warfare: Equipped to Win the Battle*. Wheaton, IL: Harold Shaw, 1997.

———. "Gaining Perspective on Territorial Spirits." 22 August 2000. *Lausanne Movement*. [Online]. [31 May 2018]. Available from: https://www.lausanne.org/content/territorial-spirits

Nunnally, W. E. "The Sins of Generational Curse." *Enrichment Journal* [Online]. Fall 2007. Available at: wavenunnally.com [Accessed 29 May 2016].

Piper, J. "How God Visits Sins on the Third and Fourth Generation." 6 March 2009. *Desiring God*. [Online]. [1 December 2017]. Available from: /articles/how-god-visits-sins-on-the-third-and-fourth-generation

Powlison, D. "Human Defensiveness: The Third Way." *Journal of Pastoral Practice* 8/1 (1985) 40–55.

Priest, R. J., T. Campbell, and B. A. Mullen. "Missiological Syncretism: The New Animistic Paradigm." In *Spiritual Power and Missions Raising the Issues*, edited by E. Rommen. Evangelical Missiological Society Series No. 3. 9–87. Pasadena, CA: William Carey Library.

Prince, D. "Seven Indications of a Curse." No date. *Derek Prince Ministries* [Online]. [Accessed 29 May, 2016]. Available from: https://www.derekprince.org/Articles/1000085722/DPM_USA/Archive_of_UK/Keys/The_Divine_Exchange/Seven_Indications_of.aspx

Rading, B. G. "How Generational Curses Affects Success." 11 March 2015. *Linkedincom*. [Online]. [30 November 2017]. Available from: https://www.linkedin.com/pulse/how-generational-curses-affects-success-biko-rading

Riddlebarger, K. "This Present Paranoia." In *Power Religion. The Selling Out of the Evangelical Church?*, edited by M. S. Horton, 265–81. Chicago, IL: Moody, 1992.

Rowley, M. "The Epistemology of Sacralized Violence in the Exodus and Conquest." *Journal of the Evangelical Theological Society* 57/1 (2014) 63–83.

Sailhamer, John H. *The Pentateuch as Narrative. A Biblical-Theological Commentary*. Library of Biblical Interpretation. Grand Rapids, MI: Zondervan, 1992.

Sande, K. *The Peacemaker. A Biblical Guide to Resolving Personal Conflict*. 4th ed. Grand Rapids, MI: Baker, 2006.

Schaff, P. *Ante-Nicene Fathers. Vol 3.* (1885). Christian Classics Ethereal Library. Available at: http://www.ccel.org/ccel/schaff/anf03.iv.vii.ii.html (Accessed 30 Nov. 2017)

———. *Ante-Nicene Fathers. Vol 7.* (1885). Christian Classics Ethereal Library. Available at: http://www.ccel.org/ccel/schaff/anf07.iii.ii.v.xx.html (Accessed 30 Nov. 2017)

Schwarz, H. "Paul Althaus (1888–1966)." *Lutheran Quarterly* 25/1 (2011) 28–51.

Shedler, J. "That Was Then, This Is Now: An Introduction to Contemporary Psychodynamic Therapy Writings." (2006) [Online]. [Accessed 3 December, 2015]. Available from: http://www.jonathanshedler.com/PDFs/Shedler%20(2006)%20That%20was%20then,%20this%20is%20now%20R9.pdf

Smith, G. R. "The Church Militant: A Study of 'Spiritual Warfare' in the Anglican Charismatic Renewal." PhD thesis, 2011. University of Birmingham.

Smith, J. K. A. "How (Not) To Change the World." *The Other Journal.* (2010) [Online]. [Accessed 16 August, 2018]. Available from: https://theotherjournal.com/2010/09/08/how-not-to-change-the-world/

Stark, R. *God's Battalions. The Case for the Crusades.* New York, NY: Harper Collins, 2010.

Stevens, D. E. "Daniel 10 and the Notion of Territorial Spirits." *Bibliotheca sacra* 157/628 (2000) 410–31.

Stott, J. R. W. *The Cross of Christ.* 3rd ed. Nottingham: Inter-Varsity, 1989.

———. *Issues Facing Christians Today. A Major Appraisal of Contemporary Social and Moral Questions.* Basingstoke, Hampshire: Marshalls, 1984.

Stowe, D. W. *Song of Exile: The Enduring Mystery of Psalm 137.* Oxford: Oxford University Press, 2016.

Taylor, Justin. "Spiritual Warfare 101." The Gospel Coalition, 2007 [Online]. [10 September]. Available from: https://www.thegospelcoalition.org/blogs/justin-taylor/spiritual-warfare-101/

Taylor, M. R. 2003. "The Cutting Edge—An Occasional Series on Doctrinal Issues Today." November. *Evangelical Times.* (2003) [Online]. [27 May 2016]. Available from: https://www.evangelical-times.org/27073/the-cutting-edge-an-occasional-series-on-doctrinal-issues-today-3/

Tidball, D. *The Message of Holiness. Restoring God's Masterpiece.* The Bible Speaks Today. Nottingham: Inter-Varsity, 2017.

van Aarde, A. "Paul's Version of 'Turning the Other Cheek': Rethinking Violence and Tolerance." In *Coping with Violence in the New Testament,* edited by J. W. Van Henten, and P. Villiers, 41–67. Leiden: Brill, 2012.

Vander Klok, D. "Breaking Generational Curses." No date. *Walking by Faith* [Online]. [Accessed 29 May, 2016]. Available from: https://walkingbyfaith.tv/breaking-generational-curses/

Wakely, M. "A Critical Look at a New 'Key' to Evangelization." *Evangelical Missions Quarterly* 31/2 (1995) 152–62.

Weiner, M. S. "This 'Miserable African': Race, crime, and disease in colonial Boston." *Common-Place,* (2004). [Online]. 4/3, 1. Available at: http://common-place.org/book/this-miserable-african-race-crime-and-disease-in-colonial-boston/ [Accessed 30 November 2017].

Wells, David F. *God in the Wasteland. The Reality of Truth in a World of Fading Dreams.* Grand Rapids, MI / Cambridge, U.K.: Eerdmans, 1994.

Wright, N. T. "N. T. Wright on Satan and Evil 3" 2009. Video recording, YouTube, viewed 24 November 2017. https://www.youtube.com/watch?v=JhrkB_55qaY

www.ingramcontent.com/pod-product-compliance
Lightning Source LLC
Chambersburg PA
CBHW071437150426
43191CB00008B/1160